Barcode in Back

# Jazz Icons

Today, jazz history is dominated by iconic figures who have taken on an almost god-like status. From Satchmo to Duke, Bird to Trane, these legendary jazzmen form the backbone of the jazz tradition. Jazz icons not only provide musicians and audiences with figureheads to revere but have also come to stand for a number of values and beliefs that shape our view of the music itself. *Jazz Icons* explores the growing significance of icons in jazz and discusses the reasons why the music's history is increasingly dependent on the legacies of 'great men'. Using a series of individual case studies, Tony Whyton examines the influence of jazz icons through different forms of historical mediation, including the recording, language, image and myth. The book encourages readers to take a fresh look at their relationship with iconic figures of the past and challenges many of the dominant narratives in jazz today.

TONY WHYTON is Reader in the School of Media, Music and Performance at the University of Salford. Prior to joining the University of Salford, he was responsible for the creation, management and strategic development of the Centre for Jazz Studies UK at Leeds College of Music. He was the founding editor of the interdisci plinary journal *The Source: Challenging Jazz Criticism* and co-edits the internationally peer-reviewed *Jazz Research Journal*.

# Jazz Icons

## Heroes, Myths and the Jazz Tradition

————

TONY WHYTON

University of Salford

**CAMBRIDGE**
UNIVERSITY PRESS

CAMBRIDGE UNIVERSITY PRESS

Cambridge, New York, Melbourne, Madrid, Cape Town, Singapore, São Paulo, Delhi

Cambridge University Press
The Edinburgh Building, Cambridge CB2 8RU, UK

Published in the United States of America by Cambridge University Press, New York

www.cambridge.org
Information on this title: www.cambridge.org/9780521896450

First published 2010

Printed in the United Kingdom at the University Press, Cambridge

*A catalogue record for this publication is available from the British Library*

ISBN 978-0-521-89645-0 Hardback

*For my parents, Irene and Wallace Whyton*

[C]ultural memory begins with death: the death of the creator. The search for meaning is left to the survivors. It is up to us to decide how to tell the story, how best to represent the struggle and achievement of artists whose lives belong to the past but whose music continues to live in the present. (Scott DeVeaux, *The Birth of Bebop: A Social and Musical History*)

[T]he history of jazz has come to be read as fabulous, in fact as a kind of Romance; and that history shows how Romance can turn readily into cult, into the regular making of icons, beginning with Buddy Bolden and going at least to John Coltrane. Jazz confirms the claim that our acts of fabulation cannot seriously be separated from the rest of our social lives … That the history of jazz has lent itself so readily to the making of myths explains much of its fascination, much of the power it has with us. (Frederick Garber, 'Fabulating Jazz')

If the study of jazz is to come of age and thrive as a discipline, criticism of canonical masters must be tolerated or, at the very least, received without rancor. (Krin Gabbard, 'Krin Gabbard Replies')

[A] jazz fan dies and reaches the other world and meets St Peter, who takes him to a club with bad lighting, crowded tables, and bored waitresses. But when he sees that the customers include Lester Young, Billie Holiday, Monk, and Bird, he cries out to St Peter, 'This *is* heaven!' Then he notices a figure sitting at the end of the bar, dressed all in black, his back turned to the audience. 'Who's that?' asks the fan. 'Oh', says St Peter, 'that's God. He thinks he's Miles Davis.' (John Szwed, 'The Man')

# Contents

*List of illustrations*   [*page* viii]
*Acknowledgements*   [ix]

Introduction: Jazz narratives and sonic icons   [1]

1 Jazz icons, heroes and myths   [15]

2 Jazz and the disembodied voice   [38]

3 Not a wonderful world: Louis Armstrong meets Kenny G   [57]

4 Men can't help acting on Impulse!   [82]

5 Witnessing and the jazz anecdote   [106]

6 Dispelling the myth: essentialist Ellington   [127]

7 Birth of the school   [153]

*Notes*   [178]
*Bibliography*   [207]
*Index*   [218]

# Illustrations

1 Still from *Collateral*, 2004; courtesy of Photofest [1]

2 Duke Ellington at the London Palladium, 1933; Max Jones Archive @ aol.com [15]

3 John Coltrane, publicity photograph; Max Jones Archive @ aol.com [38]

4 Louis Armstrong, London, 1956; Max Jones Archive @ aol.com [57]

5 John Coltrane; Max Jones Archive @ aol.com [82]

6 John Coltrane, *The Classic Quartet: Complete Impulse! Studio Recordings*; photograph by Paul Floyd Blake [88]

7 Advertisement for Donald Harrison's *Nouveau Swing*; courtesy of Universal Music [97]

8 Roy Haynes, Thelonious Monk, Charles Mingus and Charlie Parker; Max Jones Archive @ aol.com [106]

9 Duke Ellington and Billy Strayhorn; Max Jones Archive @ aol.com [127]

10 Duke Ellington and Sonny Greer, 1933; Max Jones Archive @ aol.com [153]

# Acknowledgements

Earlier versions of some of the material within this book have been published in academic journals and edited volumes as follows: 'Four for Trane: Jazz and the Disembodied Voice', *Jazz Perspectives* 1.2 (October 2007), 115–32; and 'Telling Tales: Witnessing and the Jazz Anecdote', *The Source: Challenging Jazz Criticism* 1 (March 2004), 115–31. A section of Chapter 4 appeared in my article 'Acting on Impulse! Recordings and the Reification of Jazz' in M. Dogantan-Dack (ed.), *Recorded Music: Philosophical and Critical Reflections* (London: Middlesex University Press, 2008), 155–71; and material from the opening part of Chapter 7 was published in 'Birth of the School: Discursive Methodologies in Jazz Education', *Music Education Research* 8.2 (March 2006), 65–81.

I am extremely grateful to several friends and colleagues who have offered support and advice in putting this book together. In particular, Krin Gabbard, Barry Kernfeld and Jonty Stockdale provided enthusiasm and belief in my work from the outset; without their encouragement this project would not have materialised. I have also been fortunate to have had active advice from, and critical engagement with, a number of scholars including Mine Dogantan-Dack, Nicholas Gebhardt, John Howland, Stuart Nicholson, Lewis Porter, Derek Scott, Alan Stanbridge and Catherine Tackley, all of whom offered me food for thought, encouragement and some brilliant suggestions for improvement. I would also like to acknowledge colleagues at the University of Salford and Leeds College of Music for supporting my research work; in particular, I would like to thank John Mundy, George McKay and David Sanjek for providing me with suitable working conditions to finish this manuscript. I am especially grateful to Julian Rushton for his advice and support at the proposal stage and would also like to thank Victoria Cooper, Rebecca Jones, the anonymous reviewers and staff at Cambridge University Press for their professionalism, patience and enthusiasm. Several people aided my research by providing with interesting source material. In particular, Michael Cuscuna, Paul Floyd Blake, Nick Jones, Peter Martin, Dale Perkins, Andrew Simons, and Sarah Hutchinson at Universal Music have all provided materials that have found their way into the book in one way or another. I would also like to thank all of my undergraduate and postgraduate students who have been subjected to, and actively engaged with, the development of ideas within this study. Finally, I am eternally indebted to Fiona who, from the outset, has been an incredibly understanding wife, excellent critic and enthusiastic supporter of my work.

# Introduction: Jazz narratives and sonic icons

**Figure 1**    Still from *Collateral*, 2004

MAX: I never learned to listen to jazz.

VINCENT: It's off melody. Behind the notes. Not what's expected – improvising, like tonight.

MAX: Like tonight?

VINCENT: Most people, ten years from now, same job, same place, same routine. Everything the same. Just keeping it safe over and over and over. Ten years from now. Man, you don't know where you'll be ten minutes from now. Do you?

[Vincent talks to the jazz club waitress and invites trumpeter Daniel over for a drink after his set. A short musical shot of musicians on stage cuts to Vincent, Max and Daniel sitting at the table following the set.]

DANIEL: No, now see, I was about nineteen, bussing tables right here. The money wasn't shit, but that wasn't the point. It was about being around the music. And I was. I mean, take this one night. July 22nd, 1964. Who do you think walks through that door? Miles Davis. That's right.

VINCENT: In the flesh?

DANIEL: That's right. I'm talking about, through those doors, the coolest man on the planet.

VINCENT: Jesus.

DANIEL: Anyway, he had been at a recording session up at Columbia, up on Vine. So Miles comes through that door. Before you know it, he's up on the bandstand, jamming with the band.

VINCENT: I mean it had to be …

DANIEL: Oh it was scary. I mean, the dude was so focused, man. Plus, he was a kind of scary cat anyway, man. I mean, everybody and their mama knew that you don't just come up and talk to Miles Davis. I mean, he may have looked like he was chilling, but he was absorbed. This one young, hip couple, one of them tried to shake his hand one day. And the guy says, 'Hi, my name is …'. Miles said, 'Get the fuck out of my face, you jive motherfucker. Take your silly bitch with you.' [Laughter] You know? That's … that was Miles, man. That's the way he was when he was in his musical headspace. Fierce.

VINCENT: But did you talk to him?

DANIEL: Better than that.

VINCENT: No.

DANIEL: I played for about twenty minutes.

VINCENT: Unbelievable.

MAX: How'd you do?

DANIEL: How'd I do? Well you really ain't shit when you're playing next to Miles Davis. But he carried my ass.

VINCENT: What'd he say?

DANIEL: He said one word, 'Cool'.

VINCENT: 'Cool'?

DANIEL: Yeah.

VINCENT: That's it?

DANIEL: Yeah. That meant, 'Good, but not ready.' It meant, 'Look me up when you are.'[1]

Michael Mann's 2004 film *Collateral* might seem an unlikely place to begin a book about jazz icons. And yet, although jazz only features in one scene within the entire film, the dialogue referring to the iconic jazz musician Miles Davis touches on several themes that form a central part of this study. *Collateral* is a relatively straightforward action thriller starring Tom Cruise as Vincent, a contract killer who embarks on a series of hits during one long night in Los Angeles. Hijacking taxi driver Max (Jamie Foxx) and his cab, Vincent forces Max to take him from one job to the next with their situation becoming more intense and out of control as the narrative unfolds. Vincent's third hit takes place within a jazz club where, unknown to Max, Vincent's target is the black club owner and trumpet virtuoso Daniel. The opening segment of the 'Jazzman' scene, above, is largely used to explore the relationship between Vincent and Max, Vincent being the cold, calculating, dangerous and 'improvising' killer, and Max being the safe, mundane and predictable taxi driver. Only when the gig is finished and the club is empty does it become apparent that jazzman Daniel is the next target on Vincent's hit list. Vincent, obviously an obsessive jazz fan given his insights into, and appreciation of, the music, is troubled by the prospect of killing the jazzman and so provides Daniel with the opportunity to evade execution simply by answering a jazz question correctly. At the climax of the scene, Vincent follows Daniel's anecdote about Miles Davis with the simple question 'Where did Miles learn music?' Daniel replies that he knows everything there is to know about Miles Davis, and there is a confidence in the jazzman that suggests he will walk free. And yet, when the reply comes that Miles learned music at Juilliard, Vincent immediately shoots Daniel in the head and whispers into the ear of his dead victim 'Dropped out of Juilliard after less than a year. Tracked down Charlie Parker on 52nd Street, who mentored him for the next three years.' Although fulfilling his contract, Vincent looks visibly shaken by his actions and, within the context of the film at large, the killing of the jazzman triggers the contract killer's gradual loss of control and the start of his demise.

This scene is typical of many media representations of jazz, from the sense of hysteria and otherness that surrounds the presentation of the jazz life to the hyperbolic masculine rhetoric of jazz artists; from the romanticised perception that improvisation is dangerous and on the edge to the ultimate destruction of the black jazz artist – essentially, you get the feeling that if Vincent doesn't kill Daniel the music somehow will. I suggest that, whilst these seemingly inconsequential mediations of jazz can be considered overblown, they not only reflect and perpetuate more broad-based jazz mythologies that infiltrate jazz discourse at every level, they also shed light on the signifying potential of the music and its ever-changing cultural status. Although the 'Jazzman' scene itself is less than three minutes in duration, a number of jazz tropes, representations and myth-ologies are played out in the narrative sequence that both inform, and are informed by, mainstream jazz discourse. Daniel's jazz club is stereotypical; it is an after-hours venue for a select few who 'get it', and the dialogue refers to jazz's dwindling audiences, reinforcing the impression that this music is art music and not to be consumed or enjoyed by the masses. Vincent is clearly an obsessive personality and it is through this obsession and devo-tion to the music that he has developed a passion and understanding of the music. Like Norman Mailer's problematic description of the 'white negro' who lives the jazz life, the scene presents Vincent as a non-conformist psychopath who is governed by his own rules.[2] Vincent's obsession and identification with the unpredictable, dangerous and impro-vised world of jazz becomes a model for the way in which he lives his life, as the opening dialogue with Max suggests. Crucially, the way in which jazz legend Miles Davis enters into the film narrative demonstrates his status as icon, moving between the fictional world of the film and the reality of the musician as the 'coolest man on the planet'. In effect, as an icon, Davis retains an other-worldly quality that takes him out of his historical context and invests him with symbolic meaning; he has become a trope for the romantic jazz life. The scene also uses the persona and biography of Davis to perpetuate several mythologies of jazz, from the portrayal of Davis as detached from his social environment ('the dude was so focused', 'in his musical headspace', 'you don't just come up and talk to Miles Davis'), conveying meaning through inference and non-verbal ges-ture ('That meant "Good, but not ready."'), to the fundamental assertion that true educational value can only occur on the street or bandstand. Indeed, jazzman Daniel's ultimate downfall is triggered by his suggestion that the Juilliard School was the place where Miles learned music. Daniel's failure to recognise the fact that formal education is not conducive to living the jazz life is suggestive of his own lack of abilities as a jazz artist; it is perhaps this lack of insight that contributes to his never being ready to share the stage with Davis and, therefore, he is ultimately expendable.

Film representations such as these serve to bring the broad-based mythologies of jazz to life; Davis's presence within the *Collateral* scene is all-pervasive, and anecdotal accounts of his iconic aura are a central narrative device. Moving beyond the fictional world of the film, Davis's biography is used as a means to enhance jazz myths. Krin Gabbard has discussed the use of Miles Davis's music in film to invest white characters with sex appeal and a degree of romantic depth.[3] Whilst the 'Jazzman' scene does not rob black performers of their achievements – Davis is treated with almost god-like reverence – the scene does perpetuate the Hollywood treatment of African American musicians. Daniel is perceived both as 'Other' and ultimately on a path to destruction, for within a Hollywood jazz-film context, African American musicians cannot reconcile life and music.[4]

Musically the 'Jazzman' scene is also interesting, as Miles Davis's 'Spanish Key' is heard within the film's diegesis as the music played in the club from the beginning of the scene. The choice of 'Spanish Key' is significant, as the recording is not instantly recognisable to a general audience and, although deriving from one of Davis's most commercially successful albums, *Bitches Brew*, it is not a track associated with the classic Davis sound of the 1950s to mid 1960s. From this perspective, the music not only provides the jazz club with a contemporary, electric feel, it is also symbolic as music that does not sit comfortably within the homogeneous constructed jazz tradition. Within the scene, Davis's recorded music is presented as live jazz and is embodied through the characters on screen. We are encouraged to believe that the sounds being heard emanate from Daniel on stage and, in this respect, Davis's music functions as an intertextual reference for what is to follow. Like Daniel's failure to understand the notion that jazz is learned on the street, his performance of 'Spanish Key' is also something that places him on the outside of the iconic jazz mainstream. If we assume that the sounds coming from Daniel's trumpet are improvised, and not a faithful re-enactment of Davis's music, the musical style (electric jazz/rock) lies outside the canon of masterworks created before 1970. If, instead, Daniel's performance was of Miles Davis's 'So What' from the *Kind of Blue* album, it would be instantly recognisable as an iconic recording. This would not only destroy the sense that the music was coming from Daniel's trumpet but would also signify the trumpeter as a musical genius; arguably, his association with a canonical recording might also make him less expendable.

This short scene echoes a number of key themes I explore throughout *Jazz Icons*, from the promotion of the other-worldly qualities of iconic figures to the way in which the disembodied sounds of jazz greats influence everyday jazz practice, from the use of anecdotes in communicating the story of jazz to the assertion that formal education is the antithesis of authentic jazz practice. I suggest that jazz icons occupy a complex place within contemporary culture that is evidenced through film and media representations such as this, and I have therefore adopted a multifaceted approach to understanding icons. When referring to icons, I use the word with all of its dominant definitions in mind and suggest that it is this conflation of meanings that makes jazz discourse particularly interesting and unique. Whereas conventional discussions of iconic jazz stars revolve around visual imagery, my work seeks to develop the study of icons to include the ways in which they have become symbols for the jazz life and reflect the values of the neo-traditionalist mainstream. When discussing jazz icons, then, I incorporate the following five definitions of the word into my critical methodology.

## Icon as visual image

The definition of icon as a visual image has dominated discussions of jazz musicians to date. Although still relatively limited in terms of scholarly perspectives and theoretical discussion, visual representations of jazz have played a central role in constructing an aesthetic for jazz, helping to frame the way the music is perceived and understood.[5] When considering the significance of the visual aspects of jazz as iconic art, it is perhaps no coincidence that the bebop era – widely associated with jazz's transition to serious art music – coincided with the creation of probably the most famous jazz label to date, Blue Note Records. Blue Note was established in 1939 and grew into a label that would have a significant impact on the promotion of jazz as both sonic and visual art for decades to come. From the mid 1950s on, Blue Note Records began to define jazz as quintessentially hip, acknowledging the merits of jazz as a way of life and more than just a sonic experience. Using the photography of Francis Wolff and cover art of designers such as Reid Miles, Blue Note began to develop an artistic aesthetic that would have a profound impact on the representation of jazz for decades to come. In turning album covers into works of art, Blue Note integrated iconic monochrome photography with style guidelines quite often seen within European art movements. For example, many iconic Blue Note albums bear a striking resemblance to modernist movements and pay homage to artists working within very different artistic contexts.[6] We can understand these cultural 'borrowings' as indicative of an attempt to establish a distinct experimental art aesthetic for jazz. Indeed, the success of Blue Note arguably emanated from a synergy between good music and visual representation. Furthermore, the production of liner notes helped to create the jazz life in literary form, supporting the idea of jazz existing beyond the music. Within this context, Krin Gabbard has discussed the way in which novelists, film-makers and photographers tend on the one hand to contribute to the continuation of certain mythologies bound up with the music and yet, on the other hand, have the potential to bring new life to the music, providing a new dimension to the sounds that we hear and a way into music that some might find difficult to comprehend at first.[7] Visual representations have the power both to liberate jazz and to infuse the music with new qualities but, at the same time, they can also perpetuate stereotypes of jazz and the lives that musicians lead. The visual representation of jazz, therefore, enables us to make connections with the music and feel closer to its associated figures but, paradoxically, it also plays a central role in turning musicians into icons, arguably severing connections with, and distancing artists from, the everyday world. In the same way that Jed Rasula discusses the 'seductive menace' of recordings in jazz history, I argue that the same can be said of jazz photography.[8] For example, photographers not only helped to document the history of the music but also helped to construct the media representation of jazz itself, using monochrome techniques (even when colour was available) to depict and represent jazz as art. Photographers not only document what they are witnessing, they also frame the subject in such a way that their images form part of a connotative system; jazz photography can engender feelings in us and come to stand for a multitude of cultural values. Even photographs that have a documentary purpose can be seen as framing the music in some way or encouraging a particular reading. For example, monochrome photography helps to place jazz very much in the past and also takes it out of the ordinary, creating an environment for the music that is different from our everyday world. Ironically, the monochrome world depicted in jazz photography is far from dull; there is something about this medium that pulls the viewer in and gives a richness and vibrancy to the scene that colour photography cannot. The photographic quality makes a scene look more real whilst signifying honesty, nostalgia and sentimentality, the perfect antidote to the modern day world.[9] From a professional perspective, monochrome has also become synonymous with art photography and therefore encourages the reader to take the image seriously. Visual representation is an integral part of our initial connection to any figures of history, as a means of identification and recognition; it enables us to perceive artists as real, rather than mythic. Paradoxically, visual representation is essential in the construction of iconic jazz musicians, the images themselves making a significant contribution to artists becoming iconic in the first place, moving them from the real to the hyper-real.

## Icon as symbol

Understanding the role of mediation in creating, sustaining and altering the symbolic power of icons is a central theme in this book and I explore underlying issues through the examination of different mediated 'texts', including the recording, language, image and myth. In a wider context, I argue that jazz icons have come to stand for a whole host of values beyond their visual representation. In effect, icons carry out a symbolic function in that they are continually invested with meaning and serve both to support and perpetuate jazz mythologies. Within several chapters of this book, I argue that jazz icons have taken on a symbolic quality in serving to support the authority of the jazz canon, a sense of homogenous tradition and the romantic jazz life. In addition to the canon being significant in promoting the pantheon of jazz greats, iconic representations can be viewed as part of a broader cultural sea-change in which celebrity fulfils an important role in constructing identities and reinforcing societal values. Although the growing influence of jazz icons can be viewed as part of the increasing importance of celebrity and mediated personae, their function within the constructed jazz mainstream is to appear as separate and resistant to the influence of the modern world. When jazz icons represent the values of the jazz tradition, they are presented as the antithesis of modern-day celebrity in that they purportedly preserve aesthetic values in an age of cultural and moral decline. Although this neo-traditionalist agenda is riddled with nostalgia for a bygone age, the promotion of the icon and his music as natural and unmediated remains a popular (mis-)conception. In a jazz context, then, musical greats are treated as different from celebrities; our sense of them as mediated personae is lost, and in perceiving them as symbolic icons we are encouraged to believe that they are charismatic and heroic, superhuman stars endowed with natural talent and other-worldly qualities.[10] Jazz is effectively promoted as an unmediated experience in which there is no differentiation between the star on stage and the living person backstage. Essentially, the jazz greats' fame is widely understood as a consequence of their innate ability or musical genius and not as mediated personae per se. This belief paves the way for jazz icons to be romantically perceived as at one with their instruments, leading inseparable lives from the music they perform and transcending everyday experience through improvised performance.

I would argue (as others have done within more broad-based studies of stars and celebrities), however, that it is precisely the mediated personae of icons that afford them a symbolic role, making artists seem overly charismatic and other-worldly. On a fairly straightforward level, the impact of mediation can be seen when fans get to meet a living legend in person and are either dumbstruck at coming face to face with their hero or disappointed by the normality of their experience. Moreover, consider how the perception of jazz greats would change if we didn't have access to mediating artefacts: sound recordings, monochrome photography, cinematic depictions of jazz artists, biographical accounts of musicians, a sense of homogenous tradition where one great artist influences another, literary explorations of the music, 'first hand' accounts of jazz greats and related anecdotes, and so on. Essentially, icons would cease to be iconic, jazz greats would be considered part of the everyday world and, arguably, jazz would no longer be jazz. Therefore, for jazz to be considered jazz, mediation has to occur, from the distribution of jazz 'texts' to the conveyance of meaning and a sense of the iconic. As Jessica Evans and David Hesmondalgh suggest, historically, every artist or personality that has found fame and notoriety has relied on some form of media management in order to gain acknowledgement from an audience, and it is therefore questionable to separate heroic acts (art) from forms of public expression (media).[11]

## Icon as uncritical object of devotion

'Musicians, critics and other listeners may disagree on many points, but where the music of John Coltrane is concerned there is never any argument. He was, simply, a giant.'[12] It is understandable that a canon of art requires the support of a pantheon of gods, and the greater emphasis placed on jazz as a canonical art form suggests that icons will continue to develop a central symbolic role in jazz discourse. Over recent years, jazz greats have increasingly been promoted and understood as separate from the everyday world and, partly because of the impact of the canon and its supporting pantheon of legendary figures, icons are now largely treated as objects of uncritical devotion. At several points within this study, I discuss the way in which iconic figures are treated in uncomplicated terms, so that the frictions, contradictions and problematic aspects of their lives and music are ironed out into one straightforward homogeneous narrative. In addition to discussing the consequences of canonising jazz, Gabbard has also commented on the growing wave of jazz texts devoted to treating jazz icons in uncritical terms. Indeed, he argues that there are two dominant narratives used in film to represent African American jazz musicians; the first is linked to the hysterical, sexually charged and tragic nature of Hollywood biopics, and the second is a more recent type of romanticised story that borders on hagiography.[13] Although Gabbard talks specifically about film, I argue that these dominant narratives can be applied to a wider jazz context and are not mutually exclusive. Indeed, the combination of the tragedy, masculine sexuality and hagiography summarises the representation of several jazz texts at present. As the 'Jazzman' scene from *Collateral* demonstrates, jazz can now signify a combination of sex, violence, aesthetic beauty and improvised hysteria at the same time as treating iconic musicians as saintly. Within this cinematic context, Miles Davis can obviously do no wrong; he is an object of uncritical devotion even to the extent that his antisocial behaviour ('Get the fuck out of my face, you jive motherfucker …') is considered cool and alluring.

## Icon as deity

Treating jazz greats as objects of devotion beyond criticism is only one step removed from perceiving icons as religious entities. The otherworldly and symbolic qualities of iconic jazz stars have led to a position where they perform a god-like role in certain contexts. Within this book, I examine how jazz icons have taken on a godly significance and are represented in such a way that they demand unqualified adoration and respect, bordering on a type of sacred worship and religious observance for musicians and fans alike. Jazz icons have an all-pervasive presence within mainstream jazz discourse; their influence has a more prominent place in the narrativisation of jazz as the years go by. In this way, they influence jazz practice at every level, from the way in which musicians religiously transcribe, imitate and develop techniques to sound like their jazz heroes to the role that ritual and sacrifice play in the promotion of the jazz life. Once deceased, jazz greats can be transformed into icons, and their lifestyles and the circumstances of their deaths become the subject of morbid enquiry and mythical interpretation; one only needs to consider accounts of Charlie Parker's tragic death and the creation myths associated with Buddy Bolden, or to look at the way in which John Coltrane has been transformed into a spiritual master, to understand how jazz musicians can be removed from their everyday worlds and treated as deified objects. Although initially seeking to dispel mythologies associated with the deaths of jazz artists, books such as Frederick J. Spencer's *Jazz and Death* demonstrate the market for morbid examinations of jazz musicians' lives.[14] Moreover, following the death of jazz greats, works that have a sacred theme are now revered in biblical terms; works such as Coltrane's *A Love Supreme* and Ellington's *Sacred Concerts*, for example, have been instilled with symbolic meaning and a sense of being touched by the divine.

Once deified, the icon can also become increasingly detached from the act of jazz practice itself, as if the physical qualities of musical sound are only a fraction of our experience of the god-like jazz master; in effect, we are led to believe that jazz icons transcend the very music that they have created. Take, for example, the wealth of photographs of John Coltrane that show him in a non-performative pose or the way in which Coltrane's and Parker's rarely recorded voices have been fetishised by jazz musicians and fans alike (see Chapter 2 for more on this).

## Icon as sign

This final definition of the word 'icon' highlights the way in which legendary jazz figures have become inseparable from the mythologies of jazz itself. I have already suggested that, through their representation in a variety of media, iconic figures can be invested with meaning and come to stand for a range of cultural values. Inevitably, this situation offers the potential for jazz icons to become part of what Roland Barthes discussed as a second-order sign system, their natural, uncomplicated, unquestioned place in history masking a series of mythologies. Essentially, as connotative signs, jazz icons serve the dominant values of today's mainstream, they are part of a system of representation that continually invests them with meaning in order to preserve the authority of the canon and homogenous jazz tradition. When viewing icons as a form of sign, we can understand them as socially constructed figures that appear to us as natural and unchanging; within this context, conflict and contradiction are ironed out as jazz icons appear as heroes of history, their natural authority never questioned.[15] In assuming a natural place in the history of jazz, icons support the telling of the story of jazz, from 'great man' theories, to causal narration, to the mythologies of the jazz life. These points directly relate to Barthes's writings on mythologies, and the way that cultural objects have a connotative potential and often mask underlying ideology through their supposedly natural qualities.[16] Building on this, I suggest that, within certain contexts, legendary jazz figures are gradually becoming inseparable from the underlying ideologies of the dominant social order itself and can therefore be understood as types of iconic signs, as posited by Charles Sanders Peirce.[17] In a Peircean context, the form of iconic sign clearly suggests its meaning; in other words, signs share the qualities of the object they represent. From a jazz perspective, this leads to iconic jazz stars becoming inseparable from the broader meanings within which their forms are placed. So, for example, when considering the life and music of a figure such as John Coltrane, we automatically regard him as transcendent being; Coltrane and transcendence become one and the same thing. In this respect, the growing centrality of iconic narratives within jazz discourse has led to a position where jazz figures become inseparable from the myths they represent.

When writing this book, I wanted to explore the influence of the jazz icon from a variety of perspectives. By approaching each chapter as an independent case study, I sought to blend theoretical models with practical examples and draw on several themes in the discussion of jazz icons, from advertising to anecdotes, heroic narratives to the jazz community. Through this integration of theory and practice, I wanted to develop a series of iconoclastic arguments designed to relate to everyday life, and to encourage readers to formulate critical perspectives on their own relationship to established jazz greats. My opening chapter, 'Jazz icons, heroes and myths', accounts for the way in which the jazz icon has come to dominate contemporary understandings of jazz. By examining the subtle manifestations of 'great man' theories, I explore the way in which contemporary jazz narratives present codified representations of iconic masters. Within this context I include an overview of both related and conflicting antecedents to iconic stereotypes in jazz, from classical myth to the African American trickster. This overview leads into a discussion of how iconic figures adhere to overarching and romanticised models, and yet develop distinct characteristics that set them apart from each other in broader narrative contexts. The chapter concludes with a discussion of how the mainstream jazz tradition is founded on masculine rhetoric and representation, with each iconic figure serving to support a sense of a homogenised and natural past.

Chapter 2, 'Jazz and the disembodied voice', discusses the impact of iconic recordings on contemporary performance habits and constructs a model from which to examine current trends in jazz performance that are influenced both directly and indirectly by recordings. Using examples from the work, life and music of John Coltrane, I examine ways in which a sense of iconic aura is felt by musicians and audiences alike, and demonstrate how the disembodied nature of recordings impacts on performance habits, from the Jamey Aebersold 'Play-A-Long' to albums such as Branford Marsalis's *Footsteps of Our Fathers*.

In my next chapter, 'Not a wonderful world: Louis Armstrong meets Kenny G', I explore the way in which the work of jazz icons can be viewed as sacred, beyond the bounds of criticism or revision, at the same time as promoting ritualistic acts of consumption. I discuss the way in which rituals tie into our understandings of identity and community and also create notions of universality, mysticism and transcendence found so often within jazz discourse. I examine themes related to cultural value, the ownership of jazz, authenticity and the music's relationship to popular culture, and relate ideas to Pat Metheny's outspoken response to Kenny G's reworking of Louis Armstrong's *What a Wonderful World* in 2000. Finally, by viewing jazz as a social construct, I argue that assertions of greatness in jazz often comment more on the context and position of those making value judgements than they do about musicians being valued.

Chapter 4, 'Men can't help acting on Impulse!', examines the growing importance of icons in the marketing of jazz past and present. In particular, I examine the way in which record companies set out to distinguish between everyday releases and historic reissues, and the impact this has on the jazz mainstream today. Through an intertextual reading of contemporary jazz advertising and the marketing techniques of the Impulse! label, I explore the way in which the jazz canon feeds into the consumer desire for collection, nostalgia and the deification of artists.

The study of recordings and advertising leads into a study of language in my next chapter, 'Witnessing and the jazz anecdote'. Here, I argue that conventional jazz narratives are dominated by stereotypical imagery and colourful stories that often oversimplify and romanticise issues surrounding the music. Notably, the role of the jazz anecdote is something that forms a part of any jazz musician's everyday life and yet seems to be the most uncritical of methods used to discuss the music. I examine how anecdotal accounts often form an essential part of musicians' interactions and discussions of jazz and help to distinguish jazz from other artistic discourses. The deeply social nature of the music, its celebrated oral tradition and the obsession with documentation have established anecdotal stories as a primary means of communicating historical information. I illustrate how jazz documentaries, publications and everyday conversations – between musicians and enthusiasts alike – usually contain a multitude of anecdotes ranging from the humorous to the mythological. Within this context, I examine the function of anecdote and the way in which jazz professionals and enthusiasts make use of it in the construction of jazz history and iconic figures. Although a seemingly innocent and informal method of discussing jazz, anecdote functions on a number of complicated and contrasting levels.

My penultimate chapter, 'Dispelling the myth: essentialist Ellington', revisits the ideological presentation of jazz history explored in Chapter 1, exploring the contradictory nature of mythologies and their function in jazz narratives. Specifically, the chapter uses the biography of Duke Ellington as its central focus and draws on a number of sources that illustrate how mythology in jazz is both created and perpetuated. By comparing the depiction of Duke Ellington in text form to excerpts from Ken Burns's large-scale and influential documentary *Jazz*, I establish the dominant iconic codification of the jazz icon and contrast this with other more controversial writings, most notably James Lincoln Collier's biography of Ellington published in 1989 and David Hajdu's intimate portrait of the Ellington–Strayhorn relationship.[18] Through this comparison, I demonstrate how iconic jazz narratives are often dominated by idealistic, masculine and heterosexual themes. This analysis suggests that projects that promote scholarship of Ellington as 'essential' (such as Lincoln Center's *Essentially Ellington* programme) can themselves be viewed as essentialist, through the promotion of gendered, sexualised ideology.

The final chapter, 'Birth of the school', examines the politics of music education, the implications of canon-forming and icon development in pedagogical practice, and the critical attempts to open up the field of study to broader cultural analysis. In this context, I discuss the unique problems faced by jazz education and suggest that these issues are inherently linked to the nature of the music itself. Drawing on the perspectives of musicians, critics, educators and scholars of New Jazz Studies, I examine difficult social and cultural space occupied by education and conclude by exploring the potential for educational methodologies to disrupt dominant ideologies and to uncover related cultural myths.

# 1 | Jazz icons, heroes and myths

Figure 2   Duke Ellington at the London Palladium, 1933

I know the facts. But I'm looking for something better.[1]

Albert Murray

## Introduction

The story of jazz revolves most often around the legacy of iconic figures, with a canon of masterpieces supported by a pantheon of jazz greats. Whereas other canonical arts have been subject to scrutiny in recent years, as they are inevitably bound up with discourses of power and exclusion, the recently constructed – and male dominated – jazz canon is rarely challenged or opened up to critical discussion beyond a select band of writings that constitute 'New Jazz Studies'. As the jazz tradition is constructed along canonical lines, the African American male has emerged as the embodiment of authentic jazz practice and a handful of figures play a central part not only in supporting the foundations of a linear tradition but also in providing powerful role models for present-day musicians. Figures such as Armstrong, Ellington, Parker, Coltrane and Davis can be viewed as an inter-related web of jazz geniuses, providing the story of jazz with narrative continuity through their artistic endeavours and their alignment with significant periods of jazz history. However, I argue that, in many instances, the impact of jazz greats goes beyond mere musical influence; jazz icons have developed an other-worldly quality that takes them away from everyday experience towards a symbolic, almost god-like status. Icons carry out a symbolic role that removes them from their historical and social context so that, today, they can be used to promote the values and ideals of the jazz mainstream; in effect, they come to stand for what is to be considered authentic in jazz – their canonical works providing a benchmark by which current jazz should be judged – and, in turn, for what is included and excluded from the tradition itself. Where scholars have attempted to expose the ideological nature of canonical discourses, their insights remain firmly rooted on the margins of mainstream jazz culture.[2] Within the mainstream, iconic jazz figures stand as tropes for jazz as art; their internal complexities and biographical contradictions are often removed by more straightforward, positive and simplified representations. Indeed, negative aspects of iconic personalities or biographies are often stamped out in favour of a uniform set of artistic characteristics. Similarly, works that might well have been criticised or ignored during the artist's life are subsequently reappropriated to the point where the icon's output can never be considered as sub-standard or problematic.

Within this context, even the name of the artist can come to stand for a whole series of values that embody the jazz life, from Miles the 'innovator with attitude' as explored in the introduction to this book to Coltrane the 'spiritual master' explored in Chapters 2 and 4. In promoting the pantheon of icons as a central means of telling the story of jazz, advocates of the constructed jazz tradition frequently draw upon a range of cultural influences and narrative devices to represent iconic figures, some analogous, others contradictory. This lack of straightforward representation comments on jazz's unique cultural status and its continually changing aesthetic. To demonstrate this, we can observe how the representations of jazz icons are constructed today from a composite of historical and narrative sources: from the celebration of the African American hero to the romantic genius, mythical god to trickster figure. These sources are by no means mutually supportive and often contradict each other, and yet the narrative of a homogenous tradition and its celebrated icons continues to ignite the imagination and dominate today's understandings of jazz. In this chapter, I provide examples of the subtly different, and at times contradictory, representations of iconic figures, using the writings of Albert Murray as the starting point for discussion and analysis. My observations are not designed to offer a definitive account of the cultural references for the portrayal of jazz greats but, instead, I offer ways into understanding the complexities of iconic representation today. I explore the multifaceted and often paradoxical representations of jazz icons that form current mainstream jazz culture and suggest that, in creating a convincing narrative for the jazz tradition, all iconic figures are represented as an amalgam of narrative devices and cultural mythologies in order to remain relevant to present-day needs. Through examining the jazz icon from several narrative perspectives, I demonstrate how portrayals of individual artists can be viewed as a composite of influences that serve to support an underlying ideological narrative of jazz.

## The African American hero

Since the 1990s, the jazz mainstream has been dominated by the promotion of the jazz icon as an African American hero figure. Largely influenced by the writings of Ralph Ellison and Albert Murray, and more recently by the polemics of Stanley Crouch and the work of musician and *Jazz at Lincoln Center* Director, Wynton Marsalis, this model of heroic representation seeks to move the African American artist away from the margins of American culture towards the centre of American expression. Murray's writings, for example, have been influential in countering the stereotypical representation of black Americans that serves to dehumanise its subjects, treating them as victims, and offer instead a model of heroic writing that celebrates African American experience as enriching, disciplined and intellectually complex. In his early work, *The Omni-Americans*, Murray challenged the essentialist nature of racial debates and tackled white supremacy and black separatist perspectives head on.[3] Throughout his subsequent writings, Murray not only questions the restrictive nature of categorising people along racial and class-based lines, but also explores the way in which social science language is used to reinforce stereotypes, fuelling hysteria and the perception of difference within American society. For example, Murray suggests that the idea of a 'minority group' is politically loaded, as the term could be applied to a whole range of social groupings. Within the context of American social science, the term minority is only used to connote inferior status and illustrates the underlying political potential of language; Murray, for example, suggests that geniuses are always in a minority and yet nobody would describe them in the same terms as black Americans. In response to the political agendas of social science, Murray's heroic vision is based on the charisma of the individual, and their ability to raise the aspirations of people and to provide leadership in an age of moral decline. It is in this respect that iconic artists are mainly viewed as heroic; they inspire people through the power of their personalities and exemplary behaviour. As Murray states, 'Charisma is that human quality of inspiring people to regard you as their savior, as one who can deliver, whether them or the goods.'[4]

For Murray, great African American heroes act as role models for the American public, and the blues aesthetic provides a central means of understanding American identity. Murray is also keen to assert the relationship between the quality of art and the quality of human consciousness. In championing this position, Duke Ellington is used as the model American hero, as his music not only raises the standard of the African American vernacular to that of great art, but his life and legacy can also be understood as central to the search for 'the man of the period', a hero who provides a means of expression through resilience, humanity and struggle. Ralph Ellison also refers to Ellington in heroic terms, commenting on the artist's generosity and humanitarian qualities. In a similar vein to Murray,

Ellison views the icon's work as preserving American values: 'Even though few recognised it, such artists as Ellington and Louis Armstrong were the stewards of our vaunted American optimism, and guardians against the creeping irrationality which ever plagues our form of society.'[5] For Ellison and Murray, figures such as Ellington preserved standards in an age of moral and cultural decay. These writings have had a subsequent impact on both Crouch and Marsalis, demonstrated through their work within a broad-based set of activities, from polemical writings and recordings to large-scale documentary series such as Ken Burns's *Jazz* and the broader cultural settings of arts promotion and education at Lincoln Center in New York.[6] The combined promotion of the mainstream jazz tradition, with the continued celebration and emulation of iconic figures such as Ellington, and subsequent production of new works written in the blues-oriented style, have given Marsalis and Crouch the label neo-traditionalist. In his *Is Jazz Dead? (Or Has It Moved to a New Address?)*, Stuart Nicholson offers a detailed and suspicious appraisal of the Murray–Crouch–Marsalis triumvirate, devoting two chapters of his book to the Wynton Marsalis phenomenon and the politics of Lincoln Center. Nicholson suggests that, in drawing extensively on the blues aesthetic of Murray and Crouch, Marsalis is 'seeking to influence the future course of the music through an idealized representation of the past'.[7]

Although, like Murray, Marsalis emphasises the cultural significance of the African American hero figure, Nicholson argues that the strategy of mapping the African American exceptionalism of jazz's golden era onto the pluralistic world of the present has only served to broaden racial tensions in jazz, by celebrating the authenticity of black artists, and treating white critics as adversaries and white musicians as inadequate imposters. Writer Eric Porter has also explored the African American exceptionalism of Marsalis, Crouch and Murray, discussing their perspectives within the broader context of American cultural life. In his appraisal of the canon-building of Marsalis and Crouch, Porter acknowledges the way in which the promotion of the African American hero has served to create prestige for jazz in the USA. However, he also draws attention to the irony of promoting African American exceptionalism on the one hand and denying that black accomplishment is innate on the other.[8] This last point gives Marsalis and Crouch the opportunity to have their proverbial cake and eat it, constructing a limited canon and pantheon of African American artists while celebrating the virtues of jazz as a product of discipline, intellect, training and a subservience to the tradition. Furthermore, Marsalis has drawn from Murray in developing a moral stance on jazz and its ever-distant relationship to popular culture. Porter continues: 'For close to twenty years, Marsalis has argued that an erosion of cultural values has debased American society and marginalized jazz in the process. He has been particularly critical of youth culture, commentators who have sought to locate black experience on the margins of American life, and musicians who have strayed from jazz orthodoxy.'[9] In defence of Marsalis's position, however, the resistance to racial stereotyping that pigeonholes the black artist into the category of naturally gifted entertainer should be understood in relation to the social and political context of the 1980s and 1990s. Porter, for example, suggests that Crouch and Marsalis use the heroic image not only to challenge the idea that middle-class status somehow makes African American citizens less authentically black, but also to provide a means of celebrating black contributions to society during a period that was wrought with hysteria and threatening representations of black communities.[10] With these points in mind, I argue that Murray's African American hero has become a powerful image in constructing the pantheon of jazz icons. In this respect, the Murray–Crouch–Marsalis chain of influence should not be underestimated, particularly considering their involvement in the *Jazz at Lincoln Center* programme, international education initiatives and a multitude of textual representations of jazz. The ideological implications of these influences will be explored in Chapter 6 through an examination of the iconic representations of Duke Ellington and his relationship to the neo-traditionalist agenda.

## The genius

One of the main criticisms of Murray's portrayals of the hero stems from the fact that his writings borrow heavily on references and comparisons to European and American literary works that supposedly display universal qualities. Porter, for example, questions Murray's position of opposing white supremacy and Eurocentric visions of jazz while simultaneously invoking the aesthetic standards that have been used to exclude and marginalise African American culture in the past.[11] This complexity and apparent contradiction typifies mainstream jazz discourse, as the narrative draws on a range of cultural influences to represent iconic figures convincingly. While Murray, Crouch and Marsalis resist representations of African Americans having innate abilities, their rhetoric continues to draw on broader cultural associations that often serve to contradict their position. In describing iconic figures as musical geniuses for example, the representation of African American heroes is immediately complicated, as the concept of the artistic genius has continually served to promote natural ability over training and the structured cultivation of talent. With this in mind, the values associated with Murray's hero are reversed as the romantic genius is presented as god-like, detached from his social environment and in possession of powers that are intuitive and other-worldly. This anomaly enables the jazz icon to be viewed simultaneously as a heroic role model that transforms the sterotypical image of the intuitive primitive into a disciplined intellectual, *and* a mysterious, intuitive and naturally talented god-like figure. To demonstrate this, consider Marsalis's depiction of the heroic figure summarised in his description of the 'Old Oak Tree of Men' in his book *Sweet Swing Blues on the Road*. Here, Marsalis places Murray's hero within the context of the jazz tradition, celebrating what he describes as the limited few warriors of the past who have stood tall in an age of moral decline:

They are the direct descendants of the original jazzmen, here to proclaim the majesty of the blues, the jazz blues. Tales of old are exchanged not in words but in gestures. Soul gestures. Do not misconstrue the sadness in their eyes as a sign of defeat. It is the mark of a profound loneliness, the heroic loneliness of those who sustain an intense relationship with a reality so harsh as to burn the eyes of the unprepared who chance to look upon it. Look closer and you will see a timeless joy in these oak tree [*sic*] of men. Through music, they have touched divine intelligence, and that is their identity … They bear no fancy titles or fancy positions, they are called by first name or nickname or last name alone: Dizzy, C. T., Art, Klook, Papa Jo, Pops, Lil' [*sic*] Jazz, Sweets, Frog, Trane, Pres, Jackie, Elvin, Dean, Count, Duke, Monk, Mingus, Tatum.[12]

This preacher-like prose walks a fine line between Murray's hero and evocations of the eighteenth-century genius figure. On the one hand, Marsalis describes the 'Old Oak Tree of Men' as being soulful, somewhat detached from our lives through their loneliness; they have stood the test of time and have been touched by the divine. These traits would clearly place the musicians in the world of the intuitive genius whose autonomous art is divorced from the everyday world. However, to root these men firmly within the ideology of the African American hero, their instinctive behaviour is countered by the description of artists as warriors who spend their days and nights engaged in 'practice, study and reflection'.[13] Similarly, when the above passage invokes a sense of separation and loneliness, it not only describes jazzmen as being touched by the divine, but also suggests their isolation comes from a deep-rooted understanding of the pain and suffering of broader human experience. Moreover, even when touched by the divine, there is an emphasis on this being divine *intelligence*, as if being touched by the divine in any other way is not enough; knowledge, wisdom and intellect are emphasised throughout.

Marsalis's description of the names and nicknames of the 'Old Oak Tree of Men' is also quite telling in that it deliberately omits two iconic figures from the list: Charlie Parker and Miles Davis. Here, the distinction between heroic figures and others who do not fit the mould becomes strikingly apparent and is explained further on in the text. In Parker's case, Marsalis uses the word genius as if to detach him deliberately from the previous list of names with the following brief statement: 'Charlie Parker was a genius, was a junkie. He died young.'[14] Here, Marsalis's heroes are warriors who uphold moral standards and the legacy of tradition whereas the genius is flawed to the point of self-destruction. Parker is clearly a musician too integrally involved in the development of the tradition to be ignored or written out of history and so his genius obviously cancels out the fact that he was an addict, perhaps excusing him from conforming to the heroic standards of the 'Old Oak Tree of Men'. In Miles Davis's case, Marsalis describes him as a wayward figure, 'trapped in his own fame', who felt the need to change with the times instead of standing tall, unchanging, in order to preserve the majesty of the blues.[15] Both Parker and Davis deviate from the heroic model and so their behaviour is explained away either in terms of the flawed genius or the commercial sellout. In either case, the two artists do not serve the current ideological position advocated by Marsalis yet their legacies form an integral part of the jazz tradition and so have to be included, albeit distanced from the ideals of the African American heroic construct.

In broader contexts, however, Marsalis and Crouch have frequently drawn reference to the term genius to describe iconic hero figures, and obviously do not feel the need to separate the term from the general theories of heroism posited by Murray and Ellison.[16] Consider the following example from Crouch's collection of writings on jazz, aptly named *Considering Genius*: 'Parker became a colossus of human consciousness who could process and act upon material with a meticulous lyricism at any tempo. In his finest improvisations, you hear an imagination given the wide dimension of genius, running up a hill potted and mined with obstacles, but delivering its melodies with a sometimes strident confidence in their imperishability.'[17] In this passage, there is no conflict between hero and genius. However, as if to cement the vision of African American hero, Crouch contextualises the work of Parker by describing the artist as a disciplined intellectual, emphasising Parker's 'harmonic sophistication' and stressing the need for scholarship and development of a trained ear by stating that 'only in the transcendence of the difficult can we know the intricate riches and terrors of the human soul'.[18] In describing the work of Parker and other jazz greats, there is a certain irony in Crouch's writing as he resists Eurocentricity in a musical sense and yet frequently draws on the rhetoric of the European art world. To Crouch, there seems to be no contradiction between describing jazz icons as musical geniuses and comparing Armstrong and Parker to Giotto and Piero della Francesca respectively. As previously discussed in relation to Murray's writings, European values are used to validate jazz as art when the narrative context suits.[19]

In all of these cases, it is understandable that there are inherent contradictions in the way in which the handful of icons within the jazz pantheon are discussed. Indeed, perhaps it is more necessary to adopt the rhetoric of the genius in order to take iconic jazz musicians out of the realm of the everyday and instil them with an other-worldly quality. The jazz icon is more than just a talented musician, he is often perceived as having god-like powers and abilities that cannot be acquired by learning alone. As Penelope Murray (no relation to Albert) observes, the genius defies analysis and has dominated romantic depictions of artists since the eighteenth century.[20] Within a broader jazz context, iconic figures are frequently described in terms of genius, and the notion of defying analysis is found in jazz clichés to describe the music and personae of iconic figures. Well-trodden statements such as Ellington's 'beyond category' and Armstrong's 'if you have to ask – shame on you' serve to mystify the musicians and their music, and avoid critical insight. The rhetoric of the genius ties into broader cultural associations from Greek myths to western classical music and can be evidenced in the majority of biographical writings on jazz, sleeve notes, album titles and general conversations about iconic figures.[21] Although the genius is exposed as a social construct within disciplines such as sociology and cultural studies, the presentation of the innately gifted artist remains an attractive and widespread narrative device in western musical discourses. In jazz, the romantic notion of the genius suffering for his art is a popular trope, resulting from historical representations that have focused on destructive tendencies of musicians. Indeed, the majority of writings on iconic figures celebrate their mystical qualities, portraying them either as divine messengers (as suggested by Marsalis) or reiterating a type of Faustian mythology where geniuses achieve their other-wordly talents through Mephisthophelean pacts, and are therefore cut off in their prime, paying for their supreme abilities with their lives. The synergy between the jazz narrative and genius myths also stems from the perception of the African American musician as cultural Other. As much as Albert Murray's hero is situated at the centre of American life, there is still a romantic desire among musicians and audiences to treat music as detached from everyday practices. This romantic notion also perpetuates the ideology of autonomous art, where music is understood to contain inherent qualities that transcend time and place. Janet Wolff summarises the view of the artist figure that still dominates mainstream representations of iconic artists: 'The artist is seen as outside society, marginal, eccentric, and removed from the usual conditions of ordinary people by virtue of the gift of artistic genius.'[22] The ideology of autonomous art supports the construction of jazz's canon and pantheon where great masterworks are presented as unchanging, standing the test of time. Masterworks are felt to be governed by their own internal logic and divorced from the changing values of the everyday world. In effect, canonic works transcend the social world and promote the idea of great art as being universal. Iconic artists support this ideology by being portrayed as the Outsider, either as a special being, a misunderstood figure, a social recluse or self-reflective genius. Within this world, the icon is celebrated as a conduit for divine inspiration, the jazzman who lives beyond the bounds of society. Although Wolff discusses the ideology of autonomous art as a mythical concept, claiming instead that all works of art are indeed deeply social and reflect the values of any given society, she does suggest that the perception of artist as outsider has become a popular concept both from within and outside artistic communities.[23] For example, in seeking to develop a critical stance on society or a new perspective on their subject, artists will often adopt the position of outsider in order to achieve their aims. Furthermore, the development of industrial capitalism has created a number of mediator positions in society that serve to separate the artist from his audience, perpetuating the idea that great musicians are different from ordinary people. From a jazz perspective, the iconic figure is certainly presented as detached from the everyday world; from descriptions of Ellington within the Ken Burns documentary as 'not wanting to let anyone get too close', to Coltrane's personal quest for spiritual enlightenment, iconic figures are predominantly represented as enigmatic characters who see the world differently from ordinary people.[24] Similarly, mediator positions do contribute to the perception of jazz artists as different and in need of translating. Think, for example, of the way in which agents, critics, promoters and publishers mediate between artists and their audiences, or the way in which writers seek either to explain and decipher the work of deceased icons or to protect the way in which they are represented. Developing an understanding of the role of mediation in celebrating a limited number of jazz icons and the parallel development of a single, unified and linear history helps to expose the assumed implicit power of canons, and to question their supposed 'natural' status.

## Tricksters and myths

Given that the dissolution of myths and their ideological potential has been a significant feature of critical musicology, it seems strange that the celebration of mythical trickster figures has formed an important part of new jazz scholarship in recent years. Influential writings, such as Henry Louis Gates Jr's *The Signifyin(g) Monkey*, have been adopted to celebrate the discursive and polysemic nature of jazz performance and, in several cases, to challenge previous representations of African American icons; indeed, Gates's theories have been adopted by writers to explore the signifyin(g) potential of improvisation and to revise and resist Eurocentric representations of jazz.[25] Derek Scott, for example, states that 'Signifyin(g) transforms material by troping it – using it as part of a rhetorical game or figuratively – for example, showing respect by some forms of pastiche or poking fun by parody. The device of call and response is, as its name implies, an imitation of dialogue and thus … a classic example of musical signifyin(g).'[26] By aligning African American cultural practice with that of the trickster, signifyin(g) serves to subvert white norms by using parody, wit and vernacular language to resist straightforward representations of black artists. From this perspective, the trickster serves as a trope for African American culture, exploring duality of meaning and playing with dominant codes and conventions. Robert Walser's '"Out of Notes": Signification, Interpretation and the Problem of Miles Davis', for example, uses Gates's theory of signifyin(g) to challenge previous readings of Miles Davis's improvisations that suggest the artist was lacking in technique and virtuosity.[27] Walser argues that the majority of traditional jazz analyses seek to explain away the improvisatory nature of jazz by using methodologies that have been developed to evaluate western classical music. In this context, Gates's signifyin(g), and the broader theory of intertextuality, provide Walser with an alternative methodology for analysis and evaluation. From a revisionist perspective, theories of signifyin(g) have also been used to re-evaluate works that have previously been understood as problematic. Again, Walser's study of Miles Davis serves to challenge conventional representations of the artist and the suggestion that he lacked technique, using the theory of signifyin(g) to posit an alternative reading of Davis's performance practice.

Although popular with New Jazz Studies scholars, Gates's theory can also be viewed as problematic, as there is an underlying synergy between the concept of signifyin(g) and the ideology of the jazz mainstream. For example, rather than opening up the discourse to a plurality of perspectives and resisting canonical approaches to jazz, signifyin(g) can largely be understood as a theory that promotes the construction of an equally essentialist canon of black literature and music. Furthermore, as Gary Tomlinson states, the theory of signifyin(g) has the potential to reinscribe 'the same monological, hegemonic premises that have for so long supported the white, male, European canon to which they would offer an alternative'.[28] Although the concept of signifyin(g) could be regarded as essentialist in promoting the continued existence of a collective black consciousness and self-contained indigenous canon, the theory has worked well in supporting the complex, multifaceted and often contradictory representations of iconic artists, as Walser's study highlights. Moreover, writers such as Robert O'Meally and Krin Gabbard have explored the signifyin(g) potential of Louis Armstrong in their work, challenging traditional assumptions about the icon as supposedly exploited and manipulated by the white-controlled media.[29] With this in mind, theories of signifyin(g) work well in support of different incarnations of the jazz icon but, to a certain extent, complement the neo-traditionalist mainstream's desire to resist Eurocentrism and to reinforce African American exceptionalism. To demonstrate this synergy, Albert Murray invokes the trickster as part of his theory of heroism, albeit in a solely American form. In particular, Murray draws reference to the trickster Brer Rabbit and the briar patch as analogous to his heroic ideal and the idiom of the blues respectively. For Murray, the trickster uses improvisation, humour and survival techniques to get ahead, whilst the blues has a signifyin(g) quality in its use of, among other things, repetition and revision, stylisation and the concept of the break: a means of disrupting the established narrative rhythm in order to impose one's own unique personality.[30] Murray's use of the trickster figure again highlights the complexity and contradictions of the heroic vision, particularly when we consider the essentialising connotations of signifyin(g). Similarly, both Murray's writings and Gates's theories have been described as ignoring the issue of class, representing the black vernacular as devoid of class interests and distinctions. Finally, Gates and Murray both promote stylisation and repetition as essential ingredients in African American art and the signifyin(g) process. However, whereas Gates's theory celebrates the Otherness of the African American vernacular and places the trickster in opposition to cultural norms, Murray's heroic figure is simultaneously 'Other', as trickster, and normative, in celebrating the African American hero as central to American cultural life. When scratching beneath the surface, Murray's paradoxical celebration of the African American hero – from hard-working rational role model, to innate genius, to trickster – epitomises the way in which iconic representations continually combine, conflict and contrast.

## Jazz and the frontier

And that interaction, that perpetual need to create and to face new situations on the frontier, to adapt this to that, *that's* what characterizes American society. Of course, it was overtaken by materialism, and that's our big problem.[31]

Murray's words on the African American hero are also suggestive of broader cultural narratives where jazz artists are placed within the context of American ideals. Indeed, there are striking similarities between the way in which jazz icons are represented in relation to the jazz tradition and heroic figures are portrayed within stories of the American West. Michael Jarrett, for example, not only explores the quirky synergy between jazz heroes and cowboys in his study of Sonny Rollins's album *Way Out West*, but also examines the way in which history should be revised to consider the role of African Americans in depictions of the West.[32] Leading on from this, I argue that, through examining heroic narratives of the nineteenth-century West and jazz in the twentieth century, it is possible to develop an understanding of mythologies of American life and the way in which some Americans place themselves within broader cultural narratives. Within both narratives of the West and the African American jazz hero, for example, specific values and characteristics dominate representations of American culture, including the celebration of a pioneer spirit, rugged individualism, the commitment to equality and democracy, and an inevitable sense of loss and despair about the erosion of these values. Both narratives of the West and the jazz tradition have become nostalgia-ridden, longing for a bygone era through the romantic celebration of heroic figures. In writing about the construction of frontier myths and the American West, David Hamilton Murdoch provides some interesting insights into the creation of heroic ideals that can be compared usefully to jazz discourse:

Nostalgia for the lost wilderness and the end of the frontier became bound up with nostalgia for a simpler America. This did not happen by accident: it was engineered by a handful of key figures each of whom was a deliberate and self-conscious myth-maker. They focussed attention not on the West in general, but on the last, most recent frontier and, ignoring everything which did not fit their inspiring vision, they portrayed it as the arena where all the old values fuelled heroic endeavour – a world of chivalry, honour, courage and self-reliance.[33]

Here, the adoption of the mythical frontier as a narrative device not only provides 'key figures', such as historians and politicians, with a means of homogenising a disparate and contradictory past, but also transforms musical traditions through a progressive ideology bound up with the pioneer spirit. Nicholas Gebhardt has explored the relationship between the frontier myth and jazz in his book *Going for Jazz: Musical Practices and American Ideology*,[34] drawing on the writings of Richard Slotkin and Frederick Jackson Turner in examining the way in which jazz discourse has been shaped by the progressive ideology of the frontier. Through a detailed and sophisticated analysis of bebop and the music of Charlie Parker, Gebhardt suggests that, whilst the frontier itself has long since reached its geographical limits, the symbolic nature of the frontier retains a central ideological place within American cultural life. In shifting the ground away from geographical expansion towards a symbolic ideal, the frontier became less associated with rural and unrefined country and more closely associated with a general logic of discovery and expansion. This shift in ideological focus was necessitated not only by the exhaustion of the geographical limits of the frontier itself but also by the growing importance of urban developments in the shaping of American experience. Gebhardt argues that the modern metropolis became the primary site for discourses of regeneration and rebirth and, like the frontier itself, offered a dividing line between savagery and civilisation:

The impact of such a dividing line had profound consequences for the mass of black southerners and immigrants who flooded into the northern cities in the early years of the twentieth century, but also for the development of a black underclass whose interests and identities were inseparable from the industrial advances of capitalism and the rise of the American metropolis … Jazz virtuosity substantiated a modern creative consciousness that was, in its every expansion, reconstituted as a sign of progress and refinement, mobility and adaptability, authenticity and self-possession; in other words, the structures of the jazz act were internal to the progressive logic of the state … Within this schema, Parker was heralded as a model of individualized self-expression whose 'sacrifice' to the social dynamics of the capitalist state, seemed to embody, at every turn, the conditions for a continual rediscovery and reformation of the same state.[35]

Within this context, representations of musicians such as Charlie Parker feed directly into the progressive ideology of the state, mapping the frontier myth onto the jazz life in the metropolis. Here, the Parker myth mirrors the contradictions of the frontier itself in being natural and primitive or 'bird-like' on the one hand and virtuosic, technically advanced and civilised on the other. 'Bird', in this context, acts as a symbol for renewal, transforming jazz into Art. In blending the natural with the technological world of the metropolis, jazz becomes the perfect embodiment of the state's progressive ideology. Parker's music is both tragic and liberating, he is viewed as self-destructive and yet free; he lives by his own laws. As a genius figure, his life and music have been championed by historians as a landmark in jazz history – the shape of jazz to come – and yet, as with all genius figures, his life work has largely been detached from the social conditions of its production.

When considered in their broader context, visions of both the mythical West and idealised art can largely be explained by changes in American culture during the nineteenth century. As Wolff draws parallels between the ideology of autonomous art and changes in class structure, Lawrence Levine relates the cultural and economic changes of the late nineteenth century to the sacralisation of American culture and the pursuit of an unobtainable ideal. Levine suggests that the birth of modern-day capitalism served as an organising framework for the arts, not only in terms of funding but also in establishing a hierarchy of control that helped to shape both artistic content and the way in which people think about culture.[36] As with the ideology of autonomous art, Levine suggests that the process of sacral-isation served to create the impression that music retained unique and eternal characteristics. In promoting art music as a sacred experience, there was a distinct move away from the mixing of genres and a devaluing of all things popular. In turn, sacralisation resulted in a cultural transformation of arts institutions and professional music making; European values were used as a model for asserting value, a practice that, arguably, has continued to the present day. When considering these points within a jazz context, the resistance to Eurocentrism on a musical level might seem like a politically subversive act, aiming to reinscribe the music with core African American values. However, when considered in its broader context, the rejection of Eurocentricity on a musical level only represents a small part of the prob-lem of inherited cultural values. Indeed, I would argue that once jazz entered the established musical infrastructure of the American arts the music could not help but be affected by an inherited sacralised mindset. Within organisations such as Lincoln Center, it is entirely understandable that jazz is considered and promoted as autonomous art divorced from the changing fashions and whims of the everyday world. Therefore, even though Eurocentrism is resisted within the rhetoric of the jazz mainstream, the cultural infrastructure on which current jazz practice is founded is born out of a model that celebrates art as a sacred entity shaped by European values. This largely explains the complexities and apparent contradictions of Murray and Crouch, who validate jazz through reference to the artistic and literary traditions of Europe and the promotion of a canon and pantheon. Within these writings and the work of the majority of arts organisations promoting the jazz mainstream, popular culture is presented in opposition to sacralised culture, as something that corrupts and devalues jazz music.

Levine's work comments on the ways in which America's obsession with sacralised art is only a relatively recent phenomenon and, prior to the cultural transformations of the nineteenth century, art was arguably more pluralistic and devoid of class and economic distinction. Although the subsequent shift in attitudes towards the sacred has integral links to capitalism, Levine suggests that an overall sense of corruption and cultural decay played a part in creating the ideal of the sacralised artwork. This feeds into the broader fears of societal change witnessed in the late nineteenth century and early twentieth century, with writers from Matthew Arnold to F. R. Leavis despairing at the advent of mass culture and the perceived demise of a discerning cultural elite.[37] In creating a context in which minority culture was preserved, the religious integrity of a work became of paramount importance and the singularity of the artistic creator cherished. In effect, collaboration was promoted as the domain of mass culture and its supporting industries, from which the artist was to be protected. These attitudes became embedded within a range of cultural institutions, from concert halls to public libraries and, by the beginning of the twentieth century, there was a definite move away from pluralism and the vernacular towards the pursuit of an idealised elite culture: '[Elites] left behind them ... enclaves of culture that functioned as alternatives to the disorderly outside world and represented the standards, if not the total way of life, they believed in.'[38] Levine suggests that although the celebration of the sacred remained an unobtainable ideal far removed from the obvious growth and domination of mass culture, the influence of this belief should not be underestimated as it served to shape the standards by which great art is evaluated; from the sanctity of the concert platform to the evaluation of artistry in music education, the promotion and celebration of canon and pantheon remains at the centre of supposedly high-brow artforms.

Although Levine suggests that jazz's presence in the concert hall demonstrates a blurring of cultural boundaries and the definition of culture, I would argue that the rules by which jazz is governed within these environments remains unchanged. Ironically, rather than blurring the distinction between constructions of high-brow and low-brow, mainstream jazz culture vehemently upholds the model of the sacred in art, reinforcing the values of minority culture. In other words, rather than disbanding the sense of cultural hierarchy inherited from the late nineteenth century, jazz's place within the concert hall represents a shifting of the goalposts in terms of what is considered high-brow art. The current celebration of jazz is as a music of the concert hall, detached from popular culture; a music that produces individual 'works' by singular artists, a canonical art with a supporting pantheon of masters; and as a music that downplays not only the collaborative nature of music making but also the mass-produced nature of recordings. This provides strong evidence for the upholding of European/high-brow values; all lead to jazz conforming to the standards of sacralised art.

The heroic ideals celebrated in jazz discourse can be compared directly to representations of the American frontier and, in a similar vein to Arthurian legend, can be understood as a romanticised narrative that blends historical facts and events with broader mythologies. These heroic stories and characters are often created out of a genuine need to resolve cultural conflicts and underlying tensions, and to promote idealised characters with the qualities that society needs to see. In this sense, stories of the frontier and the constructed jazz tradition can be understood as part of the same cultural phenomenon. Both narratives promote a sense of a noble bygone era, a sense of tragic loss, a desire for affirmative action and a celebration of chivalrous heroes, be it cowboys or jazzmen. When adopting this mythology, the legendary figures of the past represent a timeless world that can be mapped onto the present. In the same way that the West has been described as a 'country of the mind', the jazz tradition and its supporting icons can be understood as largely symbolic: heroic figures that are larger than life and come to stand for a particular set of idealised values. However, this constructed heroic ideal can be challenged when the uniformity of heroic figures is investigated further. As Murdoch states in relation to cowboys of the American West, 'to insist that this epic hero have the maturity of a retarded teenager, the moral outlook of a Sunday School teacher and the skills of an assassin was bizarre', and it was difficult to believe that it was 'entirely coincidental that all cowboys were brave, uncomplaining, hard-working, laconic, reserved with strangers, hospitable, chivalrous, possessed of a unique sense of humour – and all dressed the same'.[39] Interestingly, the shared and uniform characteristics of Marsalis's 'Old Oak Tree of Men' are not too far away. Within a jazz context then, iconic figures have themselves become tropes for the idealised and romantic jazz life. Although varied in certain aspects of style and biographical detail, jazz greats are universally represented as pioneering mavericks with a deep-felt knowledge and understanding of the tradition. Here, the power of these heroic narratives often has little to do with reality, reason or logic. Heroic ideals are thus created and reinforced even when historical facts provide evidence to the contrary. Indeed, figures of the West are often heralded as great role models for contemporary society even when, historically, the realities of their biographies prove deeply problematic. Hamilton Murdoch, for example, continues to describe humorously the way in which former US president Ronald Reagan drew reference to America's pioneer spirit by citing Wild West heroes Wild Bill Hickock and 'Calamity' Jane as role models by which US citizens should live their lives. However, Reagan's romanticised rhetoric obviously did not take into account the historical facts that present Hickock as a 'cold-blooded killer who spent most of his time gambling and chasing prostitutes', whereas 'Martha "Calamity" Jane Canary was a sad transvestite alcoholic, an inveterate liar who was reduced to exhibiting herself as a sideshow freak.'[40] Here, the heroic narrative ignores historical fact in favour of an idealised view of the past, a past created out of the mythologising tendencies of writers, film-makers and audiences alike. Although jazz heroes might not in reality consist of cold-blooded killers or sideshow freaks, I would argue that their iconic representations are significantly altered to convey an idealised sense of the past, in order to preserve the core values of today. This can be understood not only in relation to Albert Murray's idealism, summarised in the quotation that opened this chapter, but also by the way in which unsavoury aspects of artists' personalities are often downplayed or written out of jazz biographies. Consider, for example, the problematic aspects of Miles Davis's biography; although Davis's latter commercial exploits are criticised for not upholding the values of the heroic ideal, his violence towards women is not dealt with in any critical or analytical depth within contemporary studies of jazz. On the contrary, Davis has come to dominate mainstream representations of jazz as quintessentially hip, an innovator with attitude. Moreover, the problematic details of Davis's biography remain largely untouched or undiscussed in relation to his musical output; we are encouraged to believe that only music matters and to ignore the vices of the man, even when jazz is promoted as a deeply social music and not an autonomous art. Even within the socially grounded writings of the New Jazz Studies,

Davis's outrageous behaviour and antisocial attitude are celebrated as key ingredients that make him 'The Man'.[41] This overly positive representation of the artist might well be considered a compensatory gesture following years of negative publicity for Davis and other African American icons.[42]

However, ignoring this issue presents a problem for critical scholars who seek to develop an objective picture of jazz history, and leads to a position where the masculine dominance in society is mirrored in the musical practices of jazz. As Ajay Heble states, 'Lest our appreciation of Miles's musical genius become naturalized in ways that allow his ill-treatment of women to disappear from the critical agenda, we need to insist that gender is a necessary category in the context of the sociocultural and historical analysis of jazz.'[43] When considering the gendered nature of musical discourse, then, we must examine what part of jazz as great art enables us to excuse outrageous or ethically unacceptable behaviour. The study of the relationship between gender and ideology is, in this respect, a central theme in understanding the critical dissonances of the music.

## Rhetoric and the masculine myth

[D]isplay in jazz is much more important than devotees like to admit. Especially for male jazz artists, the music provides a unique opportunity for sex and gender display.[44]

The multifaceted representations of jazz icons discussed so far have demonstrated the fact that iconic narratives are by no means straightforward and are often developed around a composite of influences, from African American tricksters and heroes to European geniuses or American frontiersmen. These portrayals are often typified by the way in which jazz icons are described or have chosen to place themselves within the context of broader cultural mythologies. Take, for example, the rhetoric that is used to promote or describe iconic jazz artists: the jazz narrative blends the regal with the godly, Greek myth with the American West, the primitive with the modern, the natural world with the metaphysical world, the refined with the 'hot' or the 'cool' and so on. In this respect, we all become accustomed to describing jazz greats in a number of ways that suggest a multitude of influences. Thus, it seems entirely appropriate for jazz icons to be described as Dukes, Kings or Counts at the same time as being 'tenor titans' and 'saxophone colossuses', jazz warriors who slay opponents with their 'axes'. Coupled with this, jazzmen are also American pioneers, mavericks who blow opponents away, 'cutting' them off the bandstand, or who 'woodshed' and then 'shoot from the hip'. The sense of frontier also has a synergy with the wilderness of the animal kingdom where 'young lions' develop or 'cats' and 'birds' thrive in their natural habitat. However, to counter the accusation of primitivism, soulful icons are also 'geniuses of modern music' who produce masterworks; they are also quintessentially hip, in giving 'birth to the cool'. Whilst I agree with Peter Martin, who suggests that nicknames and singular surnames are employed in jazz discourse to create a sense of intimacy between artists and audiences and to strengthen the feeling of community spirit, I suggest that nicknames and metaphorical uses of surnames also demonstrate the complex and potentially contradictory nature of jazz representation.[45] The analysis of rhetoric provides a way into understanding the underlying iconic jazz narrative and the influences behind the representation of individual artists. Consider, for example, the numerous adaptations of the names Coltrane and Miles that are suggestive of the pioneering frontier spirit; titles such as *Milestones*, *Blue Train*, *Traneing in*, 'Chasin' the Trane', *Miles Ahead* etc. have been used in a number of contexts to suggest momentum and progress, innovation and the pushing of boundaries.

When seeking to understand the range of influences, rhetorical devices and representations used in the construction of the jazz narrative, it is important to note that all manifestations of iconic figures serve to support the upholding of a masculine ideal and the preservation of a patriarchal order. In this respect, although the jazz canon and pantheon celebrate the contributions of individual figures by combining cultural influences and narrative devices, all iconic jazz discourses can be understood as gendered, whether viewing jazz as frontier music or as sacralised art. The jazz tradition is created by men, largely for men, and serves to present heterosexual masculinity as the norm and the centre of creativity. If Marsalis's presentation of the 'Old Oak Tree' of jazzmen is to be believed, the preservation of standards and the integrity of the tradition itself are an exclusively masculine domain, with the pantheon serving to place the African American male at the centre of authentic jazz practice. Within this context, I argue that heroic discourses – the presentation of an unchanging jazz tradition and the influence of dead generations of great men on the present – can be understood as forming part of the 'masculine myth', the way in which the patriarchal order shapes our everyday lives with naturalised and fixed presentations of masculinity. Anthony Easthope's studies of masculinity shed light on the way in which the masculine myth has been modified and transformed historically by capitalism to produce a gulf between the work and home environments.[46] For example, Easthope suggests that where the concept of work has been masculinised, the home has typically become the idealised domain of women. More recently, the masculine myth has been challenged, wrested from its assumed authority as a natural and unchanging entity towards an awareness of its fluid and constructed potential. And yet, when the power of masculinity is disputed, compensatory devices are employed by the patriarchal order continually to assert its natural authority; this is where the celebration of a naturalised and uncomplicated linear tradition and pantheon of jazz icons becomes a useful ideological weapon. To demonstrate this in a broader context, Easthope points to the way in which Hollywood films have moved away from subtle, self-assured westerns of the 1950s to the almost hysterical assertions of masculinity found within action films post-*Dirty Harry* (1971). The increasing importance of male iconic narratives in jazz is significant when viewed against this backdrop of the masculine myth, particularly given the music's lack of belief in female geniuses, or the largely untapped discussion of homosexuality in jazz history. When considering these representations it is useful not only to explore different uses of rhetoric in the construction of iconic figures but also to consider why jazz artists are represented in this way. Scholars including Sherrie Tucker and Robert Walser, for example, have argued that it is not enough to insist on the inclusion of previously disenfranchised voices into newly constructed canons. Instead, it is important to investigate and understand why groups seek to mythologise certain artists at the expense of others. In other words, rather than just studying the life and works of great artists or attempting to bring those who have been previously excluded to the fore, asking questions about why certain artists are chosen, ignored or represented in such a way offers more meaningful insights into the motivations or ideology of various cultural groups. Within this context, the need to assert the central importance of the hero figure could again be triggered by a dominant order whose values are felt to be under threat. I have already suggested that the sacralisation of jazz results in a need to purify the music and separate high art from popular culture. This need to escape from corrupting influences can also be related to the threat to masculine norms and partially explains why neo-traditionalists such as Wynton Marsalis have been keen to assert their masculine authority and place the jazz tradition firmly in the hands of men. Consider the following statement from Marsalis:

[W]hen I first came to New York in 1979, everybody was talking about fusion. Everybody was saying that jazz was dead because no young black musicians wanted to play it anymore, and because the established cats who should have been setting an example were *bull* shittin', wearing dresses and trying to act like rock stars. So when people heard me, they knew it was time to start takin' care of business again. I wasn't playing shit no one had ever heard before, but at least I was playing some real music.[47]

As well as acting as a polemical piece of self-promotion, statements such as these give a clear indication of the gendered aspects of the neo-traditionalist ideology. From the idea that real jazzmen *take care of business* to rock musicians being corrupted by *wearing dresses*, the implications of this rhetoric clearly assert some sense of a fixed and natural masculine order on mainstream jazz discourse.[48] Although recent cultural and critical thinking have challenged fixed definitions of gender, race and identity, the African American masculine ideal continues to provide the standard by which authentic jazz performance is judged. Indeed, even when the masculine myth is understood as a construct, it engulfs jazz culture and has a coercive power that shapes the way we think about the music past and present.

It is important to explore not only the construction of icons and their cultural significance but also the similarities and subtle variations in the representation of different jazz greats. Jazz icons are portrayed in many guises, each commanding their own following and respect. However, within the confines of the mainstream, iconic figures remain integrally linked to the social and cultural ideologies of the jazz tradition. When exploring contemporary constructions of the icon, jazz masters retain many similar characteristics with necessary narrative variation and all serve to endorse the linear (or causal) development of the music and its history. For example, jazz icons are inevitably male and African American, and each figure is supported by a significant legacy of work (or significant body of myth). In serving to endorse a homogenous tradition, jazz icons align themselves not only with the oral tradition but are also cast in the form of sociological 'Other', representing either non-conformity or alternative lifestyle (albeit a culturally accepted form of 'alternative'). However, when viewing the manifestation of icons throughout the history of jazz, shared similarities give way to distinct categories of iconic codification. Deified jazz figures are united by a set of common features but each is developed into a unique iconic form, commanding their own distinct forms of adoration and worship as if to keep the jazz narrative interesting and relevant through time. Within this context, it would be useful to develop a taxonomy of iconic representation along the lines of Orrin E. Klapp's *Heroes, Villains and Fools*, and Richard Dyer's *Stars*, or to analyse iconic representation in relation to more broad-based analyses of the heroic narratives.[49] Here, jazz icons could easily be categorised into narrative type such as spiritual master (Coltrane), majestic icon (Ellington), Faustian genius (Parker) or metamorphic prince of darkness (Davis); however, where jazz discourse continues to develop and change over time, iconic representation changes too to accommodate shifting values and musical sensitivities.[50] This is best illustrated through the changing portrayal of jazz greats such as Louis Armstrong, who at one time was represented as an instinctive or primitive musical genius manipulated by the white media and who is now most often described as a politically astute, signifyin(g) artist.

Like the inevitable canonisation of jazz itself, the dominance of the iconic masculine myth is unlikely to change. However, from a critical perspective, understanding the role of the masculine ideal and other related mythologies in the celebration of jazz and the construction of its iconic artists helps to overturn naturalised assumptions about the music and to identify underlying ideology. Moreover, this kind of study enables a more comprehensive understanding of the inter-relationship between jazz icons and the broader narratives of jazz history. To illustrate this point, consider Frederick Garber's comments on Buddy Bolden:

*Jazzmen* completed a process that had begun in Bolden's time, turning the barber into an icon that centered potency. By all accounts his charisma, an extraordinary version of which is requisite for any icon, was dramatic and unforgettable. Bolden's reputed roughness and vigor echoed the qualities of Congo Square, the processes of history putting those qualities within a figure who took on (as only single figures can) iconicity.[51]

The representation of Bolden mirrors the ideals of the jazz tradition and, indeed, his mythic story facilitates the telling, and construction, of history in more profound ways than any dry, factual account. This not only feeds into a call for a more detailed investigation of the connection between icons, mythologies and the narratives of jazz, but also highlights the symbiotic relationship that has developed between icons and jazz history. The increasingly significant association between icon and history should not be underestimated; the representation of jazz greats has a fundamental impact on jazz at every level, from the preservation of idealised masculine constructs to the control of historical narratives through implicit ideology. More than at any other stage in history, icons are now arguably the primary influence on the cultural ecology of jazz.

# 2 | Jazz and the disembodied voice

**Figure 3** John Coltrane, publicity photograph

Any new art, but especially one that is also a new medium, relying on technology to bridge distances in space and time, needs icons. For if the audience is being given something, it is also being deprived of something: a human presence.

Evan Eisenberg[1]

What irony: people originally intended to use the record to preserve the performance, and today the performance is only successful as a simulacrum of the record.

Jacques Attali[2]

If there surely can be no icons without aura, there may be no fabulations without icons.

Frederick Garber[3]

## 'Aura', recordings and the disembodied voice

Jazz has a symbiotic relationship with the recording; the music's past has largely been defined by the recording, with jazz history often written as the history of important records. As the principal means of documenting jazz, recordings bring regional musics to a global audience and have enabled the work of many pioneering jazz musicians to be passed on to subsequent generations. The recording is the primary means of canonising jazz, and it has afforded jazz a level of artistic status in much the same way that the score provides western art music with something to be studied and revered. At the same time that it instils into jazz a degree of cultural capital, the recording promotes the work of alternative traditions by enabling an oral musical culture to be transmitted from one generation to the next. Records transform the musical horizons of listeners by allowing great music to reach remote audiences, and by encouraging musicians to learn, imitate, transcribe and create. On the other hand, they fix performances in time, turning the fleeting moment of improvised music into something permanent. Recordings can also allow music to be performed out of context, creating new boundaries for what can be considered physically possible. From the perspective of the jazz tradition, for example, the portability and changing formats of recordings means that we can now squeeze an entire big band into a taxi, use Charlie Parker as an accompaniment to physical exercise, or even play along with our favourite icon, as with Kenny G's infamous duet with Louis Armstrong.[4] The advent of recording enabled music to be discussed as an object, and works that were unplayable in a live setting to be written specifically for recording media. Similarly, through the release of out-takes and previously unissued material, listeners can be introduced to 'new' music by artists who have long since passed away. By their very nature, recordings are problematic, as they are essential to the study of jazz, though at the same time they present a limited perspective on jazz history.[5] Within this context, I examine the paradoxical nature of the relationship between jazz and the recording, and discuss the impact of iconic records on contemporary jazz performance practice. I argue that recordings enable musicians to gain iconic status and serve to perpetuate jazz mythologies through both their historically mediative power and their role as jazz's primary documents.

When live music and speech are recorded, sound is detached from the physical presence of the artist, which, inevitably, influences the way in which audiences listen. The impact of this kind of disembodied experience on audiences of early phonograph recordings and cinema was profound, at the time when both were new media. Within the context of early phonograph recordings, for example, Edison invented numerous ideas for bringing sound, visuals and physical 'presence' back together again in order to avoid the schism created by recordings.[6] Similarly, in his study *Capturing Sound: How Technology Changed Music*, Mark Katz describes the strategies adopted by recording companies to counter the sense of loss of physical presence when listening to music via a gramophone. In particular, Katz explores the way in which early recordings of opera were released with miniature set designs and toy characters, the physical objects being marketed to encourage listeners to interact with the music and make the performance seem more 'real'.[7] These early reactions to changes in technology and the mediation of art proved to be one of the main drivers behind Walter Benjamin's seminal essay, 'The Work of Art in the Age of Mechanical Reproduction'.[8] Benjamin argued that the concept of authenticity and the integrity of art were being destroyed by the process of mechanical reproduction. He suggested that aura is destroyed when a work is placed into situations beyond the capabilities of the original; the disembodied artwork loses its sense of unity, displacing its relationship to an authentic past. Benjamin's use of the term 'aura' in this context has been compared to the notion of the autonomous in art, the mechanically reproduced work being interpreted as an object without a clearly defined lineage, a distinct presence in time and space, or a sense of historicity.[9] Benjamin's work has been regarded as double-edged in that, on the one hand, it mourns the passing of a bygone era and the loss of artistic autonomy. On the other hand, in mechanically produced art's destruction of 'aura', Benjamin acknowledges its progressive and political potential, providing audiences with a means of creation and recreation without the hero-worshipping or fetishistic acts of reverence found within the world of European 'high' art. Although very much of its era – the mid 1930s – Benjamin's text has been cited by subsequent generations of authors in the formation of theories on recordings. Indeed, Richard Middleton suggests not only that the discourse between Benjamin and Adorno (who radically disagreed with Benjamin's conclusions) has paved the way for a whole series of writings on authenticity, technology and the culture industry, but also that the critical issues presented in these studies are yet to be superseded.[10] Moreover, Benjamin's writings on aura, technology and disembodied experience could be said to have influenced a number of different critical approaches to art and music during the twentieth century. 'The Work of Art in the Age of Mechanical Reproduction' feeds directly into debates about the role of technology as a mediating force in music, for example, and the dissolution of mythologies such as music existing as an unmediated experience. Equally, Benjamin's somewhat utopian vision of the political and progressive potential of technology provides an antecedent to discussions of music not as work or object but as textual practice and intertextual experience. Benjamin's essay feeds into discussions of the star qualities of film and recording artists, and whether artists working within mechanically reproduced media can ever lay claim to a sense of 'aura' without being described as fake or bogus. John Berger, for example, uses Benjamin's work as a blueprint to discuss the construction of 'bogus religiosity' in mechanically reproduced art.[11] For Berger, bogus religiosity has a nostalgic function that masks the mechanically reproduced nature of art. He suggests that undemocratic cultures align the spiritual with market values and create mystique and aura in artworks that can no longer be considered unique. Within a jazz context, Benjamin's essay has been used both to evidence jazz's demise in the technologically and commercially driven age (see my comments on Ted Gioia in the conclusion to this chapter) and to explore the relationship between jazz on record and mythologies of autonomous art. The latter is discussed by Krin Gabbard, who argues that the perpetuation of the myth of jazz's autonomous status is largely dependent on audiences forgetting about the limitations of technology and what it lacks, at the same time as not considering the full potential of what technology has to offer.[12] I argue, however, that jazz is a fascinating artform in that it maintains a balance between what Frederick Garber describes as a combination of 'auratic' and the textual:

Sound recordings complicate the question of the definitive in precisely the same way that they complicate the authentic. Terms like 'definitive' and 'authentic' have to be used in special ways in conditions of this sort, some special to sound recordings, some of those special to sound recordings of jazz … However good the technology, these sounds are forever Other, irrevocably past participial.[13]

For Garber, the combination of records and iconic discourses makes jazz a complex artform to understand, in that it blends discussions of the authentic (or autonomous) with the mediated world of the mechanically reproduced. Like Garber, I suggest that mythologies (or fabulations, as he puts it) serve to define jazz and our experiences of it, and cannot be separated out. Recordings, within this context, have a symbolic role to play in constructing the sense of iconic 'presence' in jazz whilst simultaneously feeding into discourses that portray technology as the antithesis of autonomous experience.

## Four for Trane

I am fascinated by the ways in which recordings have the power to separate sound from the time and space of their original creation and how the loss of physical and visual presence impacts on listening experiences. I want to demonstrate how theories of 'aura' and the disembodied voice impact on iconic jazz discourses. I begin by examining the iconic status of Coltrane's 1964 album, *A Love Supreme*, and the construction of the jazz mythologies that surround the recording. This sub-section is followed by an examination of Coltrane in interview and on camera. I then use both Andy LaVerne's 1996 *Countdown to Giant Steps* (a 'music-minus-one' or 'play-along' recording and score set)[14] and Branford Marsalis's 2002 album *Footsteps of Our Fathers* as examples of products that are influenced both directly and indirectly by historic recordings and the mythologies of jazz, albeit with markedly different approaches to interpreting Coltrane. I discuss Marsalis's album in the context of religious rites and contemporary performance practices, including the notions of ritual and sacrifice in jazz.

By exploring four examples of recorded media associated with John Coltrane – arguably, the most revered icon in jazz history – I illustrate how records can both construct and deconstruct a sense of 'mystery' through an awareness of the disembodied voice. These case studies could be viewed as examples of what Mark Katz calls the 'phonograph effect'. This term refers to the way in which recordings influence both human activities and musical discourses.[15] Katz suggests that listeners use recordings to meet various needs and aspirations, and he illustrates how societal tastes influence, and are influenced by, the development of sound recording. By treating my four Coltrane examples as phonograph effects, I argue that, through the dominance of the icon, Coltrane's recordings acquire a symbolic quality that is greater than the impact of live performance; in effect, recordings have the power not only to disseminate jazz performances but also to shape our understanding of the larger tradition itself.[16] From the outset, it should be made clear that my observations are not exhaustive and only apply to specific recordings in certain contexts. I acknowledge that recordings can fulfil a number of cultural functions. They can serve, for example, as political vehicles as much as they can be fetishised objects, and they can mobilise and empower communities, or even serve as trophies for jazz aficionados.[17] For the purposes of this study, however, I limit my discussion to the influence of John Coltrane and the impact of iconic recordings on contemporary jazz practice.

### (i)  *A Love Supreme*

A good example of the synergy between iconic artist and recording is seen in John Coltrane's album *A Love Supreme*.[18] This album has come to embody the essence of Coltrane as icon. In some quarters, this release has even elevated the artist to the status of a divine prophet. This cultish, quasi-religious status of the album is particularly evident in the performance of *A Love Supreme* during services at the Church of St John Coltrane in San Francisco, and the fact that Coltrane's liner notes have been appropriated by various fans/fanatics as a blueprint for the spiritual jazz life.[19] Several writers have commented on the significance of *A Love Supreme* and its symbolic qualities, both in terms of the album's place within Coltrane's aesthetic and its subsequent critical reception.[20] Consider this slightly romanticised comment on the synergy between Coltrane and *A Love Supreme* from journalist Ashley Kahn: 'Coltrane's canonization – his sound, his legend, his wake of influence – continues to elevate *A Love Supreme*. The album is to Coltrane what a speech on the Washington Mall was to Martin Luther King Jr, what a mountaintop sermon was to Jesus Christ.'[21] Kahn's rather extreme choice of analogies is telling, and it highlights the way in which *A Love Supreme* has moved beyond the everyday role of a mere recording and has become a complex cultural icon. *A Love Supreme* engenders a strong sense of identification between listeners and the iconic John Coltrane. Moreover, the album's elevated cultural status and its associated mythologies give the illusion of conveying both other-worldly qualities and a sense of 'mystery'. There is a real paradox at play:

iconic recordings have the ability to construct a presence around artists that divorces them from the real world even though, as listeners, we are aware of their physical place and existence in time. The unique mystery of recordings has been referred to in relation to the music of John Coltrane, both pianist McCoy Tyner and author Bill Cole describing the magic of sound on record as something different from the sound of live performance.[22] However, I argue that this type of mystery is a social construct supported and maintained by the powerful iconic presence on record. This perspective is in accordance with various writings on the ideology of autonomous art that challenge the concept of music as a mysterious, unmediated experience. Within this latter context, iconic presence can be understood as an encultured experience, born out of performative rituals and the mythologies of jazz.[23] David Ake, for example, explores the promotion of the ideology of autonomous art in jazz through several interesting case studies. His examination of 'spiritualized eroticism' in the music of Keith Jarrett offers especially useful insights into the construction of iconic presence in jazz performance. Ake suggests that Jarrett's performances are codified to feed his fans' desire for a deep and meaningful experience. In turn, those fans participate in this experience through a shared expectation that something magical will happen during each performance. Effectively, these fans are primed to react in this way through the ritualistic consumption of Jarrett's music and associated paraphernalia.[24] Part of this 'priming' is provided by writers like Kahn who promote music as having an intrinsic quality that is mysterious and indefinable.[25] This is a hotly contested debate, as the notion of 'presence' as construct challenges so many traditional approaches to music; indeed, the mysterious in music is so often celebrated by its audiences as part of their emotional and social investment in the artform.[26] From this point on, my use of the terms 'presence' and 'mystery' are qualified ones, used with an understanding of the contestations and sensitivities of different communities of interest.

The overtly spiritual nature of *A Love Supreme* offers an obvious example of how jazz on record can become enshrouded with a sense of mystery. As a professed celebration of Coltrane's relationship with God, the album has had a profound impact on many musicians, bridging the gap between sacred and secular communities.[27] In recent years, the Coltrane estate has sought to protect the spiritual integrity of *A Love Supreme*. These efforts have served to promote the album as more of a sacred artefact than a jazz recording.[28] Kahn reinforces this spiritual and religious significance in the opening of his book: 'It's difficult to write of Coltrane and not sound heavy-handed. As enticing as the inevitable Trane/train metaphors may be, so arc the Christ-like parallels. The saxophonist's life of self-sacrifice, message of universal love, death at an early age – even his initials – amplify the temptation'.[29] Kahn's observations are not investigated in any more detail. By declining to provide further commentary on these loaded comparisons, it is a matter of interpretation as to whether Kahn's work reinforces the mystical and transcendent qualities of the recording and the prophet-like status of Coltrane.

The lack of an artist's physical presence on record has the potential to diminish the impact and influence of music, as listeners do not have a visual or physical form to identify with during the act of performance. Further, in jazz, the live performance is widely regarded as the 'real thing'; unmediated and fleeting, it is akin to Carolyn Abbate's description of the 'drastic' in performance.[30] Abbate's study questions the way in which traditional musicology discusses music as a form of objective abstraction. These 'gnostic' interpretations of musical works lead to an unhealthy obsession with the deciphering of the metaphysical aspects of music and promote fixed meanings and interpretations. The 'drastic' approach, on the other hand, subverts the canonising tendencies of traditional musicology and discusses music as a real-time event, devoid of objective abstraction.

In live performance, jazz musicians have the ability to dominate the music through both the mastery of their art and the power of their personalities. Given the historically privileged view of the recording as a medium for documenting live performance, the cultural and political status of the jazz recording and its supporting industry has played a subservient role and has, by comparison, been under-researched. I argue that the influence of iconic jazz recordings such as A Love Supreme can lead us to a position where the potentially negative reactions to physical loss are reversed. Both despite and because of the lack of physical and visual presence, new forms of mystique can be created around recordings such as A Love Supreme, channelled through the power and influence of jazz icons. Finally, the void created by the absence of live and physical presence – the disembodied voice – results in listeners wanting to reclaim the physicality of the artist through associated paraphernalia, and most specifically through the need to collect.[31] In turn, then, the listener-turned-collector has moved from Abbate's 'drastic' to the 'gnostic', swapping the text-like experience of the here and now for the 'work'.[32] Within the context of Coltrane's output, one aspect of this desire for collection manifests itself in the marketing techniques of commercial recording companies reissuing materials within complete boxed sets. For example, John Coltrane's *Complete Impulse! Studio Recordings*, released in 1998, is obviously designed to appeal to the fetishistic record collector through its highly stylised packaging and extensive accompanying liner notes (see Chapter 4). These luxury trappings encourage consumers to get closer to their icon through testimony, photographs and ownership of the Coltrane Quartet's 'complete' studio output.[33]

## (ii)  *The World according to John Coltrane*

Both Swedish radio presenter Carl-Erik Lindgren's 1960 interview with John Coltrane and Robert Palmer's 1991 film documentary, *The World according to John Coltrane*, offer good illustrations of the way in which the disembodied voice can draw attention to constructed iconic presence on record.[34] On first listening, Lindgren's interview, which lasts for less than seven minutes, has the power to surprise the listener, as Coltrane's spoken voice is something that has been rarely heard on commercial recordings.[35] Through Coltrane's slightly uncomfortable and timid conversational style, the listener is encouraged to receive the icon as ordinarily human. During the interview, Coltrane is asked to respond to questions about his band, his musical compositions, his recently released *Giant Steps* album and his jazz influences. When pressed about the latter point, Coltrane states that his current musical influence is Sonny Rollins and that, as he hasn't listened to many recordings of early jazz saxophonists, he would like to acquire more early recordings to add to his collection. This comment not only places Coltrane within the category of aspiring record collector, it also dispels mythologies associated with jazz icons and their place within a linear musical tradition. By acknowledging his own inadequacies of collecting and by respecting his contemporaries, Coltrane's words display the vulnerabilities and ordinariness associated with any living artist. Furthermore, when discussing the development of his performance technique, Coltrane draws attention to his 'bag of harmonic devices' that enable him to be taken 'out of the path of the ordinary'.

Coltrane's focus on the mechanics of music and the practicalities of learning in this 1960 interview can be interpreted as being at odds with the portrayal of the artist as the conduit for divine inspiration. From this perspective, the disembodied status of the artist on record can become shockingly apparent, and some of the mystery surrounding the icon deconstructed, as the unmistakably human Coltrane is laid bare, firmly locked in time. When listening to this interview, I was surprised by the degree to which I distanced the spoken Coltrane from the iconic Coltrane (as a saxophonist) I was used to hearing on record. It was as if I needed to separate out my two experiences in order to preserve the mysteries of performance. I acknowledge that within other recording contexts, the artist's spoken voice can add to the presence surrounding artists themselves, as an extension of their musical expressivity. My comments here should also be considered within the context of writings on the desire of audiences to understand and experience the 'real' artists. For example, the film scholar Richard Dyer has discussed the way in which audiences separate out their experiences of stars in search of the 'real'. Dyer argues that all appearances of the star, whether on or off screen, manufactured and constructed or otherwise, should be considered as part of a reality, yet he observes that audiences spend the majority of the time seeking to find out what artists are 'really like'.[36] In a musical context, the listener's desire to preserve the mysteries of recorded performance can also be aligned with studies of the aesthetics of rock music and the belief that recordings have the potential to be perceived as more real than performance.[37] Conversely, an awareness of the void created by the disembodied voice can add to the mystique surrounding recordings of icons. In the 1991 documentary, *The World according to John Coltrane*, live footage of Coltrane is initially limited to a televised performance with Miles Davis and to a television broadcast of *My Favorite Things*. While the documentary builds towards its inevitable climax – an extended overview of Coltrane's spiritual obsession, his opening-up to other cultures, his period of free experimentation and his death in 1967 – footage is limited to two primary sources: a silent home movie of Coltrane on stage, and an oral testimony from his wife Alice. Though these sources would seem in keeping with most documentaries on the life and works of seminal artists, the way in which they are presented is striking and unusual, and serves to perpetuate the mystique surrounding Coltrane. First, the home-movie-style footage of him on stage shows him engrossed in a frenzied performance. The sounds used to accompany the visuals are equally frenzied, yet the music and image are unrelated. The viewer sees Coltrane performing but hears a different Coltrane playing. This disjunction could be understood simply as a piece of creative editing with a limited body of materials; however, the use of this displaced material serves to reinforce the mystique of Coltrane's free and most spiritual phase, literally separating sound from body. Second, as if to enhance this sense of separation, the presentation of Alice Coltrane's testimony is equally mysterious, as her recollections of Coltrane are heard to the accompaniment of a freeze-frame video image of her in conversation. As viewers, we hear Alice Coltrane's testimony but see a frozen image of her in interview on screen. Again, this second audio-visual disjunction highlights the schism between the physical world and recorded sound; Coltrane's wife is received as a somewhat surreal, other-worldly and, because of the quality of the freeze-frame, flickering image. Both the Coltrane interview and documentary accentuate the impact of the disembodied voice on audiences. Whether iconic presence is constructed or deconstructed, the effect of non-musical media is significant in its contrast to the primacy of the relationship between recordings and listeners.

### (iii) Andy LaVerne's *Countdown to Giant Steps*

While having the ability both to lock events in time and to rupture the relationship between original conception, time, place and performance, jazz recordings have an additional creative quality. Consider the following points:

> Recording … returns to *musica practica* something of its primacy, because it encourages imitation; and this effect is also different in different camps. In jazz, recording played a crucial role in the rapid and extremely wide diffusion of the music; many jazz musicians who grew up in the 1920s and 1930s have spoken of how they first developed their instrumental technique by copying records … The aim of jazz is to achieve a sense of the spontaneous through sophisticated and controlled improvisation, to be a music which never stands still; the record is a means to an end.[38]
>
> [W]e seriously need to develop a more complete understanding of the syntaxes of jazz. One learns how to improvise by copying, note for note, a solo that had been improvised for the moment of the recording. One learns how to make things up by playing those solos repeatedly until their radical intricacies, their on-the-spot play of texture and intertextuality, get felt in one's musical bones.[39]

These statements by Michael Chanan and Frederick Garber respectively show how the recording has the power to make musicians imitate, providing musicians with a means to learn and play the music and instilling in the listener the desire to connect with or emulate the work of the player on record. Whether this trait is linked to the need to fill the physical void left by the disembodied voice with the listener's own physical self, or whether it represents the listener's desire to get closer to the mystique and personality of the artist, imitation is a crucial feature of the musician–musician relationship enacted through the record.

In this context, the typical jazz 'play-along' recording (in the form of a recording-and-score set that has excised the performance of the solo instrument) both encourages imitation and facilitates learning through recordings. For example, the play-along publications within educator Jamey Aebersold's extensive catalogue – the 'Play-A-Long' publication series – encourage students to perform in a range of jazz styles to the accompaniment of a recording. These types of recording go back at least to the 'Music Minus One' LPs of the 1950s and, as educational tools, cover everything from jazz standards to the specific performance repertoires of major artists. Students are encouraged to internalise the core repertoire of jazz, simulating the established conventions of live performance. Additionally, most play-along recordings are made by reputable contemporary jazz musicians, providing the student with the sense of an apprentice–master relationship and the illusion of playing within a professional setting. These devices encourage the student to feel part of the community of jazz musicians, learning their craft through listening and working alongside practising musicians.[40] A prime example of an Aebersold Play-A-Long product is Andy LaVerne's *Countdown to Giant Steps*, released in 1996.[41] This Play-A-Long volume, like the majority of Aebersold releases, features a CD as well as a booklet that includes performance charts and preparatory material. *Countdown to Giant Steps* is designed to encourage student musicians to master the challenging Coltrane compositions found on the album, *Giant Steps*. In the accompanying booklet, supplementary exercises are laid out to encourage the student to 'Train for Trane'. The booklet also contains an introductory essay on Coltrane's historical innovations and a discography of other albums (by other artists) that feature tracks included in the publication. The overall aim is to prepare the student in both mind and body before undertaking the task of performing Coltrane's seminal works; paying dues starts here. The publication offers the student a lesson on the historical importance of the Coltrane album. However, the focus is on the mechanics of performance rather than a celebration of the spiritual values of Coltrane. LaVerne has developed a practice regime for musicians in the same way as a personal trainer would devise a diet for an athlete.

Aebersold Play-A-Long books employ devices that encourage the student to step into the shoes of the professional, moving from imitation towards a position where the budding musician can imagine they are the artist on record. As suggested, by presenting classic repertoires and influential musicians to play with, Aebersold products obviously encourage students to suspend their disbelief and imagine they are in a live, professional performance setting. The *Countdown to Giant Steps* compact disc features the performances of respected contemporary musicians John

Patitucci and Steve Davis, alongside LaVerne's piano, and the accompanying booklet comments on their 'inspired performances'. The publication does not give the impression that this product exists purely for student learning. Instead, the promotional copy suggests that the recorded performances *mean* something; they can stand alone as jazz recordings in their own right. Furthermore, play-along publications in general enable performers to experience a kind of becoming through the stereo-filtering of different musical performers on record. Play-alongs not only provide rhythm section accompaniment for front-line instruments, they also enable the student bassists and pianists to phase out the musician on record, physically replacing the recorded sound with their own live voice. This technical aspect of the product not only enables students to place themselves physically in the *body* of the professional, it also offers the potential to give the disembodied voice a physical presence. For example, a student can listen to the performance of John Patitucci on record, enjoy his performance, imitate his playing and finally phase out the sounds of the artist, thus *becoming* the professional, and integrating the listener-musician's own sound with those on record.[42]

In recent years, writings on imitation in performance have been dominated by theories of intertextuality and the signifying practices of musicians.[43] To align Aebersold techniques with intertextual performance practices seems a little far-fetched in this instance, as the objective of the *Countdown to Giant Steps* study aid is to teach performers how to sound like Coltrane (and the rhythm section artists on the Aebersold recordings) through the embodiment of specific technical vocabulary. This form of imitation is a far cry from the intertextual worlds of jazz artists who seek to subvert dominant codes and signify on established convention. Moreover, the type of imitation encouraged by LaVerne's *Countdown to Giant Steps* is more akin to Richard Dyer's reading of the star–audience relationships in the world of cinema, albeit most often a star–musician relationship in a jazz context. In his book, *Stars*, Dyer explores ways in which viewers identify with cinematic icons both on and off screen, through relationships ranging from general empathy and self-identification (the belief that the star is expressing the same feeling as the audience member), to the desire of viewers to imitate or *become* the screen icons through forms of projection.[44] In jazz, self-identification echoes Neil Leonard's description of musical prophets articulating for the inarticulate, the way in which the icons of jazz can be understood to appeal to the inner thoughts and feelings of musicians and fans alike, feelings that can't be expressed in everyday language.[45] In emphasising this point, Leonard draws on a quote from practising musician Gerald McKeever, who describes his experience of listening to John Coltrane: 'I was sitting there, digging ... screaming ... I *felt* so much of what he was saying, I had so much I wanted to say to the whole world ... and *I didn't know how to get it out!* He was *my God!*'[46] Imitation and projection, on the other hand, are closely related, with musicians feeling the need to recreate the work of the artist in everyday situations. By taking the act of imitation to the extreme, projection moves listener behaviour towards a form of 'becoming', thereby not only behaving like but also attempting to *think* like the star. For instance, rather than wishing to sound like Coltrane, musicians are encouraged by projection to live and think like Coltrane – performers seemingly ask the question 'what would Coltrane have done in this situation?' Although not necessarily a widespread practice, forms of projection or becoming are occasionally linked to musicians' accounts of hero worship. This can be seen, for example, in the trumpeter Rex Stewart's famous account of his relationship with Louis Armstrong: 'Then Louis Armstrong hit town! I went mad with the rest of the town. I tried to walk like him, talk like him, eat like him, sleep like him. I even bought a pair of big policeman shoes like he used to wear and stood outside his apartment waiting for him to come out so I could look at him.'[47] Ironically, and somewhat counter-intuitively, by encouraging forms of projection in students, this and other Aebersold products promote the recording as the path to an unmediated jazz experience.[48]

### (iv)  *A Love Supreme* revisited

When examining a uniquely iconic recording such as *A Love Supreme* and the power of the disembodied voice over contemporary musicians, it is easy to understand how performance practice can be transformed into a quasi-religious act. The incipit quotation from Evan Eisenberg on the impact and influence of recorded icons goes some way towards explaining the way in which recorded jazz artists have the power to transform simple listening into a form of worship. The examination of music's relationship to religion and/or the spiritual condition is by no means a recent phenomenon. For example, the obsession with art and religion permeates the literature and aesthetic of many nineteenth-century European composers and philosophers.[49] In jazz, however, this sense of awe is at its most intense around recordings such as *A Love Supreme*, where the disembodied voice not only has the potential to enhance the sense of a religious experience for the listener, but also acts as a powerful vehicle for direct contact with jazz's most revered – usually deceased – icons. Whereas other music genres have been compared to both religious and demonic practices, jazz is often set apart by the way in which musicians and their followers display an almost compulsive adherence to different forms of religious observance. Neil Leonard has made the interesting suggestion that religious compulsion in jazz is born out of a need to replace dwindling faiths and belief systems:

Jazz is more than a passive flower, a glorious cultural ornament affirming humanity, it is also a powerful social force which has cut broadly and deeply, its prophets, rituals, and myths touching not only individual souls but large groups, bringing intimations of magic and the sacred to an era whose enormous changes have depleted conventional faiths.[50]

Indeed, jazz is the ideal breeding ground for a widely spread adherence to quasi-religious rituals and obsessive behaviour. From the fetishistic world of Japanese jazz coffee shops to the jazz fan's endless quest towards the definitive record collection, many proponents of jazz seem to collude in presenting this genre as an all-or-nothing pursuit. This unusual belief supposedly rewards its devotees with some kind of deeper connection to the essence of the music.[51]

   Rituals are not the only quasi-religious observances to surround jazz, and it is thus helpful to look at other forms of behaviour in a quasi-religious context. For example, the notion of pollution in religion – and its resulting feeling of separation or fall – leads to a continued search for redemption. It could be argued that the nostalgic way in which certain jazz musicians and writers lament the music's past (implying that nothing in the present can better the past) is a form of pollution behaviour.[52] Similarly, the notion of achieving greatness through different degrees of self-flagellation is a popular mythology for many aspiring jazz musicians, and this practice could be viewed as a form of quasi-religious sacrifice. A good illustration can be seen in the wood-shedding practices of jazz musicians. This practice is built upon the belief that this type of isolation and self-imposed constraint is the best way to re-connect with the purest essence of the music.[53]

   Having established jazz's potential as a site for quasi-religious behaviour, I want to explore how certain recordings play into these mythologies and amplify them. For example, Branford Marsalis's 2002 CD, *Footsteps of Our Fathers*, moves beyond simple imitation and towards subtle forms of projection that are unusual for the jazz tradition.[54] In this release, Marsalis lays claim to a spiritual influence that connects him to the icons of jazz history. His album pays homage to four seminal recordings of the 1950s and 1960s, including Sonny Rollins's *The Freedom Suite* and Ornette Coleman's composition, *Giggin'*. The most notable and substantial recording on the album is a re-enactment of John Coltrane's *A Love Supreme*. After this album, Marsalis subsequently featured this re-enactment on tour and also released a live performance of this same project on DVD.[55] In light of my previous overview of the unique iconicity of both Coltrane and *A Love Supreme*, this type of homage might arguably be considered off-limits to those musicians wishing merely to imitate or rework jazz compositions of the past. Given the symbolic and religious associations of this album, it would not be out of keeping to suggest that such a tribute could be considered, at best, in bad taste and, at worst, blasphemous.

*Footsteps of Our Fathers* represents Marsalis's stated desire not only to pay homage to the forefathers of jazz but also to embody the techniques, values and spiritual essence of their works. The album itself promotes the idea that by internalising and then recreating the music of Coltrane, Marsalis has, in turn, received some of the wisdom and spirituality of Coltrane in performance. The supporting liner note, written by his brother Delfeayo Marsalis, endorses this project, claiming that most supposed Coltrane imitators only demonstrate technique (presumably as promoted by Aebersold) and not Coltrane's spirituality. The claim is that 'all too often, the performers who are credited as "Coltrane clones", or "owing a debt to Coltrane", actually don't play like Coltrane at all'.[56] Delfeayo Marsalis further suggests that this is where Branford Marsalis has a connection with the icon that lies above and beyond simple imitation, resulting in sounding equally like and unlike John Coltrane. The liner note implies that, through sacrifice, understanding and experience, Branford Marsalis is touched by the spirit of Coltrane, bringing the essence of the icon's most religious work into a contemporary context. The *Footsteps* album offers a good example of how iconic recordings can instil in the musician a desire for projection, a need to fill the void created by the disembodied voice with his own, historically informed, body. At the same time, the product and performers move beyond the mechanical and professional techniques encouraged by the previous Aebersold–LaVerne example, placing themselves within the continuum of jazz history on a spiritual, as well as a musical, level. By taking on the most iconic work of arguably the most iconic jazz master, we are encouraged to feel that the presence of Coltrane lives on through the work of Branford Marsalis. I am not suggesting that all recorded tributes in jazz are either simple imitations or compensatory gestures necessitated by the void created by a lack of physical or visual presence – indeed, the *Footsteps* album could be interpreted simply as a homage to the jazz canon in the same way that many other creative jazz performances draw on models from the past.[57] However, I suggest that, considering the symbolic nature of *A Love Supreme* and the presentation of the *Footsteps* album as an embodiment of both the music and spirit of Coltrane, the recording cannot be considered a simple 'reworking' of a classic album, much in the same way that Gus Van Sant's *Psycho* (Universal, 1998) was considered problematic in its scene-by-scene reproduction of Hitchcock's classic picture. While I do acknowledge that this is only one interpretation, there are other, more obvious examples of this type of morbid re-enactment in contemporary jazz practice. These include the work of the National Jazz Ensemble in the 1970s and the work of later big-band repertory groups such as the Lincoln Center Jazz Orchestra and the Smithsonian Jazz Masterworks Orchestra. This latter group was formed in the early 1990s under the guidance of Gunther Schuller and David Baker, co-directors who subsequently disagreed on the level of re-enacted literalism in performance.[58] Although these repertory groups have sparked a level of disagreement about the obeisance to the past, I would argue that their musical output is not as problematic as recorded projects that seek to re-enact improvised solos note-for-note, or that seek to produce modern versions of historic recordings in their exactitude. For example, the recorded version of 'West End Blues' performed by the British jazz repertory group on the album *The Cotton Club Band Featuring Keith Nichols* re-enacts Louis Armstrong's famous recording note-for-note, from the opening cadenza to the inflections of his vocal solo.[59] Whereas historically informed performances and period reconstructions are common to the world of classical music, re-enacting recorded jazz performances in their exactitude, such as this example, can be read as moving beyond the bounds of simple imitation, homage and historical research towards a morbid fascination with iconic records of jazz history. I argue that these types of historical tribute differ fundamentally from historical interpretations of classical music because of the way in which jazz recordings can be understood simultaneously as both 'work' and performative 'text', with the traditional roles of composer/creator and performer/interpreter merging into one entity.[60]

## Coda: jazz past and present

Jazz recordings play a central and often complex role in the shifting relationships between today's performers and listeners, and musicians of the past. Debates about value underlie these interactions, whether they concern the canonisation of certain albums or the recording's role in jazz's industry of nostalgia. The relationship between recordings and the erosion of jazz values is discussed by Ted Gioia in his 1988 book, *The Imperfect Art: Reflections on Jazz and Modern Culture.* In his opening chapter, Gioia suggests that recordings have a dehumanising effect on contemporary culture. Quoting from the work of Walter Benjamin, Gioia despairs at the erosion of the human in music, stating that reproduction in recordings leads to a loss of artistic value in current forms of music. From Muzak and Minimalism to the proliferation of electric instruments, Gioia invokes a technophobic nightmare in which the mechanised world of reproduction creates a disengaged culture in which art loses its transcendental quality. Gioia's discussion of the dehumanisation of art, caused by the distancing of audiences from the artwork's creative source, can be understood as a direct reaction to the disembodied nature of the medium. However, as a jazz fan, Gioia qualifies his position by celebrating the anomalies of jazz and the music's ability to defy the dehumanising tendencies of contemporary music. In Gioia's view, jazz (particularly the recordings of Louis Armstrong) should be celebrated, as it preserves key artistic values from nineteenth-century Romanticism, such as the promotion of the individual. Gioia states:

After Armstrong, virtually every aspect of jazz thrusts the human element into the forefront: its emphasis on the individual soloist rather than, as in earlier jazz … on the collective sound of the ensemble; its fans' and critics' fascination with – indeed their obsession with – personalities; its continued use of acoustic instruments and its reluctance to embrace many of the technological 'advances' outlined above.[61]

Here, Gioia seems to suggest that jazz enables listeners to sample the values of music from a bygone era, drawing on the sensibilities of art in the nineteenth century. This position enables him to voice his technophobia while still displaying a love of jazz; however, the comments are deeply nostalgic and fearful of the modern world. In setting up jazz as a special case, Gioia's position can be understood as a commentary on his taste and values, as his assumption that jazz is resistant to dehumanising tendencies can arguably be applied to a number of other contemporary musical forms.[62] Within this context, we come full circle, Gioia's comments echoing the incipit quotation by Eisenberg on the power of the icons of phonography to instil a sense of value into new art. However, whereas Gioia's points make a special case for jazz, I would argue that his observations are overly romanticised. Indeed, we could question both his description of other contemporary music as dehumanising and also his interpretation of nineteenth-century values as having a positive influence on musical culture. Riddled with nostalgia for the past, his promotion of core musical values creates a situation where the beliefs of a dominant ruling class, and music's autonomous and transcendent qualities, are celebrated as the norm. Ironically, in certain cases, the recording actually supports Gioia's construction of a romanticised past. Rather than countering and disintegrating this dominant culture, I argue that, in extreme circumstances, iconic jazz recordings have the power to reinforce the outmoded concepts of genius, eternal value and mystery so often challenged by critical scholars.

Recordings can perpetuate the listener's desire for mystery in music through the simultaneously intimate and distant disembodied voice; they have the ability to instil music with new ritualistic practices, encouraging the record collector's belief in authenticity through reproduction (think, for example, about the oxymoron of jazz collectors finding an *original copy*). Records can encourage creation but the dominance of the icon should not be underestimated; in certain contexts, canonical works instil listeners with the desire to imitate and project, through quasi-religious practices and the reinforcement of the mythologies of jazz history. Jazz is routinely celebrated as a live, improvisatory, performance-based art. However, through the influence of the disembodied voice and the impact of iconic recordings, the music can develop its most unique and powerful relationship with listeners at the moment when the performer is taken away.

# 3 | Not a wonderful world: Louis Armstrong meets Kenny G

**Figure 4**  Louis Armstrong, London, 1956

The increasing dominance of a handful of jazz icons at the centre of a definitive jazz canon has, I suggest, led to a more clearly defined jazz community that is unified by a set of common, shared beliefs.[1] Within this context, the development of a sense of communal belonging is essential to the promotion of what I call the three 'A's in jazz: authorship, authority and authenticity. The belief in jazz community enables musicians and audiences to feel part of a unique club, including the celebration of collective identities or the affirmation of tastes in the celebration of canonical artists and their works. Indeed, modes of identification that create a sense of community among jazz followers are often promoted through the sophisticated strategies of publishers, record companies and documentary film-makers. I argue that the growing significance of iconic readings of jazz history has not only created a position where a number of works are viewed as 'sacred texts', it has also intensified the ritualistic nature of consumption associated with jazz. Ritual creates an enhanced sense of identification in musicians and consumers alike, uniting enthusiasts in their sense of community and belonging, and also serves to promotes the three 'A's and the belief in mythological grand narratives of jazz history. When jazz icons and their works are viewed as sacred, the ritualistic consumption of their artefacts (recordings, compositions) contributes to the music's perceived religiosity. Performers and audiences are encouraged to consume ritualistically, as performance, live or recorded, must adhere either to prescribed convention or types of solemn observance.[2] Whether applauding a musician's solo in live performance or listening to the latest reissue under the watchful guidance of an authoritative liner note, ritualistic acts dominate the production and consumption of canonical jazz works.[3] Essentially, ritual enables jazz to develop a sense of common understanding and shared values, leading to notions of universality, mysticism and transcendence found so often within the music's discourse.

This chapter examines how these issues tie into the close etymological relationship between authorship, authority and authenticity in jazz, and explores how notions of jazz community and identity can be viewed at the symbolic level. This theoretical model is demonstrated practically through a discussion of guitarist Pat Metheny's outspoken response to the music of Kenny Gorelick (Kenny G) in 2000, and feeds into wider discussions on the value of jazz, its authenticity and the music's relationship to popular culture. I illustrate the important role that ritual plays in the construction of value in jazz and, by viewing jazz as a social construct, I show how assertions of greatness often comment more on the context and position of those making value judgements than they do on the musicians being valued. As I argue throughout this book, the celebration and reverence of jazz icons is widespread throughout the music's community, with the work of a select few masters providing the benchmark from which the neo-traditionalist mainstream judges itself. More significantly, however, one way of measuring the impact of iconic reverence in jazz today can be found when established great works of art are challenged or tampered with, or when their authority is called into question. In this context, the close relationship between authorship, authority and authenticity becomes strikingly apparent, with contemporary artists and audiences being outraged by the slightest threat to the iconic message; the jazz master retains a centrality to the understanding of the work and, in turn, his 'authenticity' must be preserved and celebrated. The relationship between icons, contemporary artists and consumers of art is further intensified when artists who are considered inauthentic either lay claim to the title 'genius' through promotional hype or self-publicity, or appropriate the use of an established genius's material for their own artistic development. In some circumstances, violent reactions occur when traditional artistic hierarchies are undermined and, surprisingly, new allegiances can be formed between artists and followers who would previously have been opposed aesthetically. Overall, it is possible to illustrate how iconic worship in jazz manifests itself primarily through the ritualistic consumption of recordings.

## Authorship

Over the last few years there have been several works of literature and art that comment on the importance of iconic reverence in society. Most notably, feelings of iconic ownership and allegiance are intensified when both the authority and related authenticity of a product are brought into question. I remember listening to a radio phone-in on the BBC in 1999 about the controversy over the British racing novelist, Dick Francis. At the time, an unofficial biography had been published, which claimed that Francis's wife had penned the majority of the author's works.[4] Within the text, the author's wife had confessed to writing the majority of Francis's novels but was committed to the façade, promoting works as her husband's in order to give them a degree of masculine credibility and, therefore, satisfying the needs of popular fiction audiences. Whilst Francis is not recognised as a significant literary figure, I was amazed at the outrage and disbelief among callers on the phone-in, with fans feeling cheated in not knowing who the *real* author was. For some, the literary work's meaning had changed for the public once one author was replaced by another. Furthermore, to destroy Francis's persona as the authentic voice – he had been a champion jockey with extensive 'insider' knowledge of the field of racing – was obviously too much for some fans to comprehend. This is just one example that illustrates Roland Barthes's suggestion, in 'The Death of the Author', that audiences often seek meaning and understanding in works through the biographical details of authors.[5] The Francis case not only demonstrated how the personae of artists and their works are constructed to conform to the expectations of audiences, it also commented on the mythology of authenticity, exposing the readers' assumptions that only an author who had lived through the experience of racing could offer an authentic account of the racing world. Therefore, shock among fans was not only bound up with a change to the relationship with the artist, it also made readers feel uncomfortable, exposing the limitations of their tastes and assertions of value.

More recently, the work of the controversial Brit Art brothers Dinos and Jake Chapman continues to challenge notions of artistic authorship. The Chapman Brothers' work *Insult to Injury* involved the 'reworking' of a set of eighty rare etchings drawn from Goya's *Disasters of War*, where existing heads of victims on the page were replaced with heads of clowns and puppies.[6] This act of defacing a collection of historically important etchings set out to cause maximum offence within the art world, undermining the value of the works of a great master. As a work of art, the Chapman Brothers sought to use this project to demonstrate the inadequacy of art as a protest against war. In his article 'Look What We Did', journalist Jonathan Jones discusses the outrage caused by the Chapman Brothers' actions and claims that the defacing of a work of art is one of the last taboos of the liberal art world: 'to destroy a work of art is a genuinely nasty, insane, deviant thing to do'.[7] Paradoxically, the deliberate intention of the Chapman Brothers to shock, upset and challenge traditional approaches to art is undone by the way in which many of their works are received. Indeed, the anarchic deconstruction found in the majority of their pieces has found a committed body of supporters who revere their art in iconic terms, precisely the opposite of the Chapman Brothers' intentions. This neatly illustrates the role the icon plays within society – regardless of artistic intention or the authority of the creator, iconic significance and the revering of a work are found largely in the context of reception and consumption. In other words, when seeking to understand the significance of artists and the value of their works, the social location of a work is central; an 'authentic' message not only stems from the vision of the artist but also reflects the constructed ideals of community.

Compared to the problems of authority and authenticity in art and literature, music is an artform that further complicates and problematises these issues. The popular notion of the author as the authentic, sole creator of a work maps across most readily from literature to music; indeed, the controversy over the writings of Dick Francis could be seen to correspond to the way in which jazz fans ignore the collaborative process in favour of the singularity of iconic creation. In *Lush Life: A Biography of Billy Strayhorn*, for example, David Hajdu discusses the historical anomalies that exist in the working relationship of Duke Ellington and Billy Strayhorn.[8] Throughout Strayhorn and Ellington's collaboration, and following their deaths, Strayhorn's compositional input has often been relegated in status to that of arranger or assistant through compositional credits, copyright notices or promotional materials. Hajdu describes several circumstances where Ellington had been credited as the composer or co-composer of works that were in reality penned solely by Strayhorn. One example he cites revolves around the critical acclaim received by Ellington that came at the expense of Strayhorn's involvement. In this case, the influence of Ellington's PR specialist, Joe Morgen, in shaping the opinions of the popular press, was readily apparent, as Morgen reportedly created several mythologies based around Ellington as a solo artist and singular creator. On Morgen's work, Hajdu states:

These efforts coincided, significantly, with the readiness of the mainstream to accept jazz as art and a jazz master as a cultural hero. Still, an unconventional partnership of two such heroes – both black and one gay, 'composing and arranging companions', as Ellington described Strayhorn and himself – was clearly too much, at least within Joe Morgen's sphere of influence. In several hundreds of words of description and analysis of *Such Sweet Thunder* and *A Drum Is a Woman*, the name Billy Strayhorn never appeared in *Newsweek*, *Look*, or the *New York Times*. To the contrary, Ellington was described in detail as the works' sole creator … The credits for both *Such Sweet Thunder* and *A Drum Is a Woman* acknowledged Duke Ellington and Billy Strayhorn, but nobody seemed to be reading.[9]

This example illustrates the way in which collaborative work challenges stereotypes of artistic autonomy. The romanticised ideals of jazz history dictate that, as a 'great' artist, Ellington is the sole conduit for divine inspiration. Here, the ideals of art and audience needs are mutually supportive. In giving jazz the legitimacy and credibility of other established arts, the singularity of creation is of paramount importance in promoting the romanticised ideals of musical genius. Similarly, audiences seek to experience the genius first-hand, and to be in the presence of a special individual adds both mystery and value to a musical experience. In this context, Strayhorn cannot possibly be portrayed as an artistic equal as it would dispel the myth of the music's uniqueness and singularity. In many respects, Strayhorn's contribution is received as a quirky anomaly, an eccentricity of Ellington that reinforces our vision of him as an iconic figure and the stereotype of the unconventional jazz life. The canonical history of jazz dictates that icons are the sole creators of works; Ellington is the genius not only in terms of producing the content of works but also in nurturing and channelling the creative energies of others.

Although the uncomfortable notion of icon as collaborator can be mapped across relatively easily from the world of literature to music, it is difficult to find an example comparable to the Chapman Brothers' work in music; the controversy surrounding *Insult to Injury* relies heavily on the notion of a singular, original artwork and, in music, the understanding of originality is more elusive. As discussed in the previous chapter, parallels can be drawn with issues covered in Walter Benjamin's seminal text 'The Work of Art in the Age of Mechanical Reproduction' and the politics behind the supposed loss of 'aura' when works of art are mechanically reproduced.[10] However, when discussing 'aura' in music or the nature of mechanical reproduction, it is essential to remember that, in music, an 'original' is by no means a straightforward concept. This can be illustrated through the way in which record collectors seek out different versions of the same recording. For example, one of jazz's seminal albums, Miles Davis's *Kind of Blue*, is close to becoming a fetish item for some diehard collectors, and has been released on numerous formats, digitally enhanced, adjusted in pitch to counter the problems of 1950s recording and gold-plated to improve the quality of sound.[11] Classical music revolves around the authority of the score, yet works are interpreted and revised according to artistic licence and social context. Glenn Gould's performances of Bach's *48 Preludes and Fugues*, for example, are seen as completely different from Sviatoslav Richter's; however, we retain a vision of what the original work is regardless of individual interpretations. Though classical music has an original manuscript in most cases, the score is only used as a blueprint from which to construct a musical performance; music is a temporal artform subject to change from one performance to the next.[12] The relationship of performance to an 'original' is even more problematic in jazz, as the music is perceived and discussed according to the contradictory values of a fluid oral tradition on the one hand, and the fixed world of the recording on the other. However, the concept of the recording in jazz as 'original' is now a widely accepted principle, especially given the way in which jazz history

is both articulated and understood. In the present context, we are encouraged to talk about definitive recordings, authoritative takes and original
releases, without acknowledging the fluid and ever-changing status of
recordings. The ritualistic consumption of records, coupled with the iconic
reverence in which artists are held, leads to a situation where recorded
legacies are regarded as artefacts not to be tampered with. Paradoxically,
the intensity of this feeling of preservation is heightened by the growing
emphasis on reissues, master editions and definitive collections; products
that are designed to bring the consumer closer to the original artwork
(whatever that may be) and the inner workings of the icon's mind. Whilst
the majority of releases of this type are received almost uncritically, perhaps
not even considered problematic in their own right, the changing status of
jazz and the importance of iconic legacies can be seen clearly when supposedly 'original' recordings are tampered with in some way. For example,
remixes, borrowing and sampling from 'classic' tracks, do not sit easily with
those who wish to preserve the historical legacy of great artists; you only
have to mention Jive Bunny in the UK for people to realise how the musical
legacies of musicians can be spliced, reconstituted and, arguably, devalued.

   Current trends in jazz recording seek to establish aesthetic value in the
legacies of iconic figures and to transform everyday recordings into historical treasures. By using the music of Kenny G – perhaps the most widely
criticised and ridiculed artist in jazz – as a model, it is possible to gain an
insight into jazz's uncomfortable relationship with popular culture and to
explore ways in which recordings are used authoritatively both to create
and develop a sense of jazz community and individual identity.

## Authority: the problem of Kenny G

The number of encounters between diverse musicians is great but, of course,
there are many musical meetings one wishes had taken place but which didn't:
Pharoah Sanders with Johnny Dyani, Dyani and Jarrett, Art Pepper and
Jarrett ... However, the output of musicians like these is so extensively documented
that it is not difficult to imagine what such encounters *might* have sounded like.
A task for future technology? (Geoff Dyer)[13]

By disrespecting Louis, his legacy and by default, everyone who has ever tried to do
something positive with improvised music and what it can be, Kenny G has created
a new low point in modern culture – something that we all should be totally
embarrassed about – and afraid of. We ignore this, 'let it slide', at our own peril.
His callous disregard for the larger issues of what this crass gesture implies is

exacerbated by the fact that the only reason he could possibly have for doing something this inherently wrong (on both human and musical terms) was for the record sales and the money it would bring. (Pat Metheny)[14]

Geoff Dyer's wish to hear jazz performances between different generations of artists is not as far-fetched as it might first seem. However, whereas a scenario that places legendary jazz figures with contemporary masters might appear a mouth-watering prospect for Dyer and many jazz fans, a virtual duet between Louis Armstrong and Kenny G in 1999 did not have the same impact on guitarist Pat Metheny. Although subsequently withdrawn, the Pat Metheny Group's website published an interview in June 2000 that was scattered across the pages of the jazz press owing to its outspoken nature. The interview, which attacked the merits of Kenny G, appeared to the amazement of the wider jazz community, with Metheny – a well respected, open-minded and outwardly 'laid back' jazz musician – driven to outwardly derogatory remarks on the musical credentials of Kenny G. In particular, Metheny was outraged by Kenny G's 'reworking' of the Louis Armstrong track 'What a Wonderful World', in which the saxophonist overdubs his playing onto the original recording. The track featured as part of Kenny G's 1999 release *Classics in the Key of G*, an album of easy listening and jazz standards promoted as a mark of respect to the musicians who inspired Kenny G in his formative years.[15] 'He set the standards, now he pays tribute to them' is the caption displayed on the cover of the recording, sending out a message as to the significance and stature of both artist and product. The making of such bold claims obviously invited a large degree of condemnation and disdain from the jazz community, but surprisingly, the most outspoken backlash came not from a critic or fan, but from Metheny, a reputable musician renowned for bridging the gap between experimentalism and popular culture.[16]

Within the interview, Metheny argued that Kenny G should no longer be able to get away with such products and that, when placed in the context of the jazz greats, Kenny G would be exposed as a musical fraud. Whilst the resonance of this candid outburst could not be prevented from entering the annals of jazz folklore, Metheny's words touch on many issues that surround the way in which jazz is discussed and evaluated as a cultural form. Metheny openly acknowledges that there are things in jazz that are sacred, and the music of Louis Armstrong is 'hallowed territory'. Indeed, Metheny claims that to enable Kenny G to get away with this kind of 'musical necrophilia' (his term) is to agree that nothing a musician attempts to do with their life in music has any intrinsic value. Not wanting to let this 'issue slide', as Metheny advises in his interview, it is interesting to explore the possible motivation behind both Kenny G's 'creative' efforts and Metheny's animated response. Indeed, the artistic marriage between an established jazz icon (Louis Armstrong) and the often-ridiculed 'anti-jazz' icon (Kenny G) offers an intriguing number of possibilities for comment and analysis. Moreover, the outraged reaction of Metheny to this virtual duet offers a practical way into examining current assertions of aesthetic value in jazz as well as demonstrating how musicians, critics and fans use the supposed authority of music as a form of cultural capital.

Metheny's response to Kenny G articulates many of the problems found in jazz, especially when viewing the recording as original artefact. Whilst Geoff Dyer suggests a creative use of new technology, opening up possibilities for collaboration in jazz between artists of different eras, this type of experiment could only be contemplated when the collaborating artists are of equal stature. Metheny's problem has more to do with the fact that an inferior artist has dared to share the same platform as a master of music; essentially, Kenny G does not have the authority to perform with an icon of jazz history.[17] Whilst Metheny's comments are geared towards judging Kenny G on a musical level, many criticisms of Kenny G revolve around what he has come to represent as opposed to what his music sounds like. Take the following example as a typical critical response to Kenny G:

> The origin of Kenny's G is likewise subject to theories: that he only plays in the key of G, that he is the lost son of Matthew Gee, that he has a G-spot, that he was conceived in a Petrie [sic] dish from genomes, that when told a farcical story he nods his head and murmurs, 'Geeeeee'. The truth may never be known.[18]

Here, Gary Giddins's critical reaction to Kenny G mocks the credentials of the artist by referring to an interview given in 2002 in which Kenny G made a claim as to the origin of Charlie Parker's nickname 'Bird'. Kenny G had suggested that the nickname originated from the sounds that emanated from Parker's mouthpiece. However, this criticism of Kenny G's interpretation of the nickname 'Bird' is ironic when we consider how common this type of deliberation is among jazz artists and critics. For example, although not necessarily as far-fetched and naïve as the Kenny G explanation, alternative versions of the Bird nickname have been offered in several sources.[19] Arguably, these examples suggest that value judgements in jazz are arbitrary, often linked more to personality than to music; it's not about what someone does or says but about who has the authority to do it.

Regardless of circumstance and incident, the criticism and negativity surrounding Kenny G and his credibility as a jazz artist are ongoing and still incite passion among jazz aficionados. Yet, it is interesting to question why his music is regarded with such fervent criticism and overt disrespect. Throughout his career, the musician has been regarded with contempt by the jazz community, his works considered overly commercial and lacking authentic jazz traits. Although he carries the mantle of the figure critics love to hate, the global popularity of Kenny G is indisputable. The artist has over twenty-five albums to his name and is the biggest-selling saxophonist of all time; his record sales amount to a stunning figure of seventy million over two decades. Christopher Washburne points out that at a time when jazz is being marginalised economically, Kenny G's significant market share (he commands 50 per cent of sales within jazz's 3 per cent of the marketplace) raises the stakes in terms of its impact on jazz as recognised cultural capital.[20] Building on this point, the critical reception of Kenny G and his music reflects the way in which jazz has distanced itself from popular culture and aspires to high art status whilst 'authenticity' is constructed through the portrayal of a single strand of history. This cultural condition leads to a position where jazz performers who, on the surface, appear diametrically opposed are now singing from the same hymn sheet. For example, Metheny's distress flies in the face of his previous desire to throw off the shackles of convention and encourage collaboration and experimentation with popular forms. Indeed, his keynote address at the 2001 International Association for Jazz Education (IAJE) conference laid down the gauntlet to jazz educators, encouraging them to be more open-minded and amenable to change, stressing that artistic collaboration and experimentation were essential for the development of jazz. However, Metheny's previous refusal to be pigeon-holed, and his former embracing of different jazz markets, do not fit with his response to Kenny G, which clearly has more in common with jazz neo-traditionalists.[21]

In defence of Kenny G, and within the context of the global marketplace, it is entirely understandable for a 'smooth' jazz star to interpret modern-day 'classics' of the popular canon. 'What a Wonderful World' is not only a popular hit, it is recognised globally as a track that straddles the popular, jazz and 'easy listening' marketplaces, much in the same way that Kenny G's music does. It should be noted that, historically, 'What a Wonderful World' was not considered a classic in terms of Armstrong's repertoire; therefore this outburst can be considered all the more unusual, and representative of a wider sea-change where efforts of iconic figures once considered 'mediocre' are subsequently reclaimed and celebrated as works of genius. Here we have an example of iconic figures and their works being regarded uncritically as objects of devotion. And yet, romanticism and sentimentality are key themes that embody the music of both Kenny G

and Armstrong, appealing to the nostalgic tendencies of the global consumer marketplace. Further, the techniques employed in the *Classics in
the Key of G* album do not seem too outlandish when compared to both
historic and contemporary jazz recordings. Appropriation and reinvention
of popular hits have become fundamental tenets of the performance of jazz
standards; real books, for example, come to represent the standard for
mainstream jazz players to learn their craft. Indeed, the jazz artist who has
been seen to 'pay their dues' often has to demonstrate an idiomatic awareness of jazz styles, including a sensitive grasp of transcription, interpretation and quotation. This degree of reinvention has also been taken to
another level of intensity by numerous jazz artists both past and present.
The impact of jazz icons and their recorded legacies is evident through the
vast array of tributes given by subsequent generations of artists. This
reverence takes on a number of guises, from being true to the artistic
intentions of the original creator, as with Branford Marsalis's reworking
of Coltrane's *A Love Supreme* explored in the previous chapter, to musical
quotation or the re-enactment of historical treasures in their exactitude. In
this context, Kenny G's 'What a Wonderful World' aligns itself with
existing trends. On *Classics in the Key of G*, he states:

I am very honoured to be in a position to perform these classic songs for you, and
in making this album I hope to pay tribute to the great musicians who came before me.
Recording this album was a great learning experience for me, and in doing so I now
have an even greater appreciation for the musicians who played this music originally.
    And … if you like my interpretations, I would highly recommend your checking
out the original masters who performed this great music many years ago. They are
awesome!!![22]

These words, featured in the liner notes to the album, are no more arrogant
or self-gratifying than other jazz releases. Indeed, without the association
with Kenny G and his product, the text appears incredibly humble and
respectful of the music and musicians featured on the album, typifying the
way the majority of contemporary jazz artists revere 'great masters' and
attempt to place themselves within a continuum of history. Kenny G's
closing remarks, that his fans should check out the work of the greats, reads
like an advocacy statement for the canon of jazz history and echoes many of
the altruistic statements reiterated by mainstream, if less popular, artists.
Indeed, without the Kenny G association, the wording could be mistaken
for a Jazz at Lincoln Center (J@LC) programme note.
    Interpretations of Kenny G's music comment on the wider cultural
significance of jazz and its assumed aesthetic value as an artform. In this

respect, the Kenny G–Pat Metheny opposition provides a practical example of conflict within the jazz world and articulates the way in which values in jazz tie into our sense of community and individual identity. By exploring this situation in more detail, it is possible to understand the current means of assigning value to jazz and how conflicts arise over what the 'authentic' in jazz represents. Comparing the concepts of jazz as an autonomous artform and as a fluid social construct, it is possible to get to the heart of how value in jazz is ascribed. Notably, this comparison does not itself seek to assign value to jazz, providing grounds on which to decide what should or should not be considered 'authentic'; it aims to demonstrate how cultural objects such as recordings are used in the process of assigning value to jazz, and in the formation of cultural identities.

## Authenticity

In his article 'Valuing Jazz', Robert Walser discusses the anomalies that exist within the current environment of the jazz mainstream and, by exploring alternative ways in which value is ascribed, adds a degree of complexity to readings of the music and its social context.[23] Within influential social institutions, ranging from Lincoln Center to the United States Congress, jazz is now discussed as a music that deserves to be preserved as an important cultural artefact. Such positions obviously need to be welcomed in their recognition of the importance and historical significance of jazz as a cultural artform. However, within such institutions, jazz is often promoted as a universal and transcendent music, an autonomous art with the same romanticised ideals as western art music. In this context, jazz is celebrated as a culturally significant artform, its historical canon and legacy of musicians worthy of preservation and reverence. This situation is somewhat surprising given jazz's overt links to the popular music industry throughout history, and explains the neo-traditionalist agenda of trying to separate jazz from the popular, reinforcing historical divides between high and low culture. We can therefore begin to understand why jazz's links to the commercial recording industry are actively avoided in order to preserve a sense of an authentic historical lineage. As Alastair Williams has stressed, the overtly socialised medium of popular music has appeared trivial alongside autonomous artforms in the past.[24]

In order to achieve a sense of the autonomous and authentic in jazz, then, a certain degree of historical revisionism has occurred in order to demonstrate that the music has stood the test of time and has always been regarded as art rather than as merely popular music.[25] Attempts to authenticate jazz as art in this way are deeply problematic and ideological, rooted in nostalgia and a deep-felt desire to escape from the supposedly corrupting influences of modernity. As we have seen, this positioning leads to a situation where jazz is distanced from conflict and contestation, its tradition discussed as a coherent and unified whole rather than as a discursive and problematic history. However, the celebration of jazz as an elevated artform is widespread and can be seen most clearly within texts and education programmes that seek to align jazz with western art music, ranging from Grover Sales's *Jazz: America's Classical Music* to projects featured as part of the J@LC events.[26] Wynton Marsalis, Director of J@LC, offers some of the most strongly worded and passionate arguments on the aesthetic importance of jazz:

This art has had such universal appeal and application to the expression of modern life that it has changed the conventions of American music as well as those of the world at large … To many people, any kind of popular music can now be lumped with jazz. As a result, audiences too often come to jazz with generalized misconceptions about what it is and what it is supposed to be … Despite attempts by writers and record companies and promoters and educators and even musicians to blur the lines for commercial purposes, rock isn't jazz and new age isn't jazz, and neither are pop or third stream … All the forces at work to blur the lines deplore the purist ethic in jazz … purism is considered a form of heroism – the good guy who won't sell out – but in jazz that purism is incorrectly perceived as stagnation and the inability to change.[27]

In promoting this ideal, Marsalis seeks to demonstrate the cultural significance of jazz and acts as an advocate for the music to be elevated to a higher social standing. Through the celebration of its historical legacy, the creation of cultural agencies and the dissemination of its canon, jazz can lay claim to being 'America's Classical Music', distancing itself from other, lesser, commercial pursuits. Through discipline and the pain of study, the acquisition of cultural objects such as recordings, and the reverence of iconic figures, appreciation of jazz as an artform is achieved and the music's supposedly universal appeal can be understood. Here, Marsalis's aesthetic has strong links to the writings of Albert Murray and Stanley Crouch, and the legacy of the late Ralph Ellison. As discussed in Chapter 1, Murray's writings use jazz and blues as a metaphor for American life, including the celebration of the heroic (or iconic) figure who can succeed through adversity and deliver, as saviour, through his inspiration and charisma. However, as we have seen, the neo-traditionalist universal aesthetic approach to jazz contains many inherent contradictions that need to be explored. Walser, for example, comments on Marsalis's manifesto: 'Some aspects of Marsalis's criticism seem contradictory: he is quick to decry the "aesthetic piggybacking" of those who incorrectly call their music "jazz", although he himself works to make jazz seem "classical" … Marsalis argues that jazz has universal appeal, yet he views music that actually has been popular with great suspicion.'[28] These contradictions about jazz's supposed universality sit neatly alongside Pat Metheny's outburst, as Marsalis's understanding of jazz would certainly not include the white, commercial-marketplace-oriented, global phenomenon of Kenny G. The contradictions identified in Marsalis's statements extend to the conflict between understanding jazz as a universal artform, accessible and open to everyone who devotes time and energy to playing it, and the celebration of authentic practice in music. Furthermore, as writers such as Walser, Scott DeVeaux and Stuart Nicholson suggest, the concept of authenticity can be viewed as being at odds with universality. For neo-traditionalists, authenticity in jazz is specific, focusing on a particular linearity and the promotion of African American exceptionalism; universality, on the other hand, is perceived as open to all.[29] From the perspective of universality, Kenny G's music could be seen to represent the global embodiment of jazz as a cross-cultural signifier, whereas, from a neo-traditionalist standpoint, the musician epitomises everything that is inauthentic; Kenny G is criticised for being uncool, too self-indulgent and overtly commercial. Furthermore, the music does not necessarily dictate that it needs to be studied in order to be understood, it is not about raising the aesthetic standards of jazz; functionality or 'use value' lies at the heart of Kenny G's music. When placed within the context of neo-traditionalist mythologies, Kenny G can be instantly discredited for not 'paying his dues' or working with reputable jazz sidemen. Indeed, when Kenny G has chosen to record with more reputable jazz artists, he has been described as a poor imitator; Metheny, for example, describes Kenny G as an inferior version of Grover Washington and David Sanborn, and claims that he was 'blown off the stage' by Jeff Lorber earlier in his career. Metheny is keen to place Kenny G within the framework of jazz and judge him by the standards of other jazz musicians. However, whilst Metheny is distressed at the concept of G's playing with Armstrong, it is interesting to observe the lack of discussion about the contribution of George Benson to the opening track of the *Classics* album or Bebel Gilberto's singing on 'The Girl from Ipanema'. Essentially, any potential positive artistic merit is ignored owing to Kenny G's lack of authenticity. With this in mind, Metheny's desire to judge him by the standards of the jazz community raises many questions and anomalies, especially when considering the roles both third-party endorsement and the alignment with established icons play in giving jazz musicians an air of credibility.

However, the comments surrounding community and standards rely on two fundamental assumptions: that there is such a thing as a tangible jazz community and that, within this community, there are identifiable standards by which Kenny G can be judged. These assumptions are surprising given the contradictions that appear within discussions on jazz and the ascribing of value. One such contradiction can be seen in the way in which the commercial success of a product is used either for endorsement or criticism, depending on context. Consider, for example, the way in which the record sales of an album such as Miles Davis's *Kind of Blue* are used as an indicator of artistic merit and musical genius, whereas in the case of Kenny G, commercialism is used to discredit his artistic credibility. This emphasises the fact that inherent musical attributes are secondary to the types of cultural positioning, identification and negotiation that occur within certain groups. These complexities and, at times, arbitrary judgements form the basis of how jazz is valued and understood, and also demonstrate the problematic and contradictory nature of discussing jazz authenticity and the promotion of inherent, supposedly objective, standards. Leading on from this, it is interesting to challenge underlying assumptions associated with jazz authenticity by viewing jazz as a social construct.

The commercial success of Kenny G's music presents neo-traditionalists with obvious problems, leading them to perpetuate established oppositions between art and 'popular culture' and promote jazz as aesthetically autonomous. However, these perspectives inevitably ignore the fact that Kenny G's music has a widespread and undeniable use value: in hotel lobbies, as elevator accessory, as an accompaniment to dining or as the soundtrack to love-making – the *function* of Kenny G's music is clearly recognisable. Moreover, as I suggested above, the negative reception of Kenny G within the jazz press is often concerned less with his musical product than with what the artist represents; Kenny G's music is considered bad through attacks on his character and public persona, not on the evaluation of his music. Indeed, critics find it uncomfortable to judge Kenny G's music without entering into some form of elitist positioning, promoting aesthetic appeal over popular functionality. This type of response demonstrates that value in jazz is largely constructed away from musical content and emphasises that, contrary to popular portrayals, our sense of what jazz is – and, perhaps more importantly, isn't – is socially located and subject to change according to the dominant values of a particular social order. As Krin Gabbard suggests, the notion of a 'jazz history' has as much to do with changing marketplace, writings on the subject and ideology as it does with the production of 'pure' musical masterpieces.[30] When viewing jazz in this way, we can understand that values and meanings have shifted through time to the extent where the word 'jazz' has broadened out to mean a number of things depending on context and cultural position. In this respect, jazz as 'construct' should not necessarily be defined only by those who set out to perform the music but also by the way in which the music is received and interpreted. Arguably, if the marketplace, or the dominant values of a particular social order, dictate that something is jazz, then there is a strong chance that the music will be regarded as such. To illustrate this point consider Wynton Marsalis's take on the programming strategies of jazz festival organisers: 'I recently completed a tour of jazz festivals in Europe in which only two out of 10 bands were jazz bands. The promoters of these festivals readily admit most of the music isn't jazz, but refuse to rename these events "music festivals", seeking the esthetic elevation that jazz offers.'[31] Here, Marsalis remains committed to a sense of inherent qualities in jazz and the aesthetic purity of the neo-traditionalist agenda. In contrast to this approach, I attended a forum of jazz festival organisers in Toronto in 2003 where the notion of the music's supposedly inherent qualities was challenged directly in a debate about whether Van Morrison and other 'popular' performers should be included as part of jazz festival programmes.[32] The panel, consisting of festival directors from significant Canadian jazz festivals, discussed this and continued to emphasise the fact that the marketplace dictates what jazz is. The promoters demonstrated an acute awareness of the socially constructed nature of music, stressing that if they programmed artists within a festival setting as 'jazz', for the duration of the festival (and perhaps beyond), the music would be understood as jazz.[33]

In view of this, any definition of jazz needs to encompass the broader significations that exist within an eclectic cultural climate. Shifting definitions of jazz are not only created through a blurring of distinction between established cultural boundaries; there are also many historical precedents that highlight conflict and ideology in the struggle for ownership of jazz. Bernard Gendron's article on the opposition between 'moldy figs' and modernists in the 1930s and 1940s comments on the way in which jazz, as a term, has had a far from straightforward and linear development.[34] Alan Stanbridge builds on this by challenging the notion of the authentic, linear and romanticised view of jazz history as offered by Ken Burns and Wynton Marsalis:

[T]he discursive shifts in the understanding of 'jazz' – from a 'folk' music to a 'popular' music to an 'art' music – have been neither linear nor categorical, and the discursive confusion of the 1930s and 1940s only intensified as jazz continued to expand its musical influences and resources throughout the latter part of the twentieth century, with the various discourses continuing to co-exist and clash in an often jarring and confusing manner.[35]

Both commentaries illustrate that changing cultural landscapes lead to a shifting definition of jazz. As a continually shifting cultural signifier, jazz history can be considered a site for contestation and discursive opposition. In the current dominance of the neo-traditionalist agenda – from the formation of the jazz canon to the celebration of iconic legacies – historical complexity, struggle and contradiction are often eradicated in favour of linear narratives and the myth of authenticity.

## Community, identity and ritual

Cultists demand stylistic purity of their idols and shun listeners who accept tainted music or musicians. For the most part, however, they readily tolerate other belief systems – including those of other art forms (including modern classical music) or religions (Christianity, Judaism, Islam, as well as more exotic faiths) – so long as they do not threaten the jazz life. Moreover, jazz cults, untroubled by most kinds of deviance or odd behavior, condone or even encourage them so long as they do not interfere with music or its devotions. The cult asks only that believers revere the proper music, idols, and objects, and in some instances follow tacitly approved practices of dress, vocabulary, and association.[36]

### Community

When adopting the position of jazz as construct, the belief in both an inherent aesthetic and an enduring musical description of 'jazz' is disbanded alongside other widely held assumptions such as an easily definable jazz community. The notion of a discrete jazz community, encompassing musicians, scholars and enthusiasts, has formed the basis of several studies throughout the music's history.[37] However, when searching for a tangible means of identifying jazz community, I argue that *community essence* can be viewed as largely symbolic. In other words, jazz community has as much to do with the way in which we see the world as it does with any physical or structured allegiance. Peter J. Martin promotes this sociological approach to community in challenging the stereotypical concept of jazz as a form of deviant subculture.[38] Martin suggests that, instead of jazz community existing as a fixed entity, people come to share symbolic representations of the music and musicians, and accept common values and narratives of history to suit their own needs and aspirations. In effect, a 'community of interest' is created where people place themselves in imagined narratives, with jazz taking centre stage. At a time when sociologists argue that consumption plays a major part in the construction of identities, canonical jazz provides people with a sense of stability, an identification with the values of the past. Martin comments: 'In such a situation, it is hardly surprising that an involvement with the works of Charlie Parker or Duke Ellington may provide individuals with long-term satisfactions, and a sense of security, that other areas of social life can no longer supply.'[39] Symbolic identification results in audiences feeling part of an imagined narrative or community. Martin suggests that this is why jazz people often refer to musicians by their first names even if they have never met, or talk about jazz icons as 'Bird', 'Diz' and 'Trane' even if they are born outside the musicians' lifetimes. Anthony Cohen builds on this concept:

[C]ulture – the community as experienced by its members – does not consist in social structure or in 'the doing' of social behaviour. It inheres, rather, in 'the thinking' about it. It is in this sense that we can speak of the community as a symbolic, rather than a structural, construct. In seeking to understand the phenomenon of community we have to regard its constituent social relations as repositories of meaning for its members, not as a set of mechanical linkages … Community exists in the minds of its members, and should not be confused with geographic or sociographic assertions of 'fact'. By extension, the distinctiveness of communities and, thus, the reality of their boundaries, similarly lies in the mind, in the meanings which people attach to them, not in their structural forms.[40]

Whilst community can be viewed as largely symbolic, our sense of belonging and affiliation to communities creates intense feelings that are far from imaginary, as Metheny's comments on Kenny G reiterate. However, by following both Martin's and Cohen's observations of community existing more at the symbolic level than within any physical or structural boundaries, it is important to examine how the feeling of community is created and developed in parallel with our sense of identity.

### Identity

Identity is a concept that surrounds most critical discussions on jazz and popular music and yet remains one of the most elusive, problematic and difficult subjects to tie down. As a topic for discussion, it is difficult to talk about without entering into considerations of community and ritual, alongside wider considerations about the part cultural mythologies play in our lives. I argue that identity has integral links to community, ritual and myth, and has become a central topic of discussion for cultural and critical theorists. Within a jazz context, identity remains a central issue for scholars not only because the strength of music lies in its ability to create an intense feeling of belonging – people obviously feel passionate about their association with musicians and fans – but also because it plays a key role in the way in which musicians and fans both represent themselves and are represented in society.[41] Identity is most often discussed alongside the concept of identification because in order to understand the nature of the self, or the subject, we have to think about the way in which we relate to the world and each other. In other words, in order to understand ourselves, we are inevitably measured against the norms of society or dominant modes of behaviour; this is where identity and identification become inseparable. Therefore, we must consider that identity can be considered, on the one hand, an abstracted individualised entity bound up with the self and, simultaneously, to do with how we relate to the world. Most cultural and critical theorists today refute the idea that identity can exist outside cultural discourse in some pure abstracted form.[42] Stuart Hall questions the assumption that there is some stable core of the self that forms an essential part of who we are and, instead, suggests that, in modern times, identities are never unified.[43] Therefore, we can no longer understand identity as something fixed and permanent; instead, identity is to be found within discourse, as a means of exploring, affirming and celebrating relationships and measuring ourselves against others. Here, we change and adapt our identities according to the contexts we find ourselves in and, even when we remain in the same situations, our identity is being continually appraised and renegotiated. Identity, in effect, is about how we situate ourselves in the world; it is not where we have come from but about how we would like to portray ourselves. In order to function within discourse, a certain narrativisation needs to take place where the subject situates him or herself in a cultural story – we construct narratives about who we are and why we do the things we do in order to make sense of the world around us, our movement from past to present and our relationships with others. Identity, therefore, is dependent on narrativisation and helps to explain our place in the world. There are clear links here to discussions and critiques of history – the common assumption about history is that it is born out of lived experience and is unchanging; history is in the past and tells a singular unique story. However, historiography discusses the difference between history as lived and history as represented. In other words, our telling of the story of history continually changes to suit our current desires, aspirations and values. With this in mind, books are revised, significant characters of one generation are written out to make way for the heroes of the next and, yet, the notion of history as an unchanging edifice remains resolute.

Like history, then, identity says more about who we want to be and how we relate to the world than it does about any essential core. However, the instability created in thinking this way is quite difficult for us to comprehend and so we develop communities of interest, with their associated rituals and mythologies, to make us feel part of a unified and unchanging entity. Despite the fact that concepts of identity are challenged and discredited, we cannot help but revert back to traditional ways of understanding the self.

## Ritual

Ritual is a form of organized behaviour in which humans use the language of gesture, or paralanguage, to affirm, to explore and to celebrate their ideas of how the relationships of the cosmos (or of a part of it), operate and thus of how they themselves should relate to it and to one another.[44]

Christopher Small discusses the way in which identity and community are bound together through ritual. In particular, he talks about the way in which rituals enable identity to be constructed in three ways: identity as an act of affirmation, exploration and celebration.

Regarding identity as an act of affirmation, he suggests that rituals enable subjects to confirm their sense of community-belonging, essentially making the pronouncement *this is who we are and what we are about*. As acts of exploration, rituals enable us to try on identities and discover who we are and what we would like to be. This has clear links to both the rituals of perform-ance: 'trying on' identities, and providing people with a means of exploration and experimentation.[45] Finally, he suggests that ritual is used as an act of celebration, to delight in the fact that identity is not only felt by us as individuals but can also be shared with others. Small suggests that as individuals create and develop identities, they use rituals on a daily basis to cement the feeling of movement from one social state to another. Rituals such as christenings, weddings and birthdays are linked to ceremonies that acknowledge the moving from one social state to the next. Here, the ritual metaphorically dissolves the self of the individual and then reconstitutes it into a new identity ('Oh, I couldn't drink legally yesterday but I can today …', 'I feel different now I'm married' etc.). Although largely symbolic, these ceremonial rituals can have a profound impact on the subject. Furthermore, changes in our sense of self are made all the more significant through public display, the community acting as witness to the passing of one state to the next. Within a jazz context, I suggest that ritual should be understood more as a ceremonial display of a spiritual or supernatural belief (or mythology), in that it has the power to help form identity and a sense of community. Through the use and consumption of ritualistic artefacts, communities are constructed and allegiance is made; common forms of ritualistic consumption lead to community members feeling part of a collective whole. Whether through the use of liner notes, text books, recordings or language, the subject's sense of membership is intensified through ritualistic acts of consumption. From this perspective, Metheny's comments highlight the sense of belonging that jazz and its associated industry afford us; through the process of buying and consuming records we feel an attachment to a unique club. I suggest that jazz records in particular fuel this desire to belong to a community of dedicated followers who have interest, respect and desire for the understanding of jazz. Within this context, the record becomes a sacred text that people own and consume ritualistically, to feel part of a collective whole. The role of ritual in shaping identity and constructing meaning is well documented amongst social anthropologists. For example, Small suggests that all acts of musical performance embody ritual in some way, helping to create a sense of common understanding; 'ritual is in fact an action which dramatizes and re-enacts the shared mythology of a social group'.[46] In their study of music and social movements, Eyerman and Jamison build on this concept to explain how rituals manifest themselves in modern societies and play a key role in both maintaining social order and forming collective identity.[47] Considering this, it is clear to see how our sense of community can be threatened when the role of established ritualistic acts is either challenged or undermined, and could partly explain Metheny's reaction to Kenny G's recording tampering with the 'sacred text' of Armstrong. As Roger Scruton explains: 'Changes in the ritual are disturbing, partly because they suggest that the community may be cut short by time, that the words and gestures that I employ are no better than provisional, and that we shall all be forgotten … Ritual has a timeless quality, for it affirms the community as something permanent, absolved from death and decay.'[48] When rituals are challenged, therefore, the sense of historical preservation, communal values and the very future of the community are threatened. Furthermore, the threat to established rituals illustrates that our sense of community is at its most intense when the boundaries by which we understand ourselves are questioned.[49]

Examining rituals in relation to jazz, recordings engender fetishistic tendencies in consumers by acting as a conduit for the message of the jazz icon. The recording brings the consumer closer to the icon through their recorded legacies at the same time as embodying mythologies bound up with our understanding of art; paradoxically, as suggested in the previous chapter, icons can also become ever more detached from our everyday experience through recordings. Iconic records encourage consumers to collect fetishistically in order to preserve the mysteries of jazz; they also create an intimate relationship between subject and icon. In this respect, recordings not only aid the construction of a symbolic jazz community, they also enable consumers to develop a sense of individual identity through identification. This point has close ties to John Corbett's description of contemporary modes of consumption, where individuality ('the desire to be different') and identification ('identity in mass production') coexist.[50] Through the intimate relationship created by ritualistic consumption, recordings (as well as other resources of history), assist consumers in constructing a sense of identity; they are the tools that feed our aspirations and lifestyle choices, and say as much about who we want to be as they do about the historical importance of the works themselves. Stuart Hall states:

> Though they seem to invoke an origin in a historical past with which they continue to correspond, actually identities are about questions of using the resources of history, language and culture in the process of becoming rather than being: not 'who we are' or 'where we came from', so much as what we might become, how we have been represented and how that bears on how we might represent ourselves. Identities are therefore constituted within, not outside representation. They relate to the invention of tradition as much as to tradition itself ...[51]

Hall reiterates Cohen's observation about the symbolic nature of the concepts of community and identity, yet suggests that, whilst being constructed in fantasy, the discursive, material or political effect of identities should in no way be undermined.

## Valuing jazz, fearing the inauthentic: understanding Metheny on Kenny G

The perspectives of Hall and Cohen go some way to account for Metheny's outspoken reaction to Kenny G's *Classics* album. When viewing the ritualistic consumption of recordings as helping to facilitate the construction of community and identity, the preservation of the 'sacred' (to coin Metheny's term) becomes of paramount importance. To present the fetishistic consumer with an impure or corrupt version of an accepted 'authentic' work not only challenges established codes and conventions, it intrudes on the intimate icon–subject relationship, undermining the process of identification and the way jazz fans aspire to represent themselves. In a musical context, several writers have demonstrated how music and ritual enable people to act out desired relationships in the formation of identity and sense of community.[52] Simon Frith, for example, describes how our sense of community and identity are integrally linked to understandings of what it is to be authentic, with musical practice enabling us to place ourselves within imagined cultural narratives: 'Authenticity … is a quality not of the music as such … but of the story it's heard to tell, the narrative of musical interaction in which the listeners place themselves.'[53] Identity, therefore, can be considered as an ideal, linked to understandings of the authentic, where the imagined and the real are played out in musical activities. We can consider Metheny's sense of outrage as having as much to do with how he views himself as it does with the merits of Kenny G's work. Furthermore, Metheny's knee-jerk reaction to the *Classics* album can be understood as a symptom of self-identification, the fear and dismay at recognising himself in the work of Kenny G. In this context, identification obviously works on a level of complexity that moves beyond both artists' passion for long hair and eighties clothing, towards a study of the desire to be considered authentic in jazz. For example, Kenny G's duet with Armstrong could have induced a sense of the inauthentic in Metheny, reminding him of his status on the boundary of African American art, as Metheny has frequently walked a fine line between commercial projects and progressive concept albums. This paranoia is emphasised again by Frith, who stresses that, in order to understand authenticity, it is also essential to grasp the feeling of what it is to be inauthentic. Frith argues that, in the world of the white middle class, 'American music – black American music – stands for a simple idea: that everything *real* is happening elsewhere.'[54] This point sheds a different light on Metheny's claim that we should be both 'embarrassed' about and 'afraid' of letting Kenny G get away with his *Classics* recording. Perhaps being embarrassed and afraid typifies the feelings of the inauthentic; to let Kenny G off the hook might signify that Metheny has also been let off the hook. This latter point should not be underestimated, and might explain why the Metheny interview ends with him claiming that Kenny G's music only makes *him* want to practise harder. Washburne suggests that feelings of inauthenticity such as this are widespread where Kenny G is concerned, his popularity among both black and white audiences causing concern to musicians and critics alike. Drawing on an interview between Louis Farrakhan and Henry Louis Gates Jr in which the merits of Kenny G were contested, Washburne stresses that, whilst seeking to deconstruct common assumptions about black experience and promoting alternative experiences for black Americans, audiences are still vulnerable to the charge of feeling inauthentic or disloyal:

This illustrates one cause for anxiety that some (both blacks and whites) feel about Gorelick's mass appeal within the black community at large; an appeal, which supposedly supercedes [*sic*] that of other more authentic (read black) jazz artists. On the one hand, Gorelick's economic success and popularity, I suggest, are reminiscent of previous generations of white musicians … On the other hand, Gorelick's position is a sort of double co-optation because not only has he appropriated the stylistic parameters of black music, but he has also appropriated a large black audience in the process. This raises issues of ownership and authenticity in a much more complex way than say, Benny Goodman or Elvis Presley did.[55]

This case study has sought to demonstrate the power of ritual in constructing a sense of community and identity by exploring the multiplicity of levels of interpretation of Pat Metheny's response to Kenny G's music. By responding more critically to Kenny G's place within the jazz world, it is possible to develop an understanding not only of the changing face of jazz and its relationship to popular culture, but also the way in which assertions of value in jazz are still significantly contested. My discussion of the music of Kenny G and the subsequent discussion of social construction in jazz have not sought to place his music within the framework of the jazz genius. However, this examination has highlighted the fact that the value judgements underpinning negative criticism of music predominantly lie outside the world of 'pure' musical creativity and, in many respects, can be considered arbitrary. On a musical level, it might at first seem easy to dismiss Kenny G's music as inauthentic, yet when examining the music in detail it becomes apparent that a sense of 'objective' musical understanding is problematic; musically, Kenny G's performances can be described as lacking rhythmic fluency, an original voice and perfect intonation (all terms that can be largely contested), yet record sales and the marketplace indicate that these points are inconsequential to the success of the artist. Indeed, the negative musical attributes of Kenny G could be applied to many contemporary jazz artists who are or have been given more respect within the field. Similarly, as emphasised earlier, commercialism can be used as an essential endorsement of a work's genius in one context and as a signifier of inauthenticity in another. Once we acknowledge that there is more at play in Kenny G's case than the assertion of objective musical standards to discredit the artist, the focus of critique moves towards established oppositions located in the value judgements of a particular social order; popularity is bad, and functionality is at odds with the romanticised view of music as a metaphysical and transcendent art. Once exposed, these criteria can be understood as equally problematic; in Pat Metheny's case, many of the socially located value judgements could equally apply to both artists.

Finally, when studying the close etymological link between authorship, authority and authenticity, we should also be mindful of the close link between these words and another: authoritarianism. By obsessing over a work's authority and the integrity of its production, and by adhering to fixed interpretations of the music and its authentic past, audiences should perhaps worry less about the 'G' in 'Genius' and focus more on the dangers of turning their author-worshipping communities into authoritarian regimes.

Although at the extreme end of jazz criticism, Metheny's outburst offers itself as a good case study to explore some of the broader issues surrounding iconic reverence and the significance of rituals in the construction of identity and place within a perceived community. Metheny's response to Kenny G's duet with history comments on the way in which recordings can be used as tools to assert value, and on the central role that iconic worship plays in shaping individual identities and a shared sense of community. When understood boundaries are challenged or called into question, subjects are instilled with an intense sense of community and personal identification. Rather than seeking to judge Kenny G's music, this approach contextualises the nature of value judgements in music and highlights the roles that icons play in the ritualistic consumption of jazz.

# 4 | Men can't help acting on Impulse!

**Figure 5**  John Coltrane

Over the last few years, the study of advertising and consumption has become a significant site for cross-disciplinary and interdisciplinary analysis. Indeed, within disciplines such as cultural studies, sociology and media studies, theories of consumption have now replaced theories of production when examining how products shape and reflect social identities; shopping and advertising are now considered essential ingredients in the historicising process. Consider this position from the introduction to *Buy This Book: Studies in Advertising and Consumption*:

[Shopping], until a few years ago ignored by cultural theorists, is now increasingly acknowledged as a highly complex and intellectually rewarding field of study: an essential component in the cycle of industrial production … and part of the elaborate network of significations which compose the iconography and scopic regimes of modernity, it has also played a significant part in the constitution of twentieth century ideas about citizenship and in the current politics of the environment. Shopping as one aspect of consumption is thus no trivial pursuit.[1]

Continuing on from this, we could argue that acts of consumption should be regarded as an integral part of the historicising process in jazz. Advertising is not only a crucial aid to consumption; it also provides cultural theorists with numerous possibilities for analysis, as the medium has important links to art, politics and education. From a jazz perspective, advertising and marketing strategies are important in examining the sense of societal value instilled in the music. Therefore, it is important to examine the advertising medium not only in terms of consumption but also in terms of reception and interpretation. Through textual and intertextual readings of advertising and marketing, it is possible to gain an understanding of the semiological process first-hand, examining how products convey denotative and connotative value, and how the icon can play a dominant role in consumer understanding of jazz practice. This type of analysis takes on a broader significance when considering the way in which 'serious' jazz consumers and practitioners distance themselves from the marketplace, believing they are immune to the powers of advertising. Indeed, this perspective is often referenced by the opinion that only the music matters, and that as art can speak for itself, marketing and commercial forces have little impact upon the 'true' jazz enthusiast or collector.

The belief that it is appropriate to discuss and analyse jazz in romantic, myth-laden terms without critical engagement with the music's socio-historical context is widespread, and features in a number of influential jazz texts.[2] By comparing adverts from different periods in jazz history and the marketing strategies of record companies promoting both historical and contemporary releases, it is possible to get a sense of how codes and conventions either change through time or are perpetuated from one generation to the next. Through this type of analysis, I examine the development of jazz as a historical and artistic form, to gain an understanding of its social and cultural significance through time. I have chosen examples from the Impulse! recording label as a case study, as the company was not only one of the first jazz labels to stress the cultural significance of marketing their product; it has also become synonymous with the celebration of iconic figures.

The status of jazz as a canonical artform is very much dependent on the legacy of its recorded history; the recording offers itself as the primary vehicle for the canonisation of jazz, and its history is most often used as the benchmark for standards and quality. This reliance on a mass-produced document – the recording – differentiates jazz from other artforms, such as Renaissance painting, where the appreciation of an original remains central to the discourse. In a jazz context, notions of the 'original' artwork and the singularity of authorship can prove problematic in terms of analysis and discussion, as the canonicity of jazz presents a number of variations on more established canonical discourses. For example, unlike most western art music, where a relatively fixed score offers itself to numerous interpretations and recordings, the jazz performance stands alone as an independent, unrepeatable event, through the improvisatory skills of the performer. As soon as it is frozen in time, however, the fleeting creative idea becomes a permanent artefact for subsequent generations to explore and replay. This raises interesting issues in relation to the meaning, value and context of jazz performances. I suggest below that, historically and culturally, jazz on record presents a number of challenges that differentiate it from, say, classical music or rock, and this complexity feeds back into our relationship with the music itself. In jazz, the distinction between the composer and the performer is often blurred; whether a performer is performing his own original material or adapting and improvising on the music of others, the recording solidifies and makes each improvisation into a permanent composition. Further, although jazz is often discussed and described as an artform that celebrates group dynamic and interaction, the recording encourages a focused relationship with a solo artist. The conflation of performer and composer only serves to intensify this relationship, which privileges the iconic solo artist at the expense of other group members. Finally, while the issues surrounding jazz on record may be similar to those surrounding rock music as far as its iconic recordings and obsessive record collectors are concerned, jazz is increasingly discussed in terms used to evaluate and understand classical music.[3]

Perhaps because of a lack of distinction between live and recorded jazz, and the myth that jazz is somehow an unmediated experience, jazz recordings are often celebrated as having ephemeral qualities that promote the music as improvisatory or 'in the moment'. Georgina Born, for example, has examined how jazz records can be used to undermine the concept of the musical work in western classical music, their improvisatory quality challenging fixed interpretations of music.[4] In contrast to this dominant understanding of jazz as performative 'text', I argue that the growing trend of historical jazz recordings transforms the music from a radical, fleeting and communal practice into a conformist, reified and artistically autonomous artform. This shift in status parallels the development of classical music, as critiqued by writers such as Christopher Small and Lydia Goehr, who suggest that western society became obsessed with the interpretation of works rather than events themselves, and that music started to be discussed as a reified object instead of a social activity. In effect, by treating jazz recordings as canonical artefacts, we transform the music from an action to an abstraction, from verb to noun, text to work.[5] The recorded legacy of jazz has gained a heightened significance as the desire for a definitive jazz canon has developed. Through the historical documentation of the recording, jazz is legitimised; musicians, writers and jazz enthusiasts use the recording and its history to construct a lineage of significant historical milestones. In this respect, recordings are not only essential to the study of jazz history but also problematic for writers wishing to develop an objective picture of the music's past. Jed Rasula, for example, describes recordings as a 'seductive menace', accounting for the fact that while records are essential to historians in constructing a definable and legitimate history for jazz, through their cultural dominance they at the same time have the ability to skew understandings of the past and limit our perspective on jazz history. Frank Kermode suggests that canonised artworks are complex and contradictory, in that they can be understood as fossilised, firmly locked in time on the one hand and as having the ability to transcend time on the other.[6] When viewed as permanent artefacts, I suggest that canonical records not only unlock doors into the historical environment within which they were born; they can also embody a romanticised view of history where nothing in the present can compete with the past. Ironically, this point is further complicated by the way in which jazz of the present is often defined as a broad blur of music dating from the 1970s onwards. The most notable recent example of the symbiotic relationship between jazz history and the recording is Ken Burns's PBS documentary series *Jazz*, which was accompanied by its very own collection of 'essential' jazz recordings. In his recent study of the Ken Burns documentary, Scott DeVeaux suggests that the five-CD package accompanying the series concludes with an example of nondescript fusion, demonstrating that Burns adheres to the belief that jazz died in the 1970s.[7] Canonised works are promoted as having inherent value – they are considered 'great' as they have supposedly stood the test of time. Simultaneously, and paradoxically, the canonised recording is set free of time and space; canonised art is presented as autonomous, divorced from its original context and transcendent of social forces.[8] The canonised recording serves to reinforce myths of universality and transcendence; freed from the constraints of the everyday world, the work is deemed to have a fixed worth, regardless of context. Additionally, new meanings are assigned to canonised works over time, their status gaining an enhanced significance as history is rewritten and reinscribed. What was originally a simple, average-selling recorded release can be regarded as a seminal work of masterpiece status when constructing history from the present.

When new meanings are created and canonical status is achieved, it becomes ever less likely that the recording will be received as an object of criticism. For example, in his book *Satchmo*, Gary Giddins describes Louis Armstrong's LP of Disney songs – not previously regarded as a great work of the jazz canon – as 'a masterpiece of its kind … the ultimate test of his alchemical powers'.[9] Furthermore, canonical reverence is seen throughout the jazz community on a regular basis. Take, for example, Pat Metheny's outburst at Kenny G for daring to create a track overdubbing a performance of jazz legend Louis Armstrong, discussed in the previous chapter. Similarly, people rarely discuss the music of the living jazz 'great' Sonny Rollins in the same way as iconic John Coltrane, the 'spiritual master' of jazz. This point was unwittingly alluded to in a *Downbeat* article on Sonny Rollins published in 2001. The piece, entitled 'Approaching Enlightenment', discusses the spiritual side of Rollins and his status as a jazz legend. However, as the title of the article suggests, the performer has not yet achieved the iconic status of Coltrane, suggesting that death is the only thing that divides the two artists.[10] Here, jazz mirrors the world of classical music through the reverence shown to bygone artists; as Christopher Small has maintained, for most people 'a great composer is almost by definition a dead composer'.[11]

As major players in the construction of the jazz canon, record companies have a vested interest in promoting the legacy of 'great' music, not only because reissues, bonus tracks and master editions feed the consumer desire for the 'authentic' experience, but also because a relatively small promotional budget will help sell a back-catalogue reliably and consistently. I argue that record companies, in turn, seek to exploit the importance of historical treasures through the presentation of recorded materials as masterpieces in history – each jazz recording not only represents a snapshot of a historic period but, despite its mass production, is also a unique creation. Indeed, the proliferation of transcriptions of recorded improvisations, and even re-recordings of historic recorded performances, is testament to the power and effects of reification. A good illustration of this is the way in which almost every solo of John Coltrane or Charlie Parker has been transcribed for performance and analysis.[12] Within the context of canon building, record companies set out to distinguish between everyday releases and the established 'classics' of jazz history. This has led to certain companies rationalising their output, designating specific labels to contemporary releases and others to reissues. For example, in the case of Universal Music in recent years, Verve has taken on the role of the main label for newly recorded jazz, whilst Impulse! – the label historically associated with the jazz vanguard – has produced mainly historic reissues. The promotion of jazz's recorded legacy has reached new heights, not only in the technological advances of digital remastering and editing, but also in the repackaging and promotion of original and 'authentic' products. Given this background, it is difficult at times to know where the contemporary artist fits in, as new artists are at risk of not recouping valuable investment capital. Indeed, in promoting the value of reissues, producers such as Michael Cuscuna have commented on the fragmented relationship between contemporary jazz artists and major recording companies, as major labels commit to promoting back-catalogues and celebrating jazz's iconic legacy.[13] The problems faced by record companies in this instance are very much echoed in the nature of contemporary jazz music; there is a conflict between innovation and the subservience to a defined tradition. Once again, the canon thrusts artists into a position of feeling that they need either to 'pay their dues' or to reject convention in search of the innovative or eclectic. Either way, the music's historical legacy provides the basis from which to proceed.

The following case studies examine the paradox created by recording companies who are devoted both to promoting a legacy of great recordings and to supporting contemporary artists performing 'new' works.

**Figure 6**    John Coltrane, *The Classic Quartet: Complete Impulse! Studio Recordings*

Using the Impulse! label as a case study, I explore the company's strategies in promoting iconic jazz recordings through an analysis of John Coltrane's *The Classic Quartet: Complete Impulse! Studio Recordings*, released in 1998 (see Figure 6), and illustrate how political and philosophical issues permeate jazz in everyday situations.[14] I discuss the significance of historical recordings and the consumer desire for icon worship, and go on to examine the implications and effects of canonisation for the current jazz scene. The Impulse! record label has always been heavily associated with cutting-edge marketing and design, recognising from the outset the potential for collectability in jazz recordings. The label is also particularly interesting because of its integral links to the later career of John Coltrane, arguably the most revered icon in jazz history, and his Classic Quartet, celebrated as one of the most creative ensembles. Coltrane's move to the Impulse! label coincided with his most experimental and spiritual phase, and he was still signed to the label at the time of his death in 1967. This relationship has been the making of the label, and Impulse! has continued to trade both on the success and the spirituality of Coltrane in its other recordings.

When exploring the relationship between recordings and the jazz canon, the label also provides a useful model for analysis, as many of their releases – most notably Coltrane's *A Love Supreme*, featured as part of the complete collection – were self-consciously promoted as canonical at the time of their release. In this respect, the label not only comments on current tastes and values, it has also played an explicit part in the historical construction of the jazz canon. I go on to examine the implications and effects of canonisation on contemporary jazz through an intertextual reading of an Impulse! advertisement for Donald Harrison's album *Nouveau Swing*, released in 1997.[15] I choose to contrast Harrison with Coltrane, as the former was one of the last instrumentalists to be championed by the label without an explicit link to Coltrane, whilst the latter has dominated the company's catalogue almost from the label's inception.

## John Coltrane, *The Classic Quartet*: *Complete Impulse! Studio Recordings*

### (i) Acquiring culture

Scott DeVeaux discusses the widespread desire of the mainstream jazz community to elevate jazz to the status of 'America's Classical Music', instilling the music with a degree of cultural capital.[16] Echoing this phenomenon, I would suggest that the *Complete Impulse! Studio Recordings* is an extreme example of the record company's (and consumer) desire to elevate recordings to a higher aesthetic status. The product is designed to be a definitive collection of recordings from a significant period in jazz history. The iconic status of John Coltrane is also emphasised within the release; the single word 'COLTRANE' is displayed on both spine, and outer and inner covers: acknowledgement that the surname itself has become a cultural institution. Accompanying the name on the outer cover of the release is an image of Coltrane in a typically reflective, spiritual and non-performative pose. He has become the embodiment of both the physical and spiritual quests of jazz; he represents the complete physical and emotive jazz icon whilst transcending the physicality of his art through his spirituality. The *Complete Impulse! Studio Recordings* feeds the consumer's multifaceted desire to collect, as discussed by Evan Eisenberg in his book *The Recording Angel*.[17] Eisenberg discusses the impact of recordings on western culture and draws some insights into the human desire to collect, and his ideas feed directly into the issues at play in the Coltrane release. Eisenberg suggests that recording represents the historical imperative to capture fleeting musical events in a physical form; this recording, as a supposedly definitive collection, exacerbates consumer beliefs that they own a slice of history – a passing musical event is reified and captured for eternity.

In the Coltrane collection, several devices are used to give the consumer a sense of owning a special part of history. The sleeve notes are packed with accounts and testimonies of the period, and the recordings themselves are presented to the listener as if in a pure, unadulterated form, outside the rigours of the standard post-production process. The following quotation is embossed on the inside cover of the collection: 'It felt like a perfect blend, a joy. It was always a joy, in a recording studio or a nightclub. It was the same feeling, in front of a large audience or no one at all. Music was our sole purpose' (Elvin Jones). Here, the sentiment – again considered authentic as it is spoken by one of the Quartet – reiterates the fact that these recordings were made at a special moment in Coltrane's career. Therefore the release is presented as though it is an act of witnessing; as consumers, we are encouraged to accept that it is not about money, audiences, fame or product, but is art for art's sake. Delving deeper into this idea, Impulse! use every means necessary to construct a sense of a priceless, authentic and original artefact within the release. In the past, a classic recording might well be accompanied by a third-party endorsement – by a critic or musician – or some stylish photography, but essentially the recorded sound would be required to speak for itself, the supporting material remaining implicit and subordinate to the recorded material. However, as a tactile experience, I would argue that *ownership* of the Coltrane recording engenders a sense of value as well as perceived authenticity. Unusually, the collection is bound in imitation leather and encased in metal: permanent materials that not only age well but also retain a timeless quality. When compared to a conventional plastic CD jewel case, this presentation commands both a distinct material value as well as giving the recording a physical sense of permanence. The timeless quality of the outer casing is reinforced on the inside, where the sleeve notes are printed in the format of an original recording log sheet. The chosen font is evocative of the period and the text is printed askew, as if the daily recording schedules have been pieced together for this occasion only.

This set of recordings fuels our desire for collection whilst promoting itself as an exclusive object. The metal casing shrouding the collection is deliberately aged with imitation rust and the design of the sleeve is such that opening the case requires a sense of determined effort. We are encouraged, therefore, to receive this work as if it has been taken directly from the vaults of the Impulse! archive. From this perspective, the definitive, imitation-leather-bound collection is released for the discerning jazz connoisseur as a genuine and authentic artefact of history, a trophy within the world of record collecting. Whereas record collecting as trophy hunting is perhaps more synonymous with the world of vinyl releases, many current CD releases are designed to appeal to consumers who wish to continue to set themselves apart from the everyday collector. In this way, the Coltrane collection appeals to the jazz collector on a number of levels; not only does the set have a certain high cost – obvious in its presentation – it also presents itself as something unique, not appealing to every taste.

Although the product conveys a sense of 'worth', the recording privileges content above commercial value; it defines itself as having almost archival status. This non-commercial view of the work can be seen in Elvin Jones's earlier quotation and is also apparent by the way in which the recordings are taken out of their original commercial context. Each track and recording in this set is identified firstly by name and secondly by date and catalogue number. This factual archivist information is then interspersed with either technical or aesthetic reasons as to why some recordings were chosen over others for general commercial release. The release of previously unacceptable material into a commercial context would perhaps be something to frown upon, with record companies seen as 'cashing in' on substandard material. For contemporary artists, the release of previously rejected works would signify both a lack of ability and poor judgement, and would undermine the quality of their musicianship. By contrast, Coltrane and his Classic Quartet have now reached a status where all their material is *worth* something.

## (ii) The quest for enlightenment

The significance of Coltrane's spiritual iconic status should not be under-estimated. Arguably, the artist commands the most intense spiritual persona of all jazz 'masters'. David Ake comments on how the spiritual dimension of Coltrane has been taken to extremes: '[T]he existence of San Francisco's St John's African Orthodox Church, where parishioners revere the late saxophonist John Coltrane as "the divine sound Baptist", reveals the degree to which many listeners (and not just church members) view that musician as one deeply and singularly attuned to a "higher power".'[18] Here, Coltrane is worshipped as a saint, his recorded music performed as part of weekly religious rituals. This is obviously an extreme form of reverence; however, it demonstrates the potential of jazz icons to inspire their fans to associate spiritual adoration and the quest for enlightenment with their favourite recordings.

The Coltrane collection features an altruistic commentary from executive producer Michael Cuscuna in which he discusses the previously undiscovered material of this release. Throughout his accompanying testimony, Cuscuna talks of the 'endless hours' spent listening to the Quartet and the way in which they provided him with 'ecstatic' and 'formative' experiences. As collectors, we are encouraged not only to delve into the recordings but also to devote time and energy to listening. Here, another jazz mythology is reiterated; only through time and effort will the listener be able to gain access to the hidden secrets of the recording and the musicians at play – in this world even listeners have to 'pay their dues'. The collector's quest for understanding has a deep resonance with the world of jazz scholarship, as those with the biggest and most comprehensive collections are often considered, albeit misguidedly, as the ones with the most knowledge. Within this context, definitive recordings can have the paradoxical effect of encouraging collectors to have a love of culture without having an interest in it, a love that is satisfied by ownership rather than listening.[19] This resonates throughout the presentation of the Coltrane collection; the difficulty of accessing the individual recordings gives the collector a heightened sense of reward when consuming the material. Works are not presented to the listener for their convenience or user-friendliness; this differs entirely from the world of commercial pop music, where releases are designed for immediate consumption. The current proliferation of complete recordings and boxed sets is particularly noteworthy, given the rise of the download. Arguably, the divergence between the immediacy of MP3s and the longevity of the realm of the boxed set is becoming greater, with each occupying its own space in the market. Following on from this, the determined effort required to access the individual recordings also taps into the collector's desire for displaying cultural objects. The stunning presentation of the collection serves almost as status symbol or a piece of interior design; it is easier to display than to perform. As a cultural object, the collection echoes Roland Barthes's concept of the 'work', which leads the owner into a position of worship rather than active, critical consumption.[20] Barthes's writings on 'works' help to uncover the dangers in the process of canon-forming. Within a work-like state, the artwork is a definable entity bound up with a single strand of 'authentic' history, the iconic author figure represented as a conduit for divine inspiration. In his study 'Free, Single and Disengaged', John Corbett describes the quest for an enlightened experience within recordings as a form of fetishistic audiophilia. For

Corbett, the alleviation of surface noise, scratching and hissing on contemporary recordings instils in the consumer the belief that music is detached from the everyday world; in effect, there is a purity of experience bound up with recordings. Corbett states: 'To render music free of noise is to grant it its proper musical status as sonically autonomous ... Surface noise indicates the surface, a reminder of the visible topography of recorded music objects.'[21] For Corbett, the recording presents consumers with an interesting dichotomy; the conflict between wanting to restore the visual dimension to the disembodied voice on the one hand, and creating a 'natural' autonomous sonic experience on the other. Corbett suggests that, rather than being in opposition to each other, these two fetishistic tendencies can coexist. *Complete Impulse! Studio Recordings* is a good example of this, encouraging the consumer to get closer to the artist both in physical terms, through the wealth of supporting documentary materials, and in metaphysical terms, through its simultaneous heightening of the mystery of the sonic experience.

### (iii)  Nostalgia

Recent studies of advertising and consumption have commented on the significance of nostalgia within consumer practices. In his study of nostalgia in contemporary advertising, for example, Andrew Wernick relates it both to a desire for a homecoming – born out of dissatisfaction with the contemporary world – and the need to belong.[22] The *Complete Impulse! Studio Recordings* reinforces this interpretation of nostalgia by promoting a sense of belonging, a feeling of completeness and a return to the values of the past. Not only does the collection comment on the historicising process, it also reflects Coltrane's iconic significance today. With its retro packaging, photographs, musical out-takes and testimonies, the work presents itself as a direct link to history, offering a window into a bygone era. As well as presenting itself as a historical document designed to appeal to a nostalgic disposition, the *Complete Impulse! Studio Recordings* also appeals to the fetishistic tendencies of the collector. Corbett describes the contradictions at play within this process – the desire for identification on the one hand and the need for individuality on the other – as the two modes of commodity fetishism; both fetishes remain mutually supportive within the development of the capitalist marketplace.[23] Indeed, as mentioned above, the Coltrane collection gains its own cult status and value that set it apart from the everyday consumable object; to use Eisenberg's description, 'the true hero of consumption is a rebel against consumption'.[24] In turn, the owner of the work is made to feel part of a unique set of collectors, a part of a discrete and distinguished jazz community.

The futility of the fetishistic collector's nostalgic quest for the definitive recording was demonstrated four years after the release of the *Complete Impulse! Studio Recordings* when Impulse! issued additional 'new' material as part of subsequent Coltrane releases. Ashley Kahn described the situation:

Yet there are times when the best music and best intentions are simply not enough to make the reissue business an easy one. Take, for example, the recent 'Deluxe Editions' of the 1962 albums *Coltrane* and *Ballads*, which include the original released material plus a wealth of unused takes and false starts. 'In '98, we put out the popular *Classic Quartet* box with a great booklet and eight discs', reports Ken Druker, Verve's head of catalog development, 'and called it *The Complete Impulse! Studio Recordings*'. Meanwhile, [Bob] Thiele, who passed away two years previously, had donated his collection of recordings and LPs to his New Jersey high school, which eventually passed the reel-to-reel tapes on to Rutgers University's Institute for Jazz Studies. There, Institute head Dan Morgenstern auditioned the tapes in 2000 and, realizing that some were never-heard Coltrane session masters, returned them to Verve. Adds Druker: 'So we immediately began working on them for release in 2002. They came out and of course the e-mails started – "Why did we hold these back in '98?"; "Do we know what the word complete means?" [*laughs*]. You can't win.'[25]

This account neatly articulates both consumer desire to own the definitive collection and the simultaneous futility of searching for the complete recorded experience. However, rather than viewing this type of situation as a product of circumstance, some commentators question the motives of record companies who decide to release additional material after issuing 'complete' collections. For example, historian and broadcaster Phil Schapp examined the strategies of record companies at the International Association for Jazz Education (IAJE) jazz conference in 2003, discussing both the repackaging and the 'holding back' of recordings by Louis Armstrong and Ella Fitzgerald as a means of further stimulating consumer desire to collect. As part of his presentation, Schapp read out an extensive list of Armstrong/Fitzgerald album releases, all of which were marketed as 'new material'. However, on closer inspection, all albums consisted of the same (very limited) recording material, albeit in different presentations, with the exception of one track, which did not appear on any recording.[26]

Whilst it is often stated that great music speaks for itself, there is no denying the importance of the visual appeal of recorded products.

Historically, the Impulse! label was at the forefront of album cover design; its gatefolded LPs all displayed the distinctive black and orange spine, and the company's trade exclamation mark designed to emphasise the impact of the label on the scene.[27] Indeed, many of the company's early titles were designed to build on the distinctiveness of its visual identity, carving out a unique place within the jazz recording market and embodying the values of jazz as 'art'.[28] Arguably, the arrival of John Coltrane in 1961 cemented Impulse!'s identity as an innovative and progressive label, as well as confirming its status in the jazz market. Coltrane's *Africa Brass* was only the sixth release under the new label's banner; however, the work of the artist has defined the marketing strategy for Impulse!, even up to the present day. Creed Taylor, the brains behind the identity of the newly formed Impulse!, commented on these innovations:

The gatefold was not being used except on very special albums, but all of the Impulse titles were to be gatefolds … I tried to juxtapose the visual on the album cover with the title itself, like Gil [Evans]'s *Out of the Cool* or [jazz composer/arranger] Oliver Nelson's *Blues and the Abstract Truth*. They're all combinations of words that grab you. I mean, there's nothing really abstract about the blues but it's a truth … At first there was this 'who in the heck is an Oliver Nelson and what is *Blues and the Abstract Truth*?' kind of thing. Soon enough there was a thread of 'What do you mean? It's on Impulse. It's good-looking, great-sounding stuff.'[29]

The visual impact of Impulse! recordings not only proved popular with collectors, they also provided inspiration to a host of other companies looking to develop a cutting-edge image. The Black Saint label, for example, was inspired by the Charles Mingus LP *The Black Saint and the Sinner Lady* released on Impulse!, and its spines in turn clearly paid homage to the Impulse! brand.

Within this framework, the Impulse! label offers a useful example of the paradox that exists within today's jazz marketplace, where back catalogues tend to dominate the contemporary marketing agenda. Indeed, since 1999 Impulse! has focused its output on reissues, with notable exceptions: *McCoy Tyner Plays John Coltrane* in 2001 and Alice Coltrane's *Translinear Light* in 2004, for example, show the continuing indebtedness to the Coltrane brand. Here, the dominance of the iconic Coltrane signals the demise of the label's investment in contemporary releases, with new releases such as McCoy Tyner's having to cite Coltrane in the album title.[30] Ironically, the figurehead of Coltrane, associated with cementing the vision of Impulse! as a forward-looking and at times politically charged label, can now be seen to represent the downfall of the label as a promoter of contemporary jazz. Coltrane's legacy is something that over-powers the marketplace, affecting Impulse!'s commitment to contemporary releases. Indeed, at the end of the 1990s, the music of Donald Harrison offered the only gesture towards 'new' musical creation within the label's catalogue.

## Donald Harrison, *Nouveau Swing*

In the context of Impulse!'s history and development, it is fruitful to examine how the label promotes its rare new releases. Indeed, advertisements for albums by contemporary jazz artists often situate new releases in the context of the recorded jazz canon and the label's back-catalogue. In promoting their new product, record companies attempt to create an aura around artists that is open to multiple readings. Through advertising and imagery, images of the authentic or innovative can be established alongside the reinforcing and questioning of jazz stereotypes. Figure 7 shows an advert for Donald Harrison's *Nouveau Swing*, released on Impulse! in 1997.

Although seeming fairly conventional – a simple image with a short amount of text – this advert can be interpreted on a number of levels. I have chosen to focus on four areas of interest when examining the intertextual potential of the advert. These are by no means definitive; however, they offer us an insight into the levels of signification attached to everyday jazz imagery.

### (i)  Attempts to align itself with tradition

First, it is obvious that this advert attempts to align the product with tradition, using both explicit and implicit devices. For example, Impulse!'s strap-line, 'The New Wave Of Jazz Is STILL On Impulse!', harks back to the company's recorded legacy. We are led to believe that this product is placed in line with all other 'great' Impulse! recordings of the past. The main slogan, 'Donald Harrison is no longer a young lion. *Nouveau Swing* is the work of a master', buys into the age-old cliché of the jazz artist 'paying their dues'. As an artist, Harrison is established as having served his apprenticeship; he has come of age. This statement seems a little premature bearing in mind Harrison's profile to date. As an artist, Harrison has been aligned with the new generation of jazz artists who emerged in the 1980s (hence the 'young lion' in the

**Figure 7** Advertisement for Donald Harrison's *Nouveau Swing*

advertisement). Originally performing with Art Blakey's Jazz Messengers, Harrison's career has developed steadily, the artist producing several albums that make reference to music of the past (*Nouveau Swing*, *Kind of New* etc.). However, to describe Harrison's music in master-like terms at both this stage in his career and in relation to his distinguished contemporaries seems like an overstatement. Looking at the Harrison advert on another level, the imagery itself could be seen as adhering to a classic or timeless look. Indeed, in parallel to the images of the advert, the album cover for *Nouveau Swing* aspires to classic status, from both the colours and packaging of the product to Harrison's very own zoot suit. The image of the artist here is plain and simple, perhaps aiming to transcend time in appearance.

When examining the section of supporting text, we can again extract references to the past. The text informs us that this album is not only honest but also acoustic. Honesty and integrity, coupled with the acoustic nature of performance, are obviously designed to appeal to conservative audiences seeking 'the authentic'. Musicologically, Harrison also appeals to the conservative elements of the jazz audience and has been aligned with the neo-classical jazz movement led by figures such as Wynton Marsalis, Roy Hargrove and Terence Blanchard. This isn't a dishonest, corrupt and technology-ridden contemporary jazz release. These words, although used subtly, sum up an entire approach to contemporary jazz marketing, aiming to convey to the consumer that this product is in line with authentic jazz practice. This factor is perhaps best summed up in the title of the work, *Nouveau Swing*. Here we have a direct reference to jazz of the past, albeit dressed up in a contemporary guise. When viewed alongside reissues and releases such as the Coltrane collection, the marketing of contemporary albums such as Harrison's must display a relationship to an identifiable history in order to remain relevant and meaningful. Here, the consumer who owns Coltrane will be encouraged to collect Harrison as a 'natural' continuation of values bound up with the jazz lineage. Overall, this first observation can be seen as a paradox to the second point.

## (ii)  Attempts to align itself with the contemporary

Although, on the one hand, this advert aspires to align itself with the past, there is an obvious desire to present the product at the cutting edge of the contemporary jazz scene. The body of text tells us that this album is not only fresh and compelling, but also at the vanguard of its art. At the same time, we have a comparison with Harrison's contemporaries – 'it is as good as anybody else' is effectively the sentiment. This closing comment is a little out of place within the context of the advert; on the one hand the recording is fresh, compelling and original, and yet it is as good as anybody else. The final statement appears like a closing rider to the product, a get-out clause that exonerates the company if we don't feel that the product is as fresh, compelling and original as we were led to believe. It also implies that nothing today is as good as it used to be.

The album's cutting-edge aspirations are also seen within the references to dance and physicality. Harrison has his ears to the ground, listening and sampling the music of today's world. This demonstrates that Harrison draws not only from the world of jazz, being at the vanguard of his art, but also the eclectic world of dance culture. Dance, physicality and movement are typically associated with contemporary forms of music, and this album seeks to align itself with contemporary club culture, albeit in its world-music form. The image accompanying the text reinforces the physicality and dance orientation of the music. Here, Harrison can be seen to be literally 'getting down' to the sounds of his own music. In this context, to portray Harrison as the physical master is in keeping with his contemporary image and does not come into conflict with the construction of deified artists such as John Coltrane. Finally, we are reminded of the contemporary aspirations of the album by the use of the now familiar strap-line – the New Wave of jazz is still present on this classic label.

## (iii)  Plays on established codes and mythologies

The third approach to decoding this text examines the way in which this advert plays on jazz stereotypes, codes and conventions. The image of the black male saxophonist epitomises the popular perception of the jazz stereotype. Within this context, Harrison obviously cannot change his ethnicity, gender or instrumental orientation; however, the advert seeks to build on other ingrained assumptions linked to the jazz stereotype. The combination of text and language could be interpreted as presenting the black jazz musician as musical primitive.[31] Here, Harrison is shown as an artist filled with emotion: emotion that is expressed through the physicality of performance. To be a jazz master you must be possessed by the music whilst retaining the primitive and rebellious instincts that made you a 'young lion'. Taking this imagery to another level, the sequential, descending, physical nature of the four images carries obvious links to Darwin's charts on the evolution of man. Within Darwin's world, primitive man moves through various evolutionary pathways in order to arrive at the upright and sophisticated species that we see around us. Here, the sequence is reversed; in becoming a master Harrison is turning into a primitive, moving from the refined, restrained and sophisticated to the corporeal, emotion-filled and physically unrefined. The notion of the authentic in jazz as emotion-filled rather than cerebrally inspired has clear historical precedents that are adhered to again in the body of this short text. This album is soulful and honest; there is no rational thinking here, although subtle references are made to jazz's refined and sophisticated aspirations. The text, for example, contains quasi-analytical descriptive terminology: a 'subtle integration' of things linking Harrison to jazz vanguardism.

The advert also explores other myths associated with contemporary jazz practice. In charting Harrison's progression from young lion to jazz master, the advertising copy attempts to place Harrison in the continuum of jazz masters. Indeed, the opening line, 'Donald Harrison is no longer a young lion. *Nouveau Swing* is the work of a master', is written with the implied authority of an anonymous critic. As improbable as it might seem, we, as listeners, are encouraged to accept this work as the product of genius and, in keeping with canonised works, passively to consume it without question or criticism. The myth of autonomous art in jazz establishes the artist as sole creator of the artwork, the emotionally inspired and unique individual. Within this advert, no other musicians are mentioned, the artist is photographed in the singular and the record company assumes a more passive role. Traditional power hierarchies are reinforced; the author is the sole creator, detached from his social environment; the critic is empowered by deciphering the original message of the author and audiences are treated as passive consumers.

### (iv) Plays down commercial status

Finally, the text of this advert aims to play down the commercial status of the product. The advert has a tendency to epitomise the way in which a number of contemporary jazz albums are marketed. Rather than promoting the commercial value of the album – 'go out and buy it', or '*Nouveau Swing* is the product of a master brought to you for £15.99 at all good record stores' – Impulse! seeks to thrust the consumer into a world where the album transcends these commercial traits.[32] In this sense, the need to purchase is secondary to the quality of the work. Once we appreciate that the album is the work of a genius, it follows that every jazz fan must have a copy to sit alongside their other masterworks. Building on the legacy of Impulse!'s recorded history, we are encouraged to accept the notion that great art is divorced from commercial influence. Through the integrity of the artist and his music, we are made to feel that what we are consuming is the genuine, authentic artefact. It would be a sign of bad taste to assign a commercial value to such a thing. Everything from the wording to the imagery hints at a classic status; there is no need for commercial gimmicks here. These non-commercial messages are dressed up within the altruistic words of the honest and trustworthy record company. You could imagine that the record company has gone to great lengths in bringing this artwork to our attention, and it is now available for us to witness. Once it is consumed, we will be enlightened; Donald Harrison's music is good for us. Indeed, the most typical commercial signifier, the brand-mark, is here shown almost as a third-party endorsement, and a mark of the album's authenticity.

## Impulsive behaviour: 1961

When comparing contemporary advertising techniques to the historical model of the 1960s, many subtle changes can be observed that comment on the status of contemporary jazz artists. The following quotation is taken from an Impulse! advert in the April issue of *Downbeat* magazine in 1961:

THE NEW WAVE IN JAZZ – FEEL IT ON IMPULSE!, the new force in jazz recording. The purpose of IMPULSE is as simple – and as complex – as jazz itself: to present the supreme jazzmen at the very crest of their art. IMPULSE artists are great adventurous leaders … And this IMPULSE promises: inspired performances given every advanced technical aid to insure supreme clarity and authenticity. IMPULSE records are available now. Go and get them.[33]

Here, we have the text from an advertisement by the newly formed Impulse! label that also celebrates its four leading artists. Looking at the text, the advert looks very similar to those you see in the jazz press today. As well as displaying the general text (above), the advert displays the names of its significant figures and photographs of their album covers. The familiar Impulse! logo is displayed as a corporate identification, as it is throughout the label's history. However, the advert (and others of this type around this period) promotes jazz as a contemporary and radical form, the New Wave and the newest concepts in contemporary jazz; Impulse! promotes inspired performances by adventurous leaders. The air of radicalism found in these adverts stresses the importance of forward thinking and implies that authenticity is found not in the history of jazz but in present-day performances. This fact is exemplified by the embracing of technology: Impulse! offers the promise that its inspired performances will be given every advanced technical aid to ensure supreme clarity and authenticity. Within this context, technology is something that cleanses rather than clouds, 'the new force in jazz recording' echoing the label's now famous strap-line, 'The New Wave in jazz'. This form of technological optimism is reflected in the commercial nature of the product – the advert conveys a clear sense that these records *are* products to be bought, sold and consumed. Consumption is a key tenet of contemporary music and the words 'Go and get them' encourage the materialistic tendencies of the consumer, reinforced by product pricing in the bottom left-hand corner. These points illustrate that, at this time, the commercial world of material instincts was not something to be embarrassed by or distanced from, but to be encouraged.

This situation sums up the problems faced both by record companies and jazz musicians in an age where the construction of a jazz canon has a significant impact on contemporary music and the marketing of products. Artists face the problem of conforming to constructed benchmarks whilst simultaneously aspiring to be original. Advertisers feel a real need to establish the longevity of their jazz product; unlike the understood usage and imme- diacy of pop music, jazz has to forgo its contemporaneity in order to achieve 'classic' status. Tradition, lineage and musical autonomy are essential requirements for an artwork to enter into the musical canon, and contem- porary jazz artists are thrust into a world where they feel the need to age instantly in order to be accepted. The pressures on contemporary artists to conform to established benchmarks, and the paradox this creates, impact upon jazz at many levels. Indeed, writings on jazz often reinforce the position of revering canonised works whilst criticising contemporary artists for doing the same. Take the following two quotations from the supporting essay to Geoff Dyer's literary jazz work *But Beautiful*:

In the five years it was together the classic quartet of Coltrane, Elvin Jones, Jimmy Garrison, and McCoy Tyner – the greatest creative relationship between four men there has ever been – hauled jazz to a pitch of expressivity that has rarely been exceeded by any other artform …

The long shadow of Coltrane and the question of what can still be said in the bebop idiom are part of a larger doubt facing contemporary jazz players: does any new and important work remain to be done? … Since its tradition is one of innovation and improvisation, jazz, it could be argued, is never more traditional than when it is boldly iconoclastic.[34]

Here, we have an example of overly romanticised icon worship on the one hand, celebrating the unassailable achievements of the Coltrane Quartet and, on the other, a criticism of contemporary music for not being able to escape the overwhelming influence of historical works. Within this context, it is easy to understand how contemporary artists can feel the need to live up to the masters of the past or are confused at the prospect of challenging established convention, and this feeds directly into the dominance of nostalgia within today's production and consumption of jazz. The two common definitions of nostalgia revolve around being separated from home or longing for the past; consumption of the Coltrane collection might, therefore, lead us into a position where we long for a homecoming, a desire to return to a magical age in jazz history, when jazz of the era was considered cutting-edge, progressive and political. When taken to their logical conclusion, nostalgic references in products such as these lead to a crisis in culture, by pointing to a bygone age that can never be recovered. Signifiers created in the marketing and packaging of recordings such as the *Complete Impulse! Studio Recordings* draw reference to what original music of the 1960s Impulse! label expressed; they comment on a perceived utopian moment of radicalism when art was created not by looking backwards but by looking forwards. Once this is realised, the consumer (and contemporary artist) is placed in a vacuum where there is no way back and no straightforward means of progression. The result of this crisis leads to a cocooning where the consumer can only find solace in the 'natural' values of the past. In this sense, the nostalgic impulse says as much about our relationship to the present and the future as it does to the past, representing either current dissatisfaction or fear of the future. Ironically, the opening line of the Harrison advert might have as much to say about the consumer as it does the artist; the consumer might feel like an old master but longs to be a young lion.

## From reification to deification

The Impulse! case study has shown that the issues surrounding jazz recordings are complex and relate to key themes of iconicity, collection, nostalgia, community and cultural value. I suggest that we can account for the appeal and impact of reissues such as the *Complete Impulse! Studio Recordings* on a number of levels. First, we could view these products as part of a wider cultural sea-change, where the jazz market now demands retro imagery and nostalgia, but what is presented to consumers is far from the technological optimism seen in the 1950s and 1960s. As discussed above, during its formative years, the Impulse! label promoted the technological aspects of its recordings as central to the appreciation of jazz, stressing the mediated nature of the listening experience. Today, consumers have come to expect *fidelity* as a matter of course and are seeking an intimate and direct audio experience, devoid of technological mediation. Second, consumer desire to build musical icons could be seen as the result of the postmodern condition, the decline of contemporary belief systems and a crisis of identity. Andreas Huyssen, for example, discusses the general dissatisfaction with modernity; the resultant postmodernity finds solace either in looking back (nostalgia) or looking sideways (eclecticism).[35] Third, we could view 'spiritual' and iconic products such as the *Complete Impulse! Studio Recordings* as a mode of industry manipulation; as John Berger suggests, products are instilled with a sense of bogus religiosity to mask their mass-produced and mechanically reproduced status.[36] Although I would agree that recording companies promote certain modes of consumption through the choice, presentation and packaging of their products, I believe that the overall situation is more complex than pure industry manipulation. To view the relationship as one-sided would be to deny the complex exchanges and interactions between producers and consumers. For example, I would suggest that the changes in the marketing strategies of record companies and of record store formats express a broader change in record culture, where consumption habits have become fragmented across a range of niches. Under this new regime, record companies become the exploiters of back catalogues and the creators of infinitely differentiated markets, which encourage consumers to move away from casual purchasing towards more calculated and predictable buying patterns.

Will Straw has suggested that reissues can be said to provide stability within the fragmented marketplace, and serve to ease consumer anxieties caused by the vast array of choices on offer.[37] Straw argues that reissues appeal both to the connoisseur collector – through their consistent packaging and remastered technologies – and the casual buyer (limited in their choices and collections), as they are representative samples of canonised works. The challenge for record companies, however, comes in designing products that both appeal to specialists and ease the anxieties of casual buyers. In promoting jazz, this duality of interest is most effectively catered for by marketing strategies that group products under prestigious trademarks, guaranteeing a continuity between titles. These strategies are evidenced in the promotion of the *Complete Impulse! Studio Recordings* and Donald Harrison's *Nouveau Swing*; both are clearly products of the Impulse! brand, invested with implicit associations with the label's historical legacy, and are also explicitly placed within a continuum of canonical excellence, the Impulse! strap-line and logo emphasising this continuity.

Finally, I would suggest that these types of recording comment on the cultural capital of jazz as an artform and its artistic value. Canonical recordings are not only promoted by opportunistic recording companies wishing to reissue their back catalogues by any, manipulative, means necessary. Iconic recordings are prevalent for a reason, as they appeal to, and reflect, current tastes and consumer desires. Arguably, jazz needs recording icons to help enhance the status of the artform and to separate it further from the everyday world; these icons help enable jazz to be raised to the level of an autonomous art. Equally, jazz consumers need the inherent order and focus of a select band of canonical recordings. For example, Small has commented on the way in which people both need and draw on 'great' composers as mythological heroes of culture, using them to assert values and to provide models for behaviour and relationships. He suggests that, arguably, audiences need myths more than the individual figures themselves when celebrating iconic works; artists within the musical pantheon exist outside historical time.[38] This goes some way to explaining why living artists cannot be considered 'great', as the realities of their live 'presence' subjugate the mythologies of the past. Although Small does not focus on the recording in any significant detail, I would argue that recordings play an essential part in the 'musicking' of people, i.e. the way in which they engage with music on all levels, from performing and listening, to dancing. I would also stress that, in relation to the construction of mythologies, recordings offer themselves as a two-way channel of influence, both affecting and being affected by the tastes and values of listeners.[39] In this respect, mythologies are constructed and preserved to serve the needs and desires of the present day; they say as much about current society as they explain the values of the past.

The reification of jazz fundamentally changed its development forever; indeed, the history of jazz is so deeply entwined with the history of its significant recordings that one is often written as a history of the other. Equally, the issues surrounding jazz recordings are unique to the music, and serve to amplify jazz's distinct values, codes, conventions and mythologies. It is perhaps surprising that this close and complex relationship so often goes unheard in jazz musicology. I would suggest that if, as musicians and listeners, we delve a little deeper and explore our individual relationships to jazz recordings, we can uncover the critical significance of our own impulsive behaviour.

**Figure 8**   Roy Haynes, Thelonious Monk, Charles Mingus and Charlie Parker

Language as culture is the collective memory bank of a people's experience in history. Culture is almost indistinguishable from the language that makes possible its genesis, growth, banking, articulation and indeed its transmission from one generation to the next.[1]

This will be the testimony of an eyewitness. Of course, we do have the saying, 'He lies like an eyewitness.'[2]

The beauty of any good anecdote is that in describing a specific occurrence it also describes a symptom.[3]

## Understanding anecdote

As outlined in previous chapters, the conventional jazz narrative is dominated by mythologies, chronological 'packaged' histories, stereotypical imagery and colourful stories that often oversimplify and romanticise issues surrounding the music. Notably, the jazz anecdote is something that forms a part of any jazz musician's everyday life and is an area relatively untapped in terms of critical appraisal. 'Anecdote' derives from the Greek for 'unpublished' but, unlike the more fashionable 'oral history', the word normally implies an uncritical and less academic approach. Indeed, the semantic connotations of anecdote have allowed it to slip virtually unnoticed, and without serious scrutiny, into the canon of jazz history. The boundaries between anecdote and other forms of narrative, such as oral history and testimony, are often blurred; however, I have deliberately chosen to use the term anecdote as a descriptor – and all that the term implies – to place it, for once, at the centre of critical discussions on jazz. In this chapter, I examine the function of language in jazz, focusing in particular on the way in which both musicians and enthusiasts make use of anecdotes in the construction of history and the celebration of iconic figures. Whilst I focus primarily on the reading of jazz anecdotes, my observations should be placed within the broader context of critical studies on language, anecdote and oral history.[4]

Anecdotal accounts of jazz are an essential ingredient in musicians' interactions and discussions of music. The deeply social nature of the music, its celebrated oral tradition and the obsession with documentation have established anecdotal stories as a primary means of communicating historical information. Indeed, jazz documentaries, publications and everyday conversations – between musicians and enthusiasts alike – usually contain a multitude of anecdotes ranging from the humorous to the mythological. This isn't something new; from historical accounts of early jazz history to commentary on the contemporary jazz scene, anecdote is rife and the discourse is littered with informal narratives and first-hand accounts.[5] Jazz historians often explain the music away through mythological or anecdotal stories, as if the informal biographical (and often non-musical) accounts of jazz icons can unlock doors to a single, unified meaning in the music itself. Indeed, commentators often look for the meaning of works in the romanticised biography of artists or draw conclusions from a number of strange and disparate sources. For example, if you read Ross Russell's biography of Charlie Parker, you could be mistaken for thinking that Parker's eating habits can explain his genius and unlock doors to the effect that the music has on us. Russell cites the following anecdotal account within the context of Parker's early development as a musician:

For ten cents you could buy sandwiches made up from brains or pigs' feet or pigs' snouts, or 'short thighs', which were roasted legs of chicken. That was Charlie's favourite. He'd eat two or three every night, using change his mother gave him for spending money, so that he would always have a little something in his pocket for anything that he needed.[6]

Unlike my reaction to the voice of John Coltrane in Chapter 2, Russell's text exemplifies the romanticised view of the jazz icon, reinforcing the 'great man' theory where any biographical detail is relevant by virtue of association.

In trying to get to grips with the nature and importance of anecdote in jazz practice, I searched for a critical framework in which to place my ideas and observations. In formulating my approach, I examined the function of anecdote and the way in which jazz professionals and enthusiasts make use of it. Although a seemingly innocent and informal method of discussing jazz, anecdote functions on a number of complicated and contrasting levels. As a fundamental part of jazz as social practice, anecdote remains relatively untouched in terms of critical appraisal. In the current climate of opening up the discourse critically, this fact is surprising, given the way in which anecdote presents the historian with a number of complex questions. Anecdote, particularly when it acts as a form of testimony, performs an interesting role within the historicising process. Used as a means of understanding events, anecdote contains the ability to blur boundaries around more conventional readings of the past. As a means of expression, anecdote confuses the relationship between past and present; anecdotal accounts are almost always constructed in retrospect, yet their narrative is capable of giving the recipient the sense of experiencing an event in the present. In this sense, an event that happened fifty years ago can be recounted as if it just happened yesterday. Within this context, anecdote should be regarded as problematic both historically and for the historian, as it has the capability of blurring the distinction between primary and secondary source material. Despite its obvious temporal separation from the event, it typically offers itself to interpretation as a primary source. When used as part of an oral history, for example, anecdote takes on the guise of a primary source by conveying an historical experience through a 'first-hand' account. However, given the temporal break between many an event and anecdote, regarding anecdote as if it were a primary source can be misleading. Even with our reservations about the objectivity and accuracy of 'first-hand' accounts as evidence (as seen in the Volkov quote, above), anecdote's ability to blur historical distinctions further complicates the historicising process, and helps to create many of the myths on which jazz is founded.

In attempting to explore the roots of these anomalies, and to place my observations within a wider critical context, I examine the role of anecdote within four broad categories: anecdote as entertainment, anecdote as appropriation, anecdote as mythology and anecdote as testimony. This list is not designed to be exhaustive but offers a number of perspectives on the differing functions of anecdote. From these perspectives, I evaluate its role within jazz practice and examine the influence of language on our understanding of history.

## Anecdote as entertainment

When I was a kid, that um ... My mother – we lived in an old town in Louisiana named Butte Louisiana – she sent me down to the pond to get a pail of water one day, and I came back, and my mother was on the porch, and she wanted to know 'Where's that water?' I said, 'Well momma, there's a big old rusty alligator in that water.' She said, 'Oh boy, go and get that water – don't you know that alligator's as scared of you as you is of him?' I said, 'Well, if that alligator's as scared of me as I is of him momma, that water ain't fit to drink.' [laughter][7]

The most common understanding of anecdote is that of an entertaining story, the content of which should not be taken too seriously. At a time when jazz has entered the institution and has in many ways aligned itself with classical practice, the jazz anecdote maintains the distinctiveness of the music and helps to differentiate it from other, more 'serious' artforms. Jazz musicians continue to recount the history of the music through anecdote, often under the guise of serious historical study. Anecdote serves as an important ingredient in jazz practice as, in contrast to the majority of classical music, the history of the artform is still considered recent. Historians can still draw on first-hand accounts of the music in its formative years by musicians who lived through the experience. Secondly, anecdote has a relevance to jazz practice as it ties in directly with the celebration of oral traditions. Where the recording undermines the value of oral history, crystallising fleeting musical performances into standards, anecdote maintains much of the fluidity of oral history. Anecdote tends to be altered during each recitation, according to the context in which it is delivered. Bill Crow comments on this process:

Anecdotes, arising from an oral tradition, have their own rules. A good story will often acquire modifications and improvements as it is retold. If the teller can't remember a particular detail he needs to move the story along, he will invent one and half believe in its veracity as he invents it, because it fits the situation. Things that happen to one person will sometimes be attributed to someone else who seems a more appropriate protagonist. Once a good story enters the jazz world, it takes on a life of its own.[8]

Additionally, the entertaining aspect of anecdote can be used to avoid critical readings of jazz altogether, particularly when taken together with a journalistic approach to jazz history. This feeds into Krin Gabbard's analysis of journalistic prose in jazz literature and his discussion of uncritical texts that appear under the guise of a scholarly study but that help to promote jazz's mystery and the autonomy of the jazz icon.[9] Through these informal, often entertaining journalistic accounts, anecdote is rife, with analysis of the music enmeshed in a string of subjective, voyeuristic or irrelevant stories. From this perspective, the widespread myth of jazz as a purely autonomous, natural practice is promoted, with questions surrounding the music's social function and development ignored. Gabbard's criticism illustrates this point; when the subject matter becomes too challenging or when the autonomy of the music is in danger of being questioned, authors tend to refer to their musical experience in informal or journalistic terms.[10] Mirroring this technique, anecdote functions as an essential tool in promoting an unscholarly approach to the music. The reader is engaged by the entertaining rhetoric of the text and is placed in a position where s/he is encouraged to receive the music as autonomous, and in uncritical terms.

However, the widely accepted function of anecdote as entertainment should not be discredited, as the practice is an essential and often engaging part of jazz discourse. At its best, anecdote has the power to introduce people to the music and its history through attractive prose and entertaining narrative. As a form of communication, anecdote can unlock the imagination and create a situation where events are 'relived' as if for the first time. Whether it recounts arguments in the studio or on the bandstand, or descriptions of the wood-shedding practices of jazz icons, anecdote brings the reader into the musician's world through its persuasive and entertaining value. From this perspective, anecdote, especially in its oral form, has a greater immediacy than biography or autobiography, in that it is consumed as an unmediated narrative, divorced from editorial control and reflective accounts. The Louis Armstrong anecdote recounted above appears in several texts including a reissue of the 1954 album *Louis Armstrong Plays W. C. Handy*. The reissued version includes not only musical out-takes but also studio dialogue and an interview with W. C. Handy himself. Here, anecdote is acknowledged as an important part of jazz practice. Within the framework of an historically important recorded document, anecdotal stories bring the listener into the world of the studio; the recording gives the listener a voyeuristic view into the window of the past, allowing him/her to witness an event taking place. When receiving the reissued material, we not only hear Armstrong play, but also get to listen to his interplay with other musicians and sample his humour first-hand. The story cited is humorous, and also gives the listener an opportunity to hear what one of the geniuses of jazz history has to say. This underlines the fact that when a work is canonised or a musician is mythologised, their associated paraphernalia gain an intrinsic value, almost regardless of content. This is demonstrated most clearly in the output of Armstrong, who was arguably one of the most prolific musicians to write and speak about jazz. Armstrong's output as a commentator included letters, notes and general writings on jazz that have fascinated jazz fans, collectors and historians alike.[11] As a representative example of a reissue that is considered historically important, the Armstrong/W. C. Handy 'artefact' shows how anecdotal content is now placed alongside musical content when viewing jazz in its historical context.

Anecdote can provide the collector with a useful addition to his/her recorded material, and can present the listener with a new and pleasurable way into the music. On a more critical level, however, the function of anecdote as entertainment should be treated with caution. It could be argued that, through entertainment, anecdotal narrative has the power to promote implicit ideology, precisely because it has the power to stimulate the reader in the act of consumption. In effect, anecdote as entertainment can be used as an aid to manipulation and the promotion of a dominant ideology through the lowering of the listener's critical awareness; in making assumptions about the informal nature of dialogue, we are perhaps open to influence on a subliminal level. Bill Crow cites an amusing example of the way an anecdote has become associated with the bassist Red Kelly. For thirty or forty years, Kelly had been linked with an incident where he made a mess at a party one evening and returned the next day to make amends. On his return he accidentally sat on the hostess's tiny dog, breaking its neck, and proceeded to hide the dead animal under the lid of the grand piano before making a swift exit. However, Crow contacted Kelly and received the following explanation:

The truth about that story is, I was on my way to work in Seattle one night with a trombone player named Mike Hobi, and he told me this story that he'd read someplace about the guy and the dog. I latched onto it, because I just loved it, and started telling it to people. I guess because of my erratic behavior, people said, 'Oh, you're just telling a story about yourself.' I said, 'No, it ain't me.' But they would just say, 'Ah, bullshit.' Finally you just tell the story, and everybody assumes it's you. Total strangers would come up to me and say, 'Are you the guy that sat on the dog?'

After years of going through this, it got to where I had finally resigned myself, where I didn't even deny any complicity in it at all. People would come up to me in Florida or someplace, and say, 'Are you the guy with the dog?'

'Yeah, that's me.'

So I finally come back to Seattle and run into Mike Hobi, and he says, 'Listen, tell me the story about you and the dog again.' And he's the guy that told it to me! There are some colorful things you do, but that was not one of them! It just got completely out of hand.[12]

Crow goes on to acknowledge the fact that some readers will still attribute the story to Red Kelly, even though they have read his explanation. Crow makes the important point that readers will continue to recite Kelly's story in its current form precisely because it is the sort of thing that should have happened to him.

If executed well, the telling of an entertaining anecdote results in the desire to retell: a sharing of favourite stories similar to the delivery of a joke. Through this progression, dominant ideologies can be promoted, along with their accompanying mythologies. The informal character of anecdotal narrative aids this phenomenon; if something is not perceived as 'political' or 'ideological', then there is no harm in repeating it to others. From this perspective, the function of anecdote as entertainment should be regarded as an ideological practice precisely because it is perceived as 'natural', part of our everyday lives. The fact that anecdote is described as humorous leads to its being considered insignificant, lacking in power and influence.

However, I would argue that it is precisely because of its perceived insignificance and harmless nature that the humorous anecdote has powerful ideological potential.

## Anecdote as appropriation

Unlike jazz autobiography, the function of anecdote in jazz practice has remained relatively untouched in terms of critical study. However, critical appraisals of jazz autobiography can inform discussions on the role of anecdote, as similar issues surround the two. In particular, like autobiography, anecdote can be used as a facilitator for several forms of historical appropriation. Christopher Harlos discusses the way in which, historically, jazz autobiography has provided musicians with the vehicle to seize a kind of narrative authority over the music they create.[13] In Harlos's view, personal accounts can bring the 'discursive voice' into the world of jazz history, enabling the musician to speak where only music had existed before. In effect, autobiography acts as a counter-measure against established norms and conventions of writings on jazz, breaking down the hierarchy of 'narrator' passing judgement on 'performer'. Similarly, jazz anecdote helps to give voice to the jazz musician in a more informal sense; the musician has the power to take control of the discourse through informal narrative and first-hand accounts of events as they happen. Anecdote empowers the musician through informal dialogue, functioning in many senses to undermine the value of formal, critical and mediated 'abstract' commentary. In this sense, anecdote serves as a vehicle for appropriation, giving musicians the potential to discuss the music on their own terms, to take control of the discourse and to contrast with external commentary. Arthur Taylor's seminal text *Notes and Tones* is one of the most famous collections of informal interviews with influential jazz musicians.[14] Within the text, jazz musicians have the opportunity to give voice to issues 'in their own words'. The narrative is supposedly unmediated, as musicians are talking directly to a fellow musician, someone who speaks 'their' language. The assumed 'otherness' of the musician is summed up in the foreword to the text: 'My predominant motivation in publishing *Notes and Tones* was that it was inspired by the real voices of musicians as they saw themselves and not as critics or journalists saw them. I wanted an insider's view.'[15] Here, Taylor echoes Harlos's view of musicians appropriating the historical discourse, taking control of the jazz narrative. Indeed, the text functions as a valuable medium for African

American musicians to speak on issues surrounding race, politics and media exploitation. The collection of informal interviews documents the musicians' view of jazz history, previously disenfranchised African American artists being the 'real voices' implied in Taylor's words. When viewed in this sense, a simple, explicitly unmediated agenda gives way to an implicit, political discourse that uses anecdote and informal narrative as an aid to historical appropriation.

Political and historical appropriation can be seen in a number of jazz texts. Following on from Taylor's body of work, a clear example of this kind of appropriation is cited in Howard Brofsky's 'Miles Davis and "My Funny Valentine": The Evolution of a Solo'.[16] This article aims to establish Miles Davis's recorded versions of 'My Funny Valentine' as works of genius born out of a heated racial and political context. Brofsky discusses the way in which Davis's recorded legacy of the 1950s and 1960s 'wrestles' the ballad away from the popular recordings of white jazz musician, Chet Baker. Baker's version of 'My Funny Valentine' had received tremendous popular acclaim and had been dubbed by many critics of the time as a 'jazz classic'. Brofsky analyses Davis's versions of the ballad, and describes them as stealing the limelight away from Baker, placing them firmly in the realm of the genius. In the article, the locus of both racial tension and narrative logic revolves around an anecdote cited in Bill Cole's biography of Miles Davis:

It seems more than just an accident of history that Miles should dramatically walk into Baker's [not Chet] Keyboard Lounge in Detroit with the Max Roach/Clifford Brown quintet performing and begin playing 'My Funny Valentine'. This was early in 1954, and Miles was playing single with a local rhythm section at the Bluebird Bar, not far from Baker's. Drugs had now taken their toll and pushed him near the point of no return. That night, he suddenly walked into the lounge where his competitor group was playing, interrupted the band with his own rendition of his favorite ballad, and walked out.[17]

As a backdrop to this anecdote, Brofsky describes an historical context that is laden with racial and political overtones. Through an anecdotal account of the time, Brofsky seeks to illustrate how Miles was supposedly fraught with racial tension to the point where he was overcome by emotion and driven to perform 'My Funny Valentine' as a political gesture. From this perspective, anecdotal evidence provides the key to understanding an historical event; Brofsky uses anecdote to reinforce his views on the racial, political and historical context, and to emphasise the iconic significance of Miles Davis. However, when viewing this account from Miles Davis's perspective, Brofsky's use of anecdote as appropriation comes to light. The following is stated in Miles Davis's autobiography:

> But they got the story all wrong when they say that I just came stumbling in out of the rain with my horn in a brown paper bag and walked up on stage and started playing 'My Funny Valentine'. They say Brownie – that's what we called Clifford – let me play because he felt sorry for me, that he stopped the band from playing whatever it was that they were playing, and then I stumbled off the bandstand and back out into the rain. I guess that would make a nice scene in a movie, but it didn't happen … That's just legend. I might have been a junkie but I wasn't as strung out as all that; I was on the road to kicking my habit.[18]

Although denying the incident, Miles does state that he sat in with the band. However, Davis's bemusement is taken a stage further by more recent historical developments. Bill Kirchner points out that this event could not possibly have happened as it is recounted, as not only did Miles spend a limited amount of time in Detroit in 1954; more significantly, the Max Roach–Clifford Brown group had yet to be formed.[19] This example demonstrates how anecdote can be used to appropriate historical events and help to promote a specific ideology. Brofsky's politicised reading of the event is exposed through his dependence on an inaccurate anecdote; the focal point of his argument is challenged as his main source of evidence is questioned. Here, we have a clear example of how an attractive narrative has more apparent credibility than dry historical facts when promoting a specific agenda. The use of anecdote in this context highlights how unreliable evidence can enter jazz folklore and become more significant than fact, by creating an attractive narrative that is both memorable and outside the usual boundaries of criticism. In effect, rhetoric has the power to exert influence over fact, helping to promote iconic readings of the past that are appropriated and mythologised. Perhaps more significantly, this example illustrates how history should be considered a fluid entity, concepts of 'fact' and 'truth' changing according to perspective and interpretations of cultural value.

## Anecdote as mythology

Anecdotal evidence has become synonymous with jazz practice in both practical and theoretical terms. As an example of the power of anecdote, I will recount my own anecdote of an anecdote told by the legendary jazz historian Dan Morgenstern in 2000. Morgenstern was giving an oral presentation at an international jazz conference of his life in jazz, living and working with the 'greats'.[20] Whilst acknowledging the magnitude of Morgenstern's knowledge and first-hand experience of jazz history taking shape, I was amazed at the audience's low level of critical engagement with the subject matter and the general awe-inspired response to the material being presented. The silence and total obedience of the audience were disrupted only when Morgenstern uncovered one of the great untold secrets of jazz history. A gasp ensued as, wait for it, Morgenstern confessed to witnessing Billie Holiday … 'eating chicken in a basket in a nightclub'.

This relatively funny and somewhat surreal story highlights both jazz musicians' and enthusiasts' thirst for anecdotal stories, where any account of the past is a credible and *relevant* account, as long as it fits in with established convention and is told by someone in authority. The obsession with anecdote feeds our desire for insight, information and the reliving of the past, but the fascination far exceeds simple voyeurism in its function. As a method of communication, anecdote not only provides us with a sense of entertainment but also plays a significant role in shaping our perceptions of the music and its practitioners. Anecdote can help to inform the history of the music by contextualising events whilst simultaneously constructing jazz mythologies. When listening to Morgenstern, I was struck by the way his story commented on how jazz icons are mythologised, taken out of the environment of the real to the extent where they cannot be perceived to function as human. Here, as with my distancing the voice of Coltrane from the music of Coltrane in Chapter 2, the thought of Billie Holiday eating chicken in a basket was beyond the comprehension of some audience members; a simple human act was received almost as a myth in itself. In effect, the historicising process can lead to facts being recounted with disbelief; mythology is more real than 'truth', especially when placing the autonomous artist in the realm of the social.

Anecdotal accounts not only inform and comment on jazz mythologies; they can also play an integral role in creating them. Randy Weston recites his first-hand account of an early encounter with Thelonious Monk:

When I finally discovered Thelonious, I went to his house … after hearing him the second time. I went by and asked him if I could come by to see him, and he said, 'Yes': I went to his house. And I was in his house about nine hours … I'll never forget this because he had a picture of Billie Holiday on the ceiling and he had a red light on a small piano. So, being a young musician, I started to ask him a lot of questions – he didn't answer any question, at all. And I must have stayed there about maybe one hour, asking him questions; he never said anything, you know. I stayed inside that room … close to nine hours … just with him, and all of a sudden it got very quiet, it got very silent. And finally, I said, 'Well, Mr Monk, thanks very much for inviting me, you know, I think I'd better leave, right?' He said, 'Okay, come by and see me again', and I left and I was completely perplexed, see. When I went back to see him again a month later, he played the piano almost two or three hours for me. Then I realised, because I've done a lot of reading of Sufism and mysticism – I realised, in ancient cultures a lot of the masters, they communicate without words, you see. And Monk, he was a master of that.[21]

Here, the historical event is transformed into mythology through anecdotal mediation. The entertaining narrative assists in constructing an aura around the artist that can be recounted time and time again. Weston's words are constructed in the present and placed in an historical context; we have a first-hand account of an experience with Monk that is vividly remembered, down to the colour of lamplight and the picture of Billie Holiday on the ceiling. In retrospect, however, by attempting to make sense of his unusual experience, Weston constructs a narrative that is outside the physical boundaries of his encounter. Over the course of time, new meanings have been assigned to this experience; the implication now is that Monk has been transformed into an ancient mystic, communicating through musical gestures, not words. Whilst delivered in a seemingly innocent fashion, Weston's anecdote epitomises the historical process of appropriating past events to suit contemporary narratives; Monk's genius and his link to a 'primitive' past are perceived as natural phenomena through the myth-making process. Although interpreted as a form of appropriation, Weston's words reflect the challenges of contemporary artists struggling to express difficult and sometimes contradictory relationships. In this context, Weston is clearly grappling with his experiences and trying to make sense of a complex interaction with Monk.

Anecdote not only functions as a source for the creation of myth, it can also be used to develop and perpetuate existing mythologies. The following account was given by Wynton Marsalis in Ken Burns's *Jazz*:

And out of all of this comes Buddy Bolden: a dark-skinned negro from the church. Buddy Bolden's innovation was one of personality. So instead of playing all this fast stuff, he would bring you the sound of Buddy Bolden. Buddy Bolden invented that beat that we call the big four: that skip on the fourth beat or so legend has it … [demonstrates the musical process of change from music pre-Bolden to post-Bolden] … Now I have the big four. So when I phrase it, I'm gonna sound like me and I'm gonna play with another entire feeling and groove. You're playing to not make it sound like trumpets, but like Buddy Bolden.[22]

Here, Marsalis not only talks about the legendary figure of Buddy Bolden, but also proceeds to enact mythical events and creative solos through informal conversation and performance. The result is one that places Marsalis firmly in the position of interpreter, but essentially, what is he interpreting, bearing in mind that there is no recorded evidence of Bolden's music? On several occasions, Marsalis has placed himself in the position of musical conduit for the forefathers of jazz history, enacting mythical performances and conversations between jazz artists in the pre-recorded era. Within this context, Marsalis is not just assuming the role of interpreter, he assumes the authorial position of Bolden himself whilst recounting history. Throughout the account, Marsalis flicks between the guise of historical observer and the role of creator. Through Marsalis's words, the boundary between the imaginary and the real is blurred; Bolden the legend is given a new voice that historical circumstance denied him. However, rather than dismiss Marsalis's sentiment as an act of fantasy, we are encouraged by his position of cultural interpreter to consume this as a legitimate part of the historical process. Marsalis, perceived as being firmly rooted in the traditions of New Orleans, can make the impossible appear possible. His experience and authoritative stance encourage us to take this mythological development of the Bolden legend seriously.[23] In contexts such as these, anecdote takes on greater significance both when spoken by an authority figure and when working within the framework of the serious film documentary.

## Anecdote as testimony

Taking a step back from its role as entertainment, mythology or appropriation, it is interesting to examine the context in which anecdote is created. One of the most historically important functions of anecdote is the giving of historical testimony. As an act of witnessing, anecdote provides the musician or jazz enthusiast with an opportunity to tell their story in their own words. First-hand accounts are often relayed through oral narratives, stories that are later recounted in text-based or recorded form. Indeed, there has developed a growing need for jazz musicians to record their accounts of music 'as it happened'; jazz libraries, archives and educational institutions increasingly facilitate the giving and documentation of oral testimony. However, this process is often considered essential without questioning why. As jazz historians, we know that testimony must be 'a good thing', but perhaps have not investigated the full implications of why accounts of the music in musicians' own words mean so much to us. Most obviously, testimony is seen as an essential ingredient in the telling and preservation of history, offering the recipient a direct route into the past.

It is within this context that a critical reading of anecdote as testimony can be established, examining the role of the jazz 'witness' in the historical process and uncovering the multifaceted use of first-hand accounts of the music as it happened. When searching for a critical framework in which to place anecdote and testimonial accounts, I thought of the use of witnessing in Claude Lanzmann's epic documentary *Shoah*, the powerful and disturbing film that gives voice to survivors of the Holocaust through testimony.[24] Whilst the two discourses, jazz and the Holocaust, seem far apart, both rely heavily upon testimony when accounting for, preserving and attempting to understand historical events. Within the academic environment, however, disciplines such as media studies, psychoanalysis and history have created frameworks for evaluating testimony in historical discourses, whereas jazz studies has no such formal method of analysis. Here, an interdisciplinary approach to jazz studies uncovers innovative and critical ways of approaching the subject.

## Historical testimony

When used as testimony, jazz anecdotes function primarily to support the recounting of historical events in the lives of significant musicians. Often, first-hand accounts of the music serve to support uncomplicated readings of the music 'as it happened'. Jazz musicians and enthusiasts use testimony as a primary vehicle for understanding the music and its place within society both in oral accounts and text-based readings of the past. The importance of anecdote as historical testimony is recognised throughout the jazz world and used widely by those dedicated to constructing a canonical framework for the music. Archives, libraries and jazz documentaries seek out first-hand accounts of music as it happened, and more frequently, as seen in the Armstrong–W. C. Handy release, records are released with previously unissued tracks containing studio talk and conversations with artists.[25]

In more general terms, testimony has become an increasingly crucial means of understanding and interaction within the media-saturated world, enabling people to relate external events to personal experiences. The proliferation of 'real life' documentaries and eye-witness account programmes on television epitomises this trend. Audiences seem to feel the need to understand events by hearing from those who have experienced them first-hand; from Jerry Springer to the tragedy of September 11, testimony is used as a primary vehicle for interaction and understanding. Felman and Laub's study of testimony as an historical act provides a useful framework from which to compare jazz to other testimony-dominated discourses. Within their study, they examine testimony as a literary and discursive practice, and discuss the reasons why testimony has gained a heightened cultural significance in recent times. They suggest that, as evidence, testimony is used to inform the historical process on many levels. For example, testimony may be called for when facts are not clear or when historical accuracy is challenged or in doubt. First-hand accounts of events help to set the record straight or give weight to a dominant interpretation of the past. Indeed, testimony is also called upon when truth is in doubt or an historical judgement has to be made, such as in a courtroom. Within this context, witnesses take the stand under oath, their testimony acting as evidence to uncover 'truth'.[26]

When viewing historical events such as the Holocaust, the relevance and function of testimony are easily understood. In coming to terms with events so traumatic and incomprehensible, testimony is necessary in order to piece together events in an attempt either to resolve issues or to uncover historical truth. On the other hand, within a jazz context, testimony is presented almost as a cosmetic appendage to an already defined history. Historical facts, events or, indeed, truths are already inscribed; the role of the witness is to give enhanced significance to an already written history. When comparing the two discourses, the practices of recounting and receiving testimony are poles apart. Within the world of Holocaust study, every historical account is placed under the critical spotlight, every shred of 'evidence' questioned, appraised and qualified. Indeed, the role of witnessing within the study of the Holocaust amounts to the study of the critically subjective. In the majority of cases, it is acknowledged that the full extent and depth of historical events and traumas will never truly be realised; to tell the 'whole story' would be to undermine the significance and complexity of the historical event. The discipline of Holocaust studies recognises the complexity of the historical process and understands the need to examine everything from language and narrative to the role of mediation and historical perspective. Within the now-established norms of the jazz world, every act of witnessing serves to feed into a common legacy: the supposed 'ultimate' and objective truth behind the music and its heritage.

## Clinical testimony

Once the limitations of historical accounts are acknowledged, we need to uncover alternative functions for the giving of testimony. If something is ultimately subjective, why is it still necessary or important to give testimony? Why, when a witness has seen an event that is already historically inscribed, do they still feel the desire to recount personal experiences? Felman and Laub comment on this phenomenon, '[Is testimony] a simple medium of historical transmission, or is it, in obscure ways, the unsuspected medium of a healing?'[27] Testimony, therefore, not only has an important historical function, it also serves as a vehicle for 'healing'. The saying 'a problem shared is a problem halved' has a resonance with this process, whereby bearing witness to an event creates the need to relive that experience with others. In this process, the giving of testimony acts as a form of therapy for the witness, creating not only a need to 'tell' but also a need to be 'heard'. Within the field of psychoanalysis, clinical testimonies such as these function as an essential part of the healing process, helping both subjects and the recorders of their testimony, or vendors, to come to terms with traumatic events. Clinical testimony is bound up in a complex web of relationships; to 'share' an experience not only allows the witness to 'exorcise their demons'; it also creates in the receiver a deep-felt desire to know more or to relive events. Writers on Holocaust testimonies often describe the paradoxical array of feelings attached to clinical testimony. For example, Lawrence Langer recounts an interview where the witness states 'you won't understand' and 'you must understand' in the same testimonial account.[28] Similarly, students studying Holocaust testimonies often feel the need to share their experiences with others. In effect, the act of receiving testimony instils in the vendor the desire to give testimony, thus perpetuating the process.

Within the context of jazz, the giving of testimony does not have the same traumatic historical undercurrent as Holocaust testimony; however, first-hand anecdotal accounts often function in clinical terms. Jazz musicians will express the need to tell their story, almost as if to relieve themselves of the burden of history. Once told, a testimonial account of the past is 'out there', to be witnessed by others and to be retold to future generations. The following accounts were given by the drummer Ben Riley when talking about the music of Thelonious Monk. Riley offers several anecdotes about his relationship with Monk and experiences in Monk's band, and attempts to explain why Monk chose to withdraw from performance altogether:

He was a very sensitive, I can say, a very sensitive person. And, er, I think a lot of things happened to him that he took – he held within, he never would release them. And, and I think – in the end I found it finally caught up with him, you know …

I would go back to the fact that, er, the group Sphere I was involved with. Well, our first album was dedicated to Thelonious, and the music that we wanted to play was his music. And we decided that, maybe, if this album was good enough, it would encourage him to play again. But, the morning – the day that we went in to record, he passed away that morning while we were in the studio. So we never – he never had the chance to hear the music …[29]

Riley's sadness and sense of regret is clear within this passage. Obviously, his attempt to get Monk playing again was in vain and Riley felt that a number of issues were left unresolved. Here, we have a clear example of how testimony can function in a clinical form. When Riley speaks, there is both a sense of unease in his voice and a need to share his experiences with others, as if to seek some form of resolution. In this sense, clinical testimony is used not only as an attempt to understand the past but also as an emotional release.

## Poetic testimony

When dealing with testimonies, the historian's role is to question the detail of any account and explore the extent to which the truth is articulated. As we examined earlier, oral accounts of the past often contain inaccurate readings or skewed versions of events. However, within studies of clinical testimonies, the search for complete facts and entirely accurate accounts can be a futile exercise, given the historical distance between event and its testimony, and, occasionally, the traumatic nature of the historical events. Some historians have dismissed oral testimony as unreliable when facts are omitted, changed or remembered differently. How can the historian draw a series of conclusions from inaccurate information, when something did not happen entirely in the way in which it is presented? Indeed, a traditional historical or legal reading of an inaccurate testimony would be to dismiss it as unreliable evidence. By adopting a psychoanalytic methodology, however, the problem of 'inaccurate' or fragmented testimony can be addressed by understanding the process in poetic terms. When a known participant in an historical event recounts a story with a number of anomalies, it would obviously be wasteful to consider everything the witness is saying as useless and/or insubstantial. In the foreword to his study of Holocaust testimonies, Langer states:

[S]ince testimonies are human documents rather than merely historical ones, the troubled interaction between past and present achieves a gravity that surpasses the concern with accuracy. Factual errors do occur from time to time, as do simple lapses; but they seem trivial in comparison to the complex layers of memory that give birth to the versions of the self that we shall be studying ...[30]

In this context, poetic testimony can be understood not as a statement of truth, but rather as a means of access to the truth as process. As the term suggests, poetic testimony can unlock doors in the recipient's mind, enabling the recipient to transcend the minutiae of detailed facts and attempt to understand the witness's emotion on a psychological level. When applied to jazz testimony, many of the traumas evaporate, but the need for poetic understanding can still be called upon. Take again the anecdote cited by Howard Brofsky. We have already seen how this information could be considered inaccurate as, if we believe either Bill Kirchner or Miles Davis himself, the events could not possibly have happened in the way in which they were presented. Brofsky used the anecdote as a form of testimony to reinforce his political agenda and interpretation of the racial and political context of America in the 1950s. Viewed from the perspective of poetic testimony, the initial dismissal can be re-examined or reread with the aim of tapping into Brofsky's perspective and emotions. Once moved into a position where minor details of events are ignored, access can be gained to the function of testimony on a poetic level. The anecdote, credited to the artist Richard (Prophet) Jennings, may be historically inaccurate, but opens doors not only to the experience of the witness but also to the emotion of Brofsky and his reading of the period. Here, Brofsky's citation of an historically questionable anecdote can be viewed as a useful form of poetic testimony, as it aims to articulate a mood or feeling experienced within a particular point in history. There is a word of caution here, as in order to appreciate fully the poetic function of the Brofsky anecdote, we must be aware of its factual limitations; the fact that an historical account is given in testimonial form often makes this process difficult to decipher.

Poetic testimony enables us to enter the discourse on a deeper level, trying to access given emotions and experiences of a specific historical context. In other words, although not representative of something that happened factually in its entirety, poetic testimony retains a symbolic function, unlocking doors to historical experience and emotion. Poetic testimonies give the reader access to a means of expression: not an expression of exactitude and detail, but an expression of emotion or experience. Taken in this light, the bearer of witness is not simply an historian who documents things, but is someone who retains their own cultural baggage, either in the way they experience events or recount them retrospectively. Indeed, poetic testimony could be seen as an alternative to empirical evidence by acknowledging cultural ideology and the subjective in the writing of history.

## Anecdotal language and the narrative of history

By placing jazz anecdote within the framework of disciplines such as media studies, history and psychoanalysis, the discourse is given a necessary critical perspective. Jazz narratives often concern themselves with readings of history; studies of other disciplines can inform this process, especially when they represent historical study at its most intense. For example, when comparing jazz narratives to Holocaust testimonies, the foundations on which jazz anecdotes are founded are radically questioned. Unlike conventional jazz narratives, Holocaust studies acknowledge the need to recognise the subjective; no single testimony can speak universally. History, from this perspective, can never be fully understood. Within such an environment, every text or historical account is subject to questioning and appraisal; there are no single authorial voices within history, the struggle for authorship is still a rather contentious issue. Within Holocaust studies, the acknowledgement that there are no absolutes could in turn lead to a place for Holocaust deniers to enter the discourse. However, in defence of this appraisal, current thinking would say that to deny Holocaust 'deniers' a voice would ultimately be to weaken the discourse, as complete historical appropriation can signify the ultimate form of ideological censorship. History is at its most intense when it is contested, and this active debate keeps the subject very much alive; in turn, there is less likelihood of perceiving the traumatic events of the Holocaust as something historically remote. Holocaust deniers are discredited through the strength of others' testimony, critical engagement with historical evidence and the volume and magnitude of first-hand accounts; the process of recording the history of the Holocaust is ongoing, with every testimony serving to inform the bigger picture. Unlike the world of jazz, which tends to simplify and crystallise its history into a single consumable package ('now available in a DVD boxed set'), there is a recognition in Holocaust studies that the bigger picture will never be fully realised. The role of the historian within the study of the Holocaust is a sensitive one, where duties and modes of interpretation are clearly defined; writers aim to make sense of their subject matter without laying claim to absolute understanding. The role of documentary evidence aims to be as impartial as possible, with the documentary mediator assuming a passive role. In comparing, for example, Claude Lanzmann's *Shoah* with Ken Burns's *Jazz*, the directors' roles would seem grossly opposed. However, on closer inspection, a lot of similarities can be seen in the two documentaries. Both films function on an epic scale, offering readings of events in history. The two films draw on testimonial evidence to inform historical discourses bound up with politics, trauma and oppression. However, as historical documents, Burns's narrative can be read as a closed, authorial narrative: a defined entity, depicting the frozen history of jazz in retrospect. Lanzmann's documentary, on the other hand, treats the historical subject matter as yet to be understood; the voices documented remain in the present, provoking thought and stimulating further conversation. The work invites active participation in the act of consumption, encouraging readers to use the documentary experience as a platform for further discussion. However much Burns's film sparks conversation, discussions usually focus on uncritical commentary, reflecting on a body of 'evidence' that underpins an already inscribed iconic history.

When comparing jazz to other disciplinary approaches to historical testimony, it clearly becomes apparent that jazz testimony and other testimony-dominated discourses operate at opposite extremes of the critical spectrum. When examining testimonies, the need for a sensitive, thorough and critical framework for discussion is largely self-evident when considering the extremely traumatic and devastating effects of history. 'The writer's function is not without its arduous duties. By definition, he cannot serve today those who make history; he must serve those who are subject to it.'[31] Through the examination of various functions of jazz anecdote, I have deliberately chosen examples from various contexts (film, recording, literature, spoken word) to demonstrate how widespread the use of anecdote is. As a method of conveying ideas and information, anecdote is enshrined in a number of everyday practices and media, from jazz biography and personal testimonies to discussions of musical performance and jazz practice. However, rather than treating anecdote as a purely entertaining and immaterial part of the jazz discourse, I would argue that its use influences the historical process at every level. Indeed, more attention needs to be paid to anecdote's ability to construct and perpetuate certain ideological views under the guise of entertainment and impartiality. When aiming to account for the value and function of anecdote in the jazz discourse, it is useful to consider the role of narrative and language in our understanding of history. There is a symbiotic relationship between history and narrative; narrative is the point where chronology (as a fixed list of events) ends, and history (the telling of the story) begins. As cultural subjects, we relate to and understand history through the narrative process. In turn, narrative could not exist without language; language is the means through which our identities are shaped and our understanding of history is inscribed. Poststructuralist commentaries explore the way in which our understanding of the world cannot be divorced from language and, in turn, how language defines us. In this respect, language remains central not only to the construction and representation of history but also to defining who we are, what we think and how we see the world. Within this framework, history is as reliant on narrative as narrative is on language; therefore, our sense of history and cultural identity is deeply shaped by both the power of language and narrative form. In a jazz context, the concept of language as power is embodied within the world of the anecdote and, in many cases, anecdotal language provides the key to understanding jazz identities. As a vibrant means through which the past is understood, anecdotal narrative assumes a powerful position in conveying ideas and experiences. Through attractive narrative, anecdote can enable history to be presented in a convincing form, its persuasive rhetorical power shaping both historical identity and value. In other words, if history is narrative and narrative is language, then anecdote has the potential to play a central role in the creation of jazz history. Whether used within the context of entertainment, historical appropriation, jazz mythology or testimony, anecdote serves as an essential component in the historicising process. Indeed, our recognition that anecdote plays a crucial role in the way both jazz history and practice develop should encourage us to place anecdote to the forefront of a critical jazz discourse. By moving anecdote from the margins of jazz to the centre of study, readers and practitioners of jazz can gain a heightened critical awareness of anecdote and its historical function, previous implicit ideological power can be made explicit, and its full historical and political potential realised. Indeed, the next time somebody has a tale to tell, perhaps we will consider that we are hearing more than an entertaining story; we are bearing full witness to a jazz history in the making.

**Figure 9** Duke Ellington and Billy Strayhorn

The related issue of the evolution of musical style was now questioned: if atonality was presented as an inevitable stylistic evolution, then clearly Duke Ellington was a musical dinosaur.[1]

As long as … theory remains unconscious and unthought about, it not only controls people and their musical activities, limiting and circumscribing their capabilities, but also renders them vulnerable to manipulation by those … who have an interest in doing so for purposes of power, status, or profit.[2]

The jazz world has always been filled with interesting personalities: gunslingers and saints, the beautiful and the damned. Few, however, have embodied in one personality as many contradictions as Duke Ellington.[3]

The emergence of critical musicology in recent years has enabled scholars to challenge traditional ways of discussing and understanding music. By using methodologies established within fields such as cultural and critical theory, many assumptions about music and its history have been contested and opened up to new critical perspectives. For example, within the study of music, distinctions between high and low culture have largely been broken down, and music itself is now widely understood as socially constructed, rather than having inherent qualities that constitute some essential and enduring aesthetic. This has led to writers challenging traditional approaches that promote the inherent aesthetic values of one artwork over lesser, popular, creations.[4] Similarly, the grounding of the study of art in the social has exposed and disbanded mythologies that promote art's transcendent qualities. Art is no longer discussed as the product of the 'genius' who is the conduit for divine inspiration and whose work transcends time and place, and has been replaced by discussions of art as a medium situated within a specific set of complex historical and political relationships.

When adopting this critical approach to the study of music, it is vital to have an awareness of the way in which the history of an artform is constructed and narratives are written. As several writers have suggested, there is often a confusion between history as a lived experience and history as it is represented in the present.[5] The construction of historical narratives leads to skewed and simplified accounts of the past that, more often than not, reflect the ideologies or dominant values of the present social order. This echoes the recent assertions of several jazz scholars who suggest that jazz history is written in reverse, and that a linear tradition has been constructed to fulfil a number of functions for the jazz world today.[6]

Depicting history in a linear and compartmentalised manner clearly presents problems for historians with an interest in alternative histories, or in musicians who fall between the cracks of established stylistic periods ('baroque', 'bebop' etc.). Take, for example, jazz writings that fall within categories of what Krin Gabbard describes as 'inclusionist' and 'exclusionist'.[7] Inclusionists are the types of scholar who work on the output of a single artist, concentrating on every recorded performance even when their contribution is minimal. This fetishised collection of a single artist's material does not account for the quality of work or contribution to the recording as a whole. As was the case with Louis Armstrong in the previous chapter, all material becomes valuable once an artist is regarded as iconic. Exclusionists, on the other hand, are writers who discuss music as a whole in large historical sweeps. This approach to history invests time and energy in causal narration, promoting labels such as swing, bebop, cool, hard bop etc. to explain that jazz is a neat chronology of ten-year developments. This type of historical documentation could arguably be said to suppress the kind of artist who does not play in an appropriate style or conform to the agreed narrative; if you are slightly unconventional or refuse to be pigeonholed, you are excluded or branded as an eccentric (more of this shortly). Although Gabbard uses the terms inclusionist and exclusionist in specific relation to discographers, the impact of this approach resonates within the majority of historical and biographical writings on jazz. These dominant forms of jazz writing do nothing to challenge the historical grand narrative or to promote alternative readings of the music and its social context.

As a response both to the selective view of history and the compartmentalisation of periods into easily digestible boxes, critical musicology has challenged the genealogical model of causal narratives and their teleological nature. Derek Scott's opening quotation, for example, highlights the way in which causal narratives can be problematic not only in promoting an inevitability of progress but also in offering a selected view of stylistic evolution that is presented as universal instead of context-specific. For instance, we are encouraged to consider Ellington as a compositional innovator without considering how harmonic languages differ within different musical forms. Equally, several jazz writers discuss musicians such as Ellington and Parker as great modernists when the term has very different contextual and historical connotations in relation to the aesthetic of composers of the Second Viennese School. The historically situated approach of critical musicology resists the temptation to make broad sweeping statements about history, and avoids developing romanticised theories of musical evolution and influence. Furthermore, the deconstruction of historically entrenched musical assumptions such as the high–low art divide, the promotion of the transcendent genius and causal narration has had a significant impact on jazz writings since the mid 1990s, as a new wave of critical scholars have drawn on cultural theory and interdisciplinary perspectives in evaluating the discursive nature of jazz history.[8] However, despite these engaging critical insights, within a broader cultural framework, jazz is still largely promoted and understood as a music with a causal and compartmentalised history. Indeed, even within New Jazz Studies, the linear narrative of jazz often remains unchallenged or is taken as a given. From the promotion of jazz within arts organisations such as Lincoln Center to jazz documentaries, artist biographies to the majority of jazz education programmes world-wide, many of the age-old assumptions about music not only remain intact but are encouraged to thrive. Within the context of the musical mainstream, jazz is increasingly discussed as a transcendent artform with an array of masterworks and genius figures. This development has led to a clear distancing of jazz from commerce as the historical grand narrative continues to promote jazz as an autonomous artform, detached from the everyday world. Although I suggest that this aesthetic shift is symptomatic of a broader cultural sea-change where jazz is celebrated as an artform aligned more closely with classical music, it could be argued that recent strategies that aim to instil into jazz a heightened aesthetic status are a simple continuation of an historical continuum in which jazz has been discussed as art. From this perspective, the conflict between jazz as 'art' and as a music 'of the people' has antecedents dating back to the music's inception. For example, Bernard Gendron's discussion of the conflict between 'moldy figs' and modernists demonstrates how the 'jazz as art' discourse has surrounded the music at least from the 1930s.[9] Gabbard also suggests that the resolution of factional conflicts between moldy figs and modernists was achieved by the widespread adoption of a causal narrative where one jazz style paves the way for the next.[10] Whether viewing the new aesthetic qualities of 'jazz as art' as part of a historical continuum, or as a new discourse, the genealogical model of jazz history is widespread and dominates all forms of cultural output. Just as classical music has its clearly defined (and equally problematic) historical periods, jazz can now boast its own teleological genealogy with supporting canon and pantheon; from New Orleans to the Swing Era, to bebop and beyond, causal narration has become the primary means of telling the story of jazz. When considering jazz in its wider context it is, perhaps, easy to understand why causal narratives are constructed and celebrated in this way.

First, they offer a ready-made, easily digestible account of the music and its history, in which styles and periods can be studied and celebrated in a logical and straightforward fashion. This, in turn, leads to the aesthetic appreciation of jazz and its related industry being mutually compatible through a uniform adoption of the story of jazz by a range of interest groups. Grant-giving agencies, record companies, publishers, promoters, music education programmes – the list goes on; all benefit from the categorisation of jazz in this way. Secondly, causal narratives help to distinguish jazz from other music, most notably more commercially oriented popular music forms, which are created for their immediacy and use value. A clear teleological narrative helps to promote the concept of legacy and tradition, key tenets of an authentic artform. Regardless of historical relationships or current musical associations, there is a strong desire to separate jazz from popular music in order to preserve jazz's funding and support as a marginalised artform. To align the music more closely with popular culture would jeopardise niche funding and support from arts bodies as well as, arguably, alienating its self-proclaimed 'specialist' fan base.

In this way, the promotion and celebration of the jazz tradition can be understood as implicitly ideological; in effect, the narrative history of jazz reflects the values and aspirations of the present day. To demonstrate this, consider how the adoption of a causal approach to history can present anomalies that challenge mainstream understandings of jazz, and the way in which causal narratives provide a basis for contemporary thinking based on the concept of evolutionary progress. Informed by the development of scientific understanding, where one generation builds on the work of the previous generation, causal narratives promote a view of the present day as the accumulation of all the acquired knowledge and skills to date. It is understandably easy to think about the past as if it is less refined and primitive (how did people survive without soap, electricity or email?), and to perceive the present day as the pinnacle of innovation and progress. Within jazz, though, this neat teleology is only partially present in causal historical narratives, which do not tend to regard the present day as a triumph of artistic development or the culmination of history to date. The history of jazz is therefore problematic and paradoxical in relation to this model of progress and evolution, in that causal narration only works up to a point; it is used in order to reinforce the developmental categories of the jazz tradition leading up to 1970. From the 1970s on, jazz history is widely perceived as fragmented and regressive; the past is romanticised to a point where the great historical masterworks could not conceivably be compared to the present day. These somewhat contradictory assumptions and opinions do not stack up and reflect a much broader practice of jazz historiography where, as DeVeaux suggests, a constructed jazz tradition encourages people to think of the music as governed by its own separate set of rules.[11] Further, even though we are surrounded by great living jazz musicians we still buy into the belief that jazz artists today lack innovative voices or charismatic personalities, especially when compared to the masters of the past. This promotion of great artists as a rare breed also adds a degree of status to jazz as a cultural artform; as Christopher Small suggests, rarity creates value and yet 'one is left to wonder if the scarcity of stars is not created and maintained artificially'.[12] The rooting of great jazz in the past thus serves a multitude of functions, from laying the foundations by which music is created and controlled, to instilling jazz with a degree of cultural capital. Therefore, the celebration of the causal jazz narrative serves to promote the idea of progress and evolution while, paradoxically, stifling the living in favour of the dead. In essence, the grand narrative of jazz works is an implicit ideology; the dead can be controlled and manipulated to serve as a foundation for telling the story of jazz today. In this respect, iconic figures can be represented straightforwardly, and function at the symbolic level to reinforce the central themes of the jazz tradition (for example, jazz is an autonomous artform, jazz is not popular music, jazz is an unmediated spiritual performance art, jazz has an authentic lineage and so on). This explains why living artists cannot possibly be understood in the same way as dead icons, for there is a certain safety and security in mythologising the past. Once written into the historical narrative, jazz masters provide the foundation for artistic practice today and are rarely challenged or criticised. Jazz greats are, in turn, *reduced* to mythological figures who remain uncomplicated and unchanging, not like the living who are vulnerable, complex and prone to contradiction. I suggest that this acceptance of a causal narrative up until 1970 sheds light on the ideological nature of jazz history, where the concept of tradition is naturalised, received as a given and not a cultural construct. In this context, the jazz canon remains a dominant and controlling force.

Ideology in jazz can also be seen in the way that certain figures have been written out of history. Examples of historical revisionism in jazz demonstrate that the development of history is by no means straightforward; indeed, the discursive nature of music can be understood most clearly by the ever-shifting boundary of what is considered jazz. Examples of how the jazz narrative has been rewritten over time range from the numerous battles over the ownership of jazz – both in terms of performance practice and music criticism – to the way in which historically significant figures have been downplayed or erased from present-day portrayals of the music. In developing an understanding of how jazz history is constructed to serve the needs, and reinforce the values, of the present day, it is therefore just as important (if not more so) to study what is excluded as what is included, from promoting jazz as art in opposition to commerce, to constructing history along racial, gendered or geographical lines. Writers such as David Ake, Ajay Heble and Scott DeVeaux have discussed how present-day histories have been shaped by idealised notions of what jazz represents, resulting in a gradual shift away from the music's roots in popular culture. DeVeaux, for example, examines the absence of certain musicians in historical studies of jazz and suggests that figures such as Slim Gaillard have been misrepresented or erased from present-day writings on bebop in order to maintain the purity of jazz as 'art'.[13] Even though Gaillard was widely known as a bebop artist during the period, his role as entertainer does not fit within present-day narratives of jazz of the forties and fifties. In response to this, DeVeaux puts together a convincing account of why the musician should be considered a bebop artist; from his artistic interactions with Charlie Parker and subsequent billing with both Gillespie and Parker to his music being the first to be mentioned on the KMPC radio ban of bebop, Gaillard should play a more significant role in the reading of bebop than present-day histories would allow. Building on DeVeaux's point, consider the following passage from Jack Kerouac's *On the Road*:

Dean stands in the back, saying, 'God! Yes!' – and clasping his hands in prayer and sweating. 'Sal, Slim knows time, he knows time.' Slim sits down at the piano and hits two notes, two Cs, then two more, then one, then two, and suddenly the big burly bass-player wakes up from a reverie and realizes Slim is playing 'C-Jam Blues' and he slugs in his big forefinger on the string and the big booming beat begins and everybody starts rocking and Slim looks just as sad as ever, and they blow jazz for half an hour, and then Slim goes mad and grabs the bongos and plays tremendous rapid Cubana beats and yells crazy things in Spanish, in Arabic, in Peruvian dialect, in Egyptian, in every language he knows, and he knows innumerable languages. Finally the set is over; each set takes two hours … Now Dean approached him, he approached his God; he thought Slim was God; he shuffled and bowed in front of him and asked him to join us. 'Right-orooni', says Slim; he'll join anybody but he won't guarantee to be there with you in spirit. Dean got a table, bought drinks, and sat stiffly in front of Slim. Slim dreamed over his head. Every time Slim said, 'Orooni', Dean said, 'Yes!' I sat there with these two madmen. Nothing happened. To Slim Gaillard the whole world was just one big orooni.[14]

Although beat writings have been criticised for their romantic appropriations of blackness, this passage is written with the same degree of reverence as Kerouac's depictions of iconic jazz musicians such as Charlie Parker.[15] Kerouac's writings obviously situate Gaillard within a fictional literary context; however, the deification of Gaillard in this passage serves as an indicator of his significance at the time. These observations illustrate how the constructed grand narrative cannot consider musicians to be simultaneously serious virtuosic artists and commercial entertainers, therefore, characters such as Gaillard are inevitably relegated to alternative histories that do not impact on the significance of jazz as 'art'.

The constructed tradition serves to detach jazz from the everyday world; if the social aspects of a musician's life figures in the jazz narrative, it can be understood either as of secondary importance to the underlying mythologies of jazz, or to serve as a symbolic indicator of the icon's genius. Whether it is Miles Davis's record sales that come to symbolise the underlying aesthetic qualities of his music, or Duke Ellington's ability to look beyond the vices of dysfunctional band members to bring out the *magic* of their artistry, the social aspects of the jazz narrative feed into a bigger story; jazz icons cannot exist purely for pleasure, entertainment and commercial gain.

## Myth and ideology

In jazz, the promotion of a teleological, causal narrative leads to history gaining an overblown, romanticised and mythical character. Yet, despite the anomalies and contradictions identified above, it is interesting to examine why jazz history continues to be constructed and celebrated in this way. One explanation centres on the role that cultural mythology plays in shaping our understanding of the world around us. When exploring the use of myth in constructed historical narratives, we should first consider how mythologies do not just represent deviations from the truth and historical 'facts', they can also provide people with models for behaviour. When viewed in this way, myths provide a means by which relationships can be explained: between individual subjects and communities, the physical and the metaphysical worlds, and so on. As discussed in Chapters 2 and 3, there is an integral link between myth and ritual that helps bind communities together. Mythologies endure because they resonate with us today; they provide a cultural function, outlining codes and conventions by which we live our lives. Essentially, mythologies are used as paradigms for human values and experiences and, as several writers have pointed out, they have played a part in shaping artistic life since the Middle Ages.[16] Small, for example, claims that mythologies are essential to forms of human behaviour not because they offer people accounts of how things originated but because they provide a blueprint for how things ought to be:

A myth, therefore, no matter how ancient its origins or its subject matter, is always concerned with contemporary relationships, here and now. Whether or not it is historically true is beside the point; its value lies not in its truth to any actual past whose reality we can establish or disprove but in its present usefulness as guide to values and to conduct.[17]

Mythology, therefore, is an inevitable part of life, and helps to shape identity and communal values. Whether artistic icons are understood as heroes, villains or divine messengers, mythological paradigms can be mapped across to constructions of the jazz life. However, when mythologies themselves are treated as forms of natural law, they have the potential to indoctrinate, limiting the possibilities for alternative forms of existence. Small continues:

We have been taught, and seem to need, to assert the absolute historical truth of our myths if we are to believe in them, whereas members of most other cultures seem to be able to live with the idea that they are at the same time both true (in the sense of being valid) and untrue (in the historical sense) without feeling any strain.[18]

Although Small's study relates primarily to a critique of the European concert tradition his observations on the usage of myth in western culture can interestingly be compared to the constructed jazz tradition. Arguably, the treatment of mythologies as forms of historical fact goes some way to explaining current obsessions with authenticity in jazz and the celebration of the single-strand causal narrative. The prospect of considering alternative histories or the possibility of a discursive approach to the study of iconic figures would only serve to make the underlying mythologies of jazz explicit. Within the present climate, to conceive of jazz in a different way would undermine the power, status and profit of the myth-makers themselves and so the presentation of a relatively uncontested tradition remains of paramount importance. When understood in this way, the promotion and celebration of jazz mythologies as forms of historical fact lead to the position advocated by Marxist and structuralist writers, where mythology is understood as a form of cultural ideology.

Mythologies do not just impact on jazz at the level of the constructed tradition; they are prevalent throughout the music's discourse, from the anecdotal language explored in the last chapter to the stereotypical representations of artists seen in Chapter 4. Even within live performance settings, the mythologies of jazz are widespread and underpin many codes and conventions of jazz practice. For example, consider the way in which improvisation is championed as mysterious, musicians supposedly 'pulling lines out of the air'; this rides against the reality of improvised music as a codified system that appeals to the expectations of performers and listeners alike.[19] Similarly, when music is notated, musicians are encouraged to internalise the music, memorising the notes on the page, as if to demonstrate that the music flows through the veins, even though music created 'behind a score' might sound more assured and creative. The perception of musicians being possessed by music is intensified further by other subtle codes and conventions and their signifying potential – for example, the way in which performers close their eyes and look up to the heavens, or take in a deep breath as if to signify inspiration. Furthermore, the uncontrollable urge of some instrumentalists to sing out during their improvised solos can be seen as an indication of the musician being possessed by a spirit from within (one only needs to see the priest-like performances of Keith Jarrett to witness all of these codes in action). In all cases, we are encouraged to buy into the idea that the musicians are possessed by music, and the mythology that jazz is both unmediated and other-wordly is continually reinscribed in performance practice itself. When we understand mythology as ideology in jazz, the significance of icons today becomes all the more apparent; icons provide stability and assurance to a community whose values have been under threat historically, and who now have a relative degree of power and influence within the dominant order. Heroic figures are portrayed as fixed entities beyond critical discourse; they are divorced from the complexities and contradictions of the present day. In this respect, icons serve the needs of the present, by maintaining stability and control within the existing social order.

## Jazz and classical music

The use of mythology to promote a fixed ideological view of jazz history is symptomatic of a much broader cultural sea-change where the aesthetic status of jazz is aligned more closely with classical music. Historically, jazz's relationship to classical music has been wrought with friction and contradiction. On the one hand, there have been concerted attempts to bring jazz in line with classical music ranging from the symphonic jazz of Paul Whiteman in the 1920s to experiments in Third Stream music in the 1950s. On the other hand, classical pretentions have been rejected through the development of an independent jazz aesthetic that celebrates the virtues of the African American tradition and the music as a truly American artform. These portrayals resist the Eurocentric descriptions of jazz as well as promoting analytical methodologies that are designed specifically for jazz contexts. From the 1960s onwards, black authenticity has remained central to the perceived ownership of jazz, from the Black Nationalist writings of Amiri Baraka to the heroic idealism put forward by Albert Murray and, latterly, strongly polemic writers such as Stanley Crouch. The frictions surrounding the relationship between jazz and classical music have formed a central part of jazz discourse since the music's inception. However, as writers such as Peter Townsend have claimed, there is a certain inevitability about jazz and its comparison to classical music: 'Between jazz and classical music the lines of demarcation are increasingly hard to draw, as older jazz compositions are performed by repertory orchestras dedicated to the faithful recreation of earlier work, and as jazz players receive commissions to write and perform music for ensembles in concert settings.'[20] Here, changes in cultural status have blurred the boundaries between jazz and classical music; composers such as Duke Ellington are now widely accepted as art composers and have their works performed in traditional concert settings.

Regardless of the historical struggle over the ownership of jazz and its independence from other music, when jazz is discussed as art, the shift in aesthetic status results in an inevitable comparison and alignment with classical music. I argue that, even when the discourse of jazz as art is resistant to Eurocentric understandings of music, when seeking to validate the music as a canonical artform, ironically there is frequently a borrowing of the cultural positioning, rhetoric, performance practices and analytical techniques found within the western concert tradition. As stressed in Chapter 1 when discussing the sacralised culture of art, in order to achieve a shift in aesthetic status, jazz cannot avoid being compared to, and evaluated in relation to, classical music; the jazz canon, pantheon and linear-causal-historical grand narrative combine to create America's Classical Music. Whereas jazz has a long history of performance in concert hall settings, the proliferation of jazz concerts today also demonstrates a shift in cultural status for jazz. On the one hand, Scott DeVeaux suggested that the term 'jazz concert' could at one stage have been considered an oxymoron and yet, within our current context, the proliferation of jazz in concert settings offers a demonstration of how jazz is changing as a cultural signifier. Furthermore, I am interested in the way in which cultural practices found within the concert hall are now readily adopted within informal jazz settings. In this respect, the alignment of jazz with classical music not only occurs within the cultural practices of the music but also in the physical environment of several new jazz venues. Venues such as the Bimhuis in Amsterdam or the several jazz venues at Lincoln Center in New York provide purpose-built jazz spaces within arts organisations that have traditionally been associated with high culture. Stuart Nicholson discusses the political hotbed that surrounded the development of Jazz at Lincoln Center and questions the association with other arts organisations such as the New York Philharmonic, Metropolitan Opera and New York City Ballet. He suggests that the growth and investment in Jazz at Lincoln Center only serve to promote a limited tradition constructed along race lines, the power and influence of such organisations inevitably having a detrimental impact on jazz as a vibrant and ever-changing modern music. In reaction to the general concerns about Jazz at Lincoln Center becoming a powerful museum for jazz, Director Wynton Marsalis defended the cultural shift towards venues traditionally associated with high art, stating that: 'It's just another setting, and what better setting than a place where the other arts are being celebrated?'[21] Although the placement of jazz within the context of broader arts institutions allows the music to be opened up to new audiences through shared marketing opportunities and the creation of arts centres, I argue that the physical attachment to organisations traditionally associated with high art should not be viewed as a geographical accident. Indeed, rather than viewing the architectural alignment as a postmodern blurring of high- and low-brow, we can understand these partnerships at a symbolic level, seeing them to reflect the broader cultural changes occurring within jazz. As Nicholson suggests, jazz's cultural capital is increased by these associations, and the prestige of jazz as art is celebrated above the desire to bring the vernacular into spaces traditionally associated with high art. Indeed, while Marsalis's position is clearly understandable in seeking to gain respect for the ongoing work of jazz musicians, the alignment of jazz within organisations such as Lincoln Center does not represent a breaking down of previously entrenched cultural positions; jazz has not witnessed a disbanding of boundaries between art and popular culture. On the contrary, in this context jazz *is* high art and serves to reinforce the ideology of autonomous art so often reflected in the practices of classical music. With this in mind, Christopher Small's analysis of the rituals and practices of the western concert hall provides many useful insights into changes in the aesthetic of jazz and the motivations behind promoting music as high art. Small suggests that the concert hall of the western concert tradition represents the power and wealth of the cultural elite; it is a physical manifestation of an underlying ideology. The architecture of the concert hall is designed to reinforce values and modes of behaviour and establishes performance as an important activity in its own right, not just as part of another ceremony or event. Small continues by discussing the way in which, as a nineteenth-century innovation, the concert hall is designed to convey an impression of opulence and sumptuousness at the same time as denying the audience the opportunity to socialise: 'The very form of the auditorium tells us that the performance is aimed not at a community of interacting people but a collection of individuals, strangers even, who happen to have come together to hear the musical works. We leave our sociability behind at the auditorium doors.'[22] Drawing on Small's observations on the symbolic nature of the concert hall, it is enlightening to observe how jazz venues that align themselves with high culture either appropriate or modify the codes and conventions of classical music. From the physical design of the auditorium to audience behaviour, the jazz concert clearly treads an uncomfortable path between promoting the music as deeply social on the one hand and artistically autonomous on the other.

Purpose-built concert venues such as those at Lincoln Center signify that what happens inside is to be taken seriously; venues are sanctified spaces where audiences adopt certain codes, conventions and formal behavioural patterns. In effect, the architecture signifies wealth and power, and this, in turn, has an impact on behaviour. Small suggests that in soundproofing performance spaces so that no sound can escape or get in, the design of western concert halls cuts off the music from the outside world; venues are purposely designed to promote the idea that music exists in a time and space outside the real world. Essentially, the ideology of autonomous art is reinforced within the architecture and design of the building. Purpose-built jazz venues function in a similar way but with subtle differences. Although, on the one hand, these venues can be viewed as sanctified spaces encouraging modes of behaviour, their architectural design and layout would on the surface appear to promote the informalities of jazz performance and social aspects of the music's reception. For example, the architecture of both Lincoln Center venues and the Bimhuis in Amsterdam draw reference to the outside world through glass backdrops – façades that allow access to the cityscape beyond. Taken at face value, this architectural feature of new jazz venues rides against Small's notion of the concert hall separating music from the everyday world; we are encouraged to believe that jazz in this environment is not hermetically sealed art for art's sake but a reflection of the sound of everyday life. We could almost be encouraged to imagine that jazz provides the soundtrack for the city scene beyond, connecting the music explicitly to everyday life. However, these design features can be understood as constructing an idealised view of the social, much in the same way as a travel agent would sell a trip to New York. The urban environment is mediated through glass, the transparent façade signifying the 'real world' while the music remains cosseted in the safe, sterile and opulent world of the concert hall. Ironically, the marketing pitch for Lincoln Center's Allen Room promotes the space as being modelled on a Greek amphitheatre. The symbolism here is quite telling; the venue not only connotes high culture and spectacle, it is also a space where myths are created, performed and developed.

Cultural signifiers attached to new jazz venues create a complexity of relationships not found in classical music. Jazz's shifting aesthetic status, its underlying mythologies and social narrative create a discourse in which many signifiers are in direct opposition to one another. Most obviously, the promotion of jazz as an autonomous artform on the one hand and as a deeply social music on the other seems to come to a head within formal concert settings. I will explore this complex relationship in more detail in my final chapter.

## Essentially Ellington?

[T]he existence of composers like Ellington provokes a whole series of mismatches with categories … Ellington's experience, as a composer, bandleader and performer, somewhere between jazz and 'serious music', had a wholeness and unity which defy the theoretical problems of category that swarm about it. Ellington's case illustrates perfectly the ways in which the actualities of jazz … are fragmented and made problematic by the antinomic concepts that are applied to them.[23]

When seeking to get to grips with the impact of mythologies of jazz discussed so far, it is necessary to take some of these observations and to examine how iconic figures fit within the constructed ideals of the neo-traditionalist mainstream. For example, examining how a figure such as Duke Ellington has been portrayed in a range of jazz contexts, from biographies to documentaries to jazz education programmes, can raise a number of thought-provoking insights into iconic representation. Arguably, Ellington is an icon who embodies the values of the constructed jazz tradition more than any other artist; he is widely understood as a jazz legend, and spanned the majority of the music's history until jazz's supposed demise in the 1970s. Within the constructed jazz tradition, Ellington is most often presented as an uncomplicated figure, an elder statesman of jazz who has played the most significant role in asserting jazz's value as an American artform; more than any other iconic jazz figure, he fits into the promotion of jazz as America's Classical Music. Equally, more than any other jazz great, Ellington has come to represent the ideals of the African American hero construct as advocated by writers such as Albert Murray and Ralph Ellison. And yet, as Townsend's quotation above suggests, when scratching beneath the surface, Ellington is a figure who resists simplistic representations and challenges the reductive categorisation of icons found so readily in constructed jazz histories. While I am not dismissing Ellington's stature and significance, the homogenising effect of the jazz canon leads to a position where complex figures are represented as uncomplicated beings, narrativised beyond the point of criticism. Jazz icons are now portrayed in a uniform and straightforward manner to serve the needs and values of the present. Limiting the complexity of iconic figures particularly grates with Ellington's biography, as not only was he acutely aware of the potential implications of pigeon-holing music, but he also consciously set out to problematise the discourse surrounding jazz and its relationship both to art and popular culture. As the numerous writings produced within Ellington's lifetime suggest, the discourse surrounding the icon has always been colourful and, to a certain extent, riddled with complexity and political intrigue.[24] Although the methods of portraying Ellington, or the forms of narrative representation, were largely created during Ellington's lifetime (and to a large extent, fuelled by Ellington himself), biographical accounts following his death have served both to intensify and crystallise dominant representations of the icon's life and music. After surveying a variety of sources on Ellington, from biographies to testimonials and retrospectives, educational pamphlets to critical articles, a dominant narrative emerges that, whether intended or not, has a tendency to reinforce a unified and uncomplicated reading of Ellington's life and music. To illustrate this, the following themes are examples of narrative traits that support the mythologies of the neo-traditionalist jazz world and that leave little room for conflict and contradiction.

## Ellington as great American composer

'There is a true need to look at Ellington as we look at Mozart or Schubert; as a composer … Perhaps we could make a start by giving him something approaching the nature of K (Koechel) or Opus numbers. It always seems to give a composer respectability.'[25] Although differing in authorial perspectives and relative detail of investigation, the celebration of Ellington as a great American composer has now emerged as one of the dominant themes within the iconic jazz narrative. From insider biographies of writers and musicians who encountered Ellington first-hand, to more recent hagiographic accounts, Ellington is frequently portrayed as having the status of a great composer, his works placed within the company of classical composers from Mozart to Stravinsky.[26] Indeed, even when authors appear to be motivated by different ideological positions, there is an apparent inevitability about representing Ellington in this way; for example, authors such as Gunther Schuller and Albert Murray have discussed the significance of Ellington and his deserved place within 'the pantheon'.[27] Ellington is firmly celebrated as a composer of *works* that can be studied, reproduced and revered; within Murray's writings, for example, Ellington is the exemplary composer of America's Classical Music. Even for writers who have tried to argue for jazz's autonomy from classical music, the assertion that Ellington is a composer to rival the classical masters remains central. For example, Schuller has stressed that he is troubled by 'those who feel the need to dignify jazz by equating it with "classical" music', and yet frequently validates Ellington's work by reference to classical music, suggesting parallels to sonata form and the concerto grosso.[28] Derek Jewell's biography of Ellington, first published in the 1970s, not only draws reference to classical music by comparing Ellington to Bach, Delius, Debussy and Mozart but also contrasts his statements by stressing that Ellington had a total disdain for rock music.[29] These rhetorical strategies are not exclusive to a handful of writers, but dominate the literature on Ellington; there remains a continual evocation of classical music and comparisons to high culture stereotypes, alongside the distancing of the icon's music from the popular. As explored in the opening chapter, figures such as Wynton Marsalis have repeatedly sought to distance jazz from the classical tradition on a musical level but continue to adopt artistic positions borne out of the sacralisation of American art and the influence of European high culture. This paradox leads Marsalis on the one hand to insist that jazz music has a totally different history and aesthetic quality and, on the other hand, to suggest that Ellington's compositions had a sophistication that had only previously been found within European music.[30] In Marsalis's case, however, comparing Ellington to European masters and asserting the icon's greatness as an American composer says as much about jazz's distancing from popular culture as it does about comparisons to classical music. Take, for example, Lincoln Center's *Essentially Ellington* education programme, an initiative that celebrates the success of delivery to over 275,000 students across 4,500 schools. This programme should obviously be viewed as a major initiative, bringing historically important jazz works to a new generation of musicians and audiences. However, the publicity materials for *Essentially Ellington*, yet again, adopt a reductionist stance where the icon is compared to classical composers, his biography simplified to a two-page handout for teachers and students.[31] These materials not only serve to place Ellington within the context of the western concert tradition but also, inevitably, eradicate the complexity and multifaceted nature of his musical life. As a musical figure, Ellington can be heralded as a proud African American who was not tarnished by accusations of 'selling out' and, in many ways, his career trajectory can be seen to echo the shifting cultural status of jazz (moving from entertainment to 'art'). Mirroring his own transition from the Cotton Club to the cathedral, Ellington is represented as an artist who has transformed the aesthetic qualities of jazz to its present cultural status. These simplified and reductive representations of Ellington can be viewed as a type of ideology in action, particularly when used in educational settings.

The separation of Ellington from the everyday world, and the distancing of his output from the popular are also implied within representations that claim that *only the music* mattered to him. For example, Jewell states 'But nothing mattered to him except his music. *Music*, as his book declared, *Is My Mistress*. And in music his greatness is founded.'[32] Here, we have a typical attempt to portray Ellington as lost in music and divorced from his social context; Ellington is an art composer who produces autonomous works in isolation. As with most iconic discourses, Ellington's biography and musical outputs have also served to support cultural mythologies. For example, the increased significance of religion and spirituality towards the end of Ellington's life reinforces the sense that iconic jazz transcends the everyday world. Here, Ellington's late sacred compositions provide romantics with an idealised narrative: the artist's final works being explicitly linked to the divine, a final expression of the icon's god-like genius. The pursuit of the divine or spiritual in Ellington's late works ties the artist in with other romanticised readings of genius figures, from Mozart's Requiem to Einstein's late, near-discovery of the secrets of the Universe.[33]

## Ellington as African American hero and a leader of men

Ellington's life and music have featured heavily in writings that celebrate jazz and the African American hero, from the work of Albert Murray and

Ralph Ellison to more recent polemics by Stanley Crouch and Wynton Marsalis.[34] Ellington is a crucial figure in Murray's writings in particular, representing the pinnacle of African American achievement and the centrality of the blues aesthetic in American cultural discourse. This adoration is understandable, given that Ellington is widely accepted as one of the most enduring and successful jazz icons in history, a role model for the current generation of aspiring artists. During his lifetime Ellington was not associated with drugs or reckless living, but perceived instead as a role model promoting African American pride, and a responsible approach to business and artistic endeavour. Indeed, the fact that Ellington was not a great virtuoso with destructive tendencies in the spirit of Charlie Parker means that he can better represent the heroic African American ideals of discipline, rigour and responsibility. The Ellington legacy serves to emphasise this fact; there is a significant body of work produced on record and transcribed in score form and, from an early point in his career, Ellington himself remained complicit in portraying himself as the great Amercian composer of the twentieth century. This is reinforced by his son, Mercer Ellington, who describes how Ellington and his management had an acute awareness of the way in which the artist should be represented.[35] Equally, Ellington's resistance to categorisation and his constant problematising of the discourse surrounding jazz and its relationship to both classical music and popular culture can easily be interpreted as forms of signifyin(g) practice, playing with dominant codes and expectations. Indeed, in promoting Ellington as hero figure both Murray and Ellison comment on Ellington's signifyin(g) potential, his ability to preserve the integrity of jazz whilst putting down young pretenders through his inimitable style.[36] As an African American hero, Ellington is often portrayed as an idealised masculine stereotype; he is widely understood as a great leader of men, not passing judgement on the vices of his musicians, at the same time as embarking on innumerable sexual conquests. Here, the portrayal of Ellington blends the different forms of iconic representation as discussed in Chapter 1; he is simultaneously African American hero, genius, signifyin(g) artist and idealised masculine role model, and there is frequently an interchangeable rhetoric within accounts of Ellington that moves seamlessly between assertions of his musical greatness and descriptions of his sexual charisma. In supporting the masculine myth, Ellington provides leadership by example; he is portrayed as chivalrous and charismatic, exuding charm and panache, but is also laid back and tolerant of the people around him. Indeed, his close mentoring of Strayhorn could also be interpreted as an indicator of his masculine prowess: Ellington is at one with his sexuality and generous in his understanding of others.

## Ellington as an enigma

For all of Ellington's adherence either to the African American heroic ideal or the paradigms of European classical music, it is clear that the majority of representations fail to bring out the anomalies, contradictions and controversies of the artist's life. Although biographies of Ellington describe the icon as enigmatic and difficult to interpret, and his life as being full of contradictions, the majority refuse to engage in critical discourse and instead choose to perpetuate an uncomplicated story with varying degrees of detail. Consider, for example, the following passage from Jewell's biography of Ellington, published in 1977:

> He was, in truth, as easy a man to misunderstand as to comprehend. Set down just some of the paradoxes and contradictions his life contained, and his elusiveness becomes clear. He was both showman and serious artist. He was a stunning innovator, yet extremely conservative, never deflected from his chosen path by the treacherous tides of popular fashions like bebop or rock 'n' roll.[37]

Jewell's biography, like so many other writings on Ellington since the 1970s, fails to engage in a discussion of why the artist is so enigmatic to begin with or how it is easy to misunderstand him. Instead of interrogating the biographical complexities and contradictions of Ellington, studies such as Jewell's are reduced to a straightforward narrative that perpetuates the mythologies of jazz as both mysterious and divorced from the everyday world of popular music, as Jewell's comments on the 'treacherous tides' of fashion suggest. With this in mind, rather than viewing the ambiguities of Ellington's life as irrelevant tangents to a much bigger picture, I would argue that the problematic aspects of the artist's life could provide access to a deeper understanding of his place within the social, hence making history more immediate and relevant to the everday world. Simultaneously, challenging the preconceived and predigested narratives of the constructed jazz tradition would serve to expose the ideologies of present-day myth-makers and the reasons for representing Ellington in this way.

The complex and contradictory nature of Ellington's life and career have been discussed in detail by recent studies. Graham Lock's *Blutopia*, for example, examines the way in which Ellington's music is underpinned by racial discourses and debates about the traditional – albeit misguided – binary opposition between high art and popular culture. Lock explores the context and reception of Ellington's *Black, Brown and Beige*, where the composer was accused of getting above his station in attempting to write 'serious' music, and also perceived as turning his back both on dance music and the black tradition. Lock suggests that racial motivations provide a backdrop to this entire discourse, from Ellington wishing to rid himself of the jungle or minstrel stereotypes, to critics – driven by a need to restrict the representation of black jazz artists – suggesting he should return to writing dance music. Equally, among white supporters of Ellington, the prospect of their hero moving away from his perceived authentic black lineage towards concert music denied them the opportunity to revel in the experience of jazz as 'other'. Lock states: 'These well-bred youngsters, very proper in look, manner and dress, wanted jazz to flagellate their sense of propriety … their taste ran to the blues, "low down" blues, and when Duke escaped from the tyranny of that limited jazz form … they beat a quick retreat from their earlier position of fawning admiration of Ellington.'[38] Here, Lock suggests that white critics and fans appropriated the black music of Ellington in order to celebrate the soulful, corporeal and sensual characteristics of jazz. However, this type of revelling denied the music an intellectual or spiritual dimension; even if the intentions were to glorify the music of Ellington, the result was essentialising, restricting the representation of their idol. Building on this, I would suggest that the construction of the jazz canon and the more recent celebration of Ellington as great composer serve to counter the primitivising tendencies of white critics from the early part of the twentieth century. Ellington is now clearly represented as an intellectual and spiritual leader, which could be seen to challenge the earlier racially motivated representations of the artist. However, within the jazz main-stream, Ellington's life and works are portrayed in one-dimensional terms, devoid of complexity and controversy. Even Ellington's overt commercial enterprises are now used as a signifier of artistic credibility and not an end in themselves, as if to demonstrate that the jazz icon has always been a spiritual and autonomous artist. This strategy serves to mystify the life and music of Ellington, avoids any critical engagement with the artist's place in jazz history and, ultimately, creates a reverse essentialism that denies the artist a complexity of representation. It is almost impossible to find a representation of the life of Ellington where the cerebral and corporeal, artistic and commercial coexist; as Townsend suggests above, antinomic concepts are problematic in simplifying jazz discourse. Drawing on the work of Lock, George Burrows suggests that even when Ellington's music is labelled as 'beyond category', this description is used more often than not to perpetuate the mysteries of jazz as autonomous art rather than to open up the discourse to alternative perspectives. In exploring the signifying potential of Ellington's music, Burrows suggests that the description of Ellington as 'beyond category' underplays his mediating position in relation to race issues, 'fixing him in a new category, one of his own'.[39] In effect, to use the label 'beyond category' is a way of avoiding critical discussion of a complex figure in the same spirit as Armstrong's assertion that 'if you have to ask – shame on you'.

## Biographical accounts play down controversy

The dominant themes of the Ellington narrative tend to promote a homogeneous and simplified picture of the icon's life where controversial points are often ignored, glossed over or framed in such a way that they do not appear central to the understanding of Ellington's life and music. When writers past and present have strayed from the official line, their works have either been heavily criticised or largely ignored. One obvious example of the desire to control the Ellington discourse was evidenced in the critical reaction to James Lincoln Collier's controversial Ellington biography, published in 1987.[40] Collier's work made several judgements relating to Ellington's life, proposing a reading of the icon that, among other things, challenged his status as a great American composer and suggested that his musical career was in decline from the mid 1940s onwards. Moreover, Collier portrayed Ellington as manipulative – exploiting, controlling and dominating the people around him – and suggested that he was neither an intellectual, an accomplished pianist or particularly interested in racial issues. Collier raised the issue of musical ownership, citing several instances where musicians had felt aggrieved at not being credited as composers, and concluded by comparing Ellington to a master chef, arguing that we should view him as a great compiler of music and not a composer in the traditional sense. Collier suggested that Ellington's large-scale works would pale in comparison to European classical music and firmly placed his most creative output within the popular domain, the songs and cabaret numbers produced pre-1945.

Collier's work received a large amount of negative press among jazz writers and musicians, ranging from reviewers labelling the biography 'sloppy' and 'problematic' to assertions that the text displayed a fundamental lack of respect for Ellington – one critic even compared the author to Hitler.[41] However, the extent to which the biography was criticised seemed disproportionate in relation to Collier's controversial observations, and the more extreme responses to Collier's work can be understood as examples of trying to control the narrative of jazz ideologically. Although all jazz criticism, including my own text, can be understood as ideologically loaded, the character assassination of Collier following the publication of his Ellington biography demonstrated the extent to which the jazz world polices its own discourse and the representations of its icons. One of the most extreme public reactions to Collier's work came from Wynton Marsalis, who wrote a letter to *The New York Times* claiming that Collier was, among other things, a 'poseur', 'a pompous social scientist' and a 'viper in the bosom of blues and swing'.[42] This critical outpouring led to an open debate between Marsalis and Collier at Lincoln Center a few years later, where Marsalis sought to expose several musical inaccuracies within Collier's text. Collier, on the other hand, attempted to question Marsalis's programming and commissioning policy at Lincoln Center and, in defence of his Ellington biography, stated: 'The problem that we have in jazz today, and this exemplifies exactly what's wrong with jazz criticism, is that you're not allowed to say anything about a jazz musician except what's very nice.'[43] No consensus was reached in the discussion about the ideological control of jazz discourse, owing no doubt both to the gladiatorial setting for the debate and the entrenched positions of both speakers. Indeed, the resultant discussion was far from satisfactory in examining some of the underlying critical issues to do with the positive representation of iconic artists and the impact of hagiography masquerading as historiography. However, the Collier biography sparked some heated dialogues between respected scholars within the field of New Jazz Studies. Krin Gabbard and Lawrence Gushee, for example, exchanged views about ideology within jazz discourse, with Gabbard suggesting that the desire to control the iconic jazz narrative is a sign of the infancy of jazz studies and that scholars need to mature and come of age in order either to embrace or accept revisionist perspectives.[44] However, from today's perspective twenty years on, I would argue that the desire to control the jazz narrative runs deeper than a mere discipline in its infancy and greatly reflects the quasi-religious aspirations and desires of the jazz mainstream in American culture, from scholars to musicians to audiences. Why, for example, should it remain a taboo for authors to challenge existing representations of jazz icons or to explore some of the more controversial or unsavoury aspects of their biographies? Indeed, interrogation of representation and the revision of interpretations of the past has formed the bedrock of critical and cultural theory, and is an expected mode of criticism within the majority of academic contexts outside jazz; the now firmly established world of New Jazz Studies should be able to draw on such methods.

## Moving beyond category: the controversial Ellington

Although several recent studies have done much to reinvigorate the study of Ellington with discursive elements, there is still a reluctance to explore subjects that could pose a threat to the authority of the constructed jazz tradition and its iconic figures. For example, although he seeks to problematise the representations of Ellington, Lock plays down Mercer Ellington's perception of his father as having a deep-felt hatred of women, as if to preserve the icon's status as a heroic African American 'ladies' man'.[45] To consider Ellington as a misogynist would destroy the idealised image of the artist; this degree of realism would inevitably lead to either a devaluing of the artist's status or, more typically, a divorcing of the artistic genius from his everyday vices. This latter outcome can be seen clearly in the portrayal of Miles Davis, a figure who openly acknowledged his abuse and mistreatment of women. Despite his open admission of social taboos, Davis continues to be represented as a cultural icon; in books, films and advertisements, he has come to stand as a role model for aspiring innovators.

When viewed in social terms, then, the jazz narrative must adhere to a number of romanticised traits in order to remain valid and acceptable; to ride against this trend would result in ridicule, or in accusations of being overly ideological, or in undermining the artistic contribution of iconic figures. Consider the way in which Ken Burns's PBS documentary *Jazz* (2001) offers significant air time to social context when the narrative describes the violence, social degradation and substance abuse suffered by significant jazz artists or, more significantly in Ellington's case, the heterosexual exploits of the masculine icon. When discussing the contentious relationship between Duke Ellington and Billy Strayhorn, however, the documentary avoids any meaningful commentary on stories of the 'closeness' of their relationship beyond professional collaboration as had been reported in other sources around the time. In an article for *Vanity Fair* in 1999, David Hajdu speculated on Ellington's sexuality, following the discovery of an intimate photograph of Strayhorn inside Ellington's bible.[46] Hajdu suggested that the close working relationship of the two artists might well have moved beyond a professional relationship to something more intimate. The article drew on a range of evidence as part of the discussion, ranging from personal testimony of family members to an analysis of Ellington's behavioural patterns following the death of Strayhorn. Hajdu even cited testimony from Ellington's son Mercer when discussing the sensitivity and mystery of the Ellington–Strayhorn relationship, with

Mercer Ellington suggesting that his father's sense of adventure probably led to some sexual experimentation with Strayhorn. In contrast to the response to Collier's biography, Hajdu's thought-provoking study was largely ignored by jazz critics, scholars and musicians alike, proving a subject too far for the mainstream jazz community to engage with. Regardless of whether Hajdu's study has any basis of truth, the issue of bisexuality in jazz remains a taboo, especially where iconic personalities are concerned. The refusal to entertain the prospect of an intimate relationship between Ellington and Strayhorn again demonstrates the ideological control of iconic representation, especially given that the majority of writings on Ellington are littered with references to his heterosexuality. This highlights the centrality of the masculine myth in jazz and a refusal on behalf of the mainstream to engage with conflicting and controversial subject matter. For example, the Ken Burns documentary, produced around the same time as Hajdu's study, does not touch upon the complexities of the Ellington–Strayhorn relationship, and the film continues to represent Strayhorn's homosexuality in a typical way; the artist's homosexuality is tolerated, presented both as a matter of 'objective truth' without narrative gloss or embellishment, and established in clear opposition to Ellington's being a 'ladies' man'. Indeed, the Burns narrative avoids any discussion of the inner workings of the Ellington–Strayhorn relationship, and commentary is steered clearly towards a celebration of their music. The words of Ellington's granddaughter, interviewed as part of the documentary, are not developed either through further testimony, anecdotal accounts or conjecture: something that can be identified as unusual in the context of the rest of the documentary:

There were maybe two people that Duke Ellington valued above all others. I believe that one of them was his mother and the other one was Billy Strayhorn. You must know that they loved each other. Basically, I think the joy of them finding each other was the core of their mutual creativity – they brought out the best in each other … It was very private. I think that, that only the two of them knew what their relationship was like. (Mercedes Ellington)[47]

Ken Burns's *Jazz* has received a plethora of negative commentary since its initial broadcast in 2001, as it was seen by many critics as a missed opportunity to examine the complexity and impact of jazz both past and present.[48] Here, as with other jazz texts that support the constructed jazz tradition, the social remains relevant as long as it reinforces the reverence of the autonomous icon and the stereotypical portrayal of the jazz artist. Rather than expose jazz to scrutiny at multiple levels of the social, jazz narratives retain a taboo on certain subjects; the Burns documentary, for example, discusses the great collaboration between Strayhorn and Ellington but fails to comment on the significance of Strayhorn's sexuality, implying that such an investigation would detract from the significance of the music and tarnish Ellington's reputation as a 'ladies' man'. While again reinforcing the autonomous nature of music, the adoption of this approach could seemingly be understood if applied to *all* sexual relationships, profiles and characteristics of musicians and their influence on music. However, a significant body of the documentary – and a large number of other conventional jazz narratives – remain devoted to the assertion of heterosexual masculinity (the 'norm') as the centre of creativity. These types of anomaly lie just beneath the surface of many jazz texts and can be usefully deconstructed through critical analysis. Indeed, the significance of the Burns documentary should not be underestimated, as the narrative commentary reflects directly on the issues, stereotypes and ideologies discussed so far. One clear illustration of these points is offered in Episode 8 of the documentary, 'Dedicated to Chaos 1943–1945'. The first eight minutes of the sub-section, 'We Need to Be Free', present an introduction to the music and working practices of Duke Ellington. In such a short section of film, many of the common tropes of the jazz narrative are introduced that draw attention to the way the canon presents jazz as both autonomous art and a deeply social music. Notwithstanding the earlier commentary on the relationship between Ellington and Strayhorn, the footage typifies the way the jazz icon is discussed within popular narratives, drawing attention to many of the critical issues bound up with understanding jazz practice. Descriptions of Ellington clearly set him apart from the rest of the group; the sentiment 'he never let anyone get too close' has resonances with the notion of the artist working in isolation, the autocratic genius figure detached from the 'real' world. Coupled with this comes the portrayal of the artist 'working incessantly, as if possessed by the music'. Indeed, there are no workings, reworkings or controlled rational thinking here; the work of the jazz genius is inspired, 'natural', individual and God-given. The description of Ellington's character blends the autonomous genius with the traits of the masculine jazz stereotype. When we read the footage with knowledge of the critical response to Collier's work and the sexual taboos explored by Hajdu, the documentary clearly illustrates how the conventional jazz narrative seeks to control the representation of Ellington and is dominated by assertions of heterosexual masculinity. Wynton Marsalis's opening words on Ellington, for example, discuss him as 'a great flirter', almost to stress the importance of masculine norms as a key to iconic success; within this context, sex and music are conflated, the genius is idolised by women for his sexual prowess and by men both for his music and his sexual conquests. However, the antithesis of the genius is displayed in the excesses of Ellington's band members. Drugs, violence, alcohol abuse and kleptomania are themes central to the group: jazz stereotypes that root the musicians firmly in the degraded and corrupt world of the social. But as iconic genius, Ellington is able to see beyond the social reality of his times and bring out the magic in the musicians; it is not the personalities that count but the 'music that matters'. These points clearly demonstrate the way in which the popular jazz narrative blends the worlds of the autonomous and the social, discussing the music and icon as autonomous, while the context is markedly 'real'. However, the social *is* romanticised, drawing on themes that help to perpetuate the jazz stereotype and distance the musicians from real life. This approach enables the commentator to forgive the artist his sins of reality; it is not the behaviour of the artist that counts, only the beauty and transcendent quality of the music he produces. As a case study, the Burns narrative offers a good example of a conventional portrayal of jazz history as an ideological construct and, when placed in relation to the body of writings on Ellington, can be considered a valuable tool for both constructing and deconstructing the jazz tradition, demonstrating how narratives police iconic representation to reinforce dominant ideologies.

# 7 | Birth of the school

**Figure 10** Duke Ellington and Sonny Greer, 1933

For this final chapter, I examine the politics of education and the implications of canon-forming and icon worship within jazz studies programmes. Leading on from this, I suggest a critical methodology that both opens up the field of study to broader cultural analysis and promotes strategies that encourage us to reflect on our relationship to iconic jazzmen. In this context, I discuss the unique problems faced by jazz education and suggest that these issues are inherently linked to the nature of the music itself. I focus on two areas of significance that feed off opposing positions in jazz: the 'value' of jazz education and the perceived difference between jazz practice and social theory. My examination of the difficult social and cultural space occupied by education highlights the potential for educational methodologies to disrupt dominant ideologies, and to uncover related cultural myths. I conclude with some suggestions as to how these critical methodologies might usefully be employed.

As the study of jazz gains increased legitimacy in academic circles, I would argue that jazz educators need to become more critically aware. Traditionally, the narrative of jazz, including textbooks, biographies and documentaries, has been very limited, with the history of the music being defined in terms of names, dates and anecdotal evidence. As jazz has gained a foothold in academia, the need for a critical understanding of the subject has become a primary concern. Over recent years, jazz as an academic discipline has grown in volume and stature; indeed, jazz studies now play a significant role in a number of higher education music programmes within the university and conservatoire sector. The proliferation of jazz education programmes has, inevitably, brought about the publication and development of specific pedagogical methodologies; from the development of the Associated Board of the Royal Schools of Music (ABRSM) jazz examinations in the UK to the widespread dissemination of Jamey Aebersold jazz 'play-alongs' (a business that has now transformed itself into Jamey Aebersold summer schools and a university programme), jazz pedagogy is big business. The extent to which jazz education is a significant industry was demonstrated by the work of the International Association for Jazz Education (IAJE), which, until its dissolution in 2008, welcomed over 7,000 delegates to its annual convention, ranging from educators to musicians, promoters to jazz enthusiasts. Although they provide musicians with opportunities to cultivate and benchmark their skills, the majority of pedagogical publications on jazz do not encourage critical engagement with the educators' techniques or underlying methodologies, or, indeed, offer dialogues on the nature of jazz education itself.

## Context: music education

The profound connection and … disconnection between formal education and culture is a problematic one. It is hardly controversial to state that most classroom teachers abide by a select compendium that represents our culture's best ideas and greatest works. Disagreements occur when the education we receive serves to reinforce one greater culture or heritage at the expense of another. Thus, differing voices who wish to compete in this landscape must argue that *their* culture's best works are valid and worth engaging in.[1]

Where music is often criticised as slow to catch on in terms of applying cultural and critical theory to the subject, it could be argued that jazz studies remains one of the last musical disciplines to open its doors to revisionist methods. Randall Allsup's comments above not only focus on the framework of music education and the politics behind canon-forming, they also feed into the wider discussion of education's broad cultural significance. In his article 'Transformational Education and Critical Music Pedagogy: Examining the Link between Culture and Learning', Allsup comments on the interesting cultural space that education occupies, and outlines the potential conflict that exists between Marxist social theory and more aesthetic-based readings of arts education. Marxist readings, he argues, display a deep-rooted suspicion of the ideological potential of education and its powers to indoctrinate. I would suggest that Antonio Gramsci's concept of hegemony, or a type of domination by consent, best describes this power relationship and its underlying scepticism, where a ruling class uses education as a weapon to promote and perpetuate existing value systems and political hierarchies. In certain debates on post-colonialism, for example, education has also been singled out as one of the last remaining bastions of imperial rule, traditional belief systems being perpetuated from one generation to the next through the perceived 'natural' pedagogical order.[2] In this way, educators promoting art of 'inherent' greatness or beauty can be viewed as implicitly reinforcing the value systems of a particular social order.

Allsup argues that some middle ground needs to be found between ideological scepticism and the belief in art's transcendent nature, in which aesthetic beauty can be celebrated within the context and ideology of a dominant culture. Whilst this position could be construed as ideological in its own right, Allsup's commentary echoes the way in which musical scholarship has opened itself up to a broader historical and cultural debate, exploring the ideological potential of musical discourses. Indeed, it is now established practice for western classical music courses to introduce discursive elements into the discipline that seek to question music's previously assumed universal and transcendent values. In his groundbreaking text, *Music, Society, Education*, first published in 1977, Christopher Small describes the traditional abstracted reading of classical music and puts forward an argument for the social context of music to take centre stage:

[M]usic is cut off even more effectively from any disturbing function by being placed firmly in a time, and often a place, set aside from everyday life, becoming thus an antidote to, rather than an exploration of, our lives, a relaxation after our struggles to maintain ourselves in what seems an uncaring or even hostile society. In addition, the majority of those who regard themselves as music lovers are essentially passive in their attitude … They have no part to play in the creative act, but content themselves with the contemplation of the finished musical work as it is presented to them, the work itself having an abstract existence apart from themselves as listeners … The parallel between this abstract view of the musical work and the abstract view of knowledge held in our culture is clear; both are thought to exist 'Out There', independently of the listener and of the knower, and both are thought to be essentially unchanged whether or not any individual, as it were, plugs himself in to them (where 'Out There' is remains a mystery).[3]

Writings such as this spearheaded a new approach to musical scholarship, where musicologists aimed to move their study away from music as 'ideologically autonomous' towards the realms of the social, exploring power relationships between different musical genres. In this sense, the creation of community music courses, music business programmes and arts industry modules within traditional music courses can be seen as logical by-products of this approach; these educational developments serve to embrace the social in some form, and aim to reconnect 'art' with 'reality'. In addition, the questioning of artistic canons has also enabled previously disenfranchised voices to enter into the educational framework. For example, popular music studies has now broadened its field to encompass not only the social function of the music but also the development of an aesthetic model for valuing popular music and its cultural significance.[4] These major shifts in music education have also resulted in new approaches to the study of classical music, together with the introduction of new disciplinary fields, such as popular music and jazz studies. Whilst there are commonalities between the critical frameworks for each discipline, there are also unique issues associated with each artform. Within this context, I suggest that the problems of jazz education are inseparable from the underlying codes, conventions and mythologies at play in the music.

## The polarities of jazz: understanding jazz education

Although they violently disagreed on the definition of jazz, critics in the 1940s tacitly agreed to fight their battles around a set of dualisms – black versus white, art versus commerce, nature versus culture, technique versus affect, European versus native – on which claims about jazz as art have been built ever since.[5]

Although critical jazz scholarship has secured a place within education and research environments, writings on jazz arguably remain dominated by journalistic prose that tends to oversimplify the narrative into binary oppositions. Indeed, binary oppositions govern both the theory and practice of jazz at every level, whether centring on discussions cited by Gabbard above, or championing the cerebral–corporeal, masculine–feminine, recorded–live; polarities are present throughout. Against this backdrop, writer Stuart Nicholson asked me to comment on the differences between American and European approaches to jazz education for his book *Is Jazz Dead? (Or Has It Moved to a New Address?)*, published in 2005.[6] In particular, I was invited to explore approaches to teaching jazz in Britain and to compare European jazz education to what was assumed to be the more mainstream American pedagogical model, using bebop as its centre-piece. At the very outset, this line of questioning neatly illustrated the way in which jazz commentators seek to polarise the debate, in this case assuming that European jazz is more pluralistic. In general terms, the suggestion was that many European jazz courses have a much looser approach to jazz education, not rooted in one particular style, and that there is a willingness to incorporate aspects of local culture into shaping the music, as well as an emphasis on individuality. My response to this perspective was that generalisations such as these create an unhealthy environment, where musicians, academics and enthusiasts feel they have to take sides or make a choice.

Using Nicholson's questions as a starting point for my own investigation of jazz education, however, I felt compelled to take a step back and examine the complex framework within which jazz education operates, as it is central to understanding the underlying issues. Discussions of the value and significance of jazz education engulf the discipline from the inside out, and the response to the growing area of jazz pedagogy typifies the issues at stake. Primarily, arguments about the value of jazz education tend to centre on the question of whether or not jazz can be taught. However, when examining this fairly well-trodden debate, it is clear that this question is rarely answered and instead tends to raise a host of other issues. Indeed, when discussing the effectiveness of jazz education, respondents' answers are telling, and echo assumptions central to the nature of the music itself. Although the question itself invites an antithetical response, rarely are non-educators put on record celebrating the benefits of jazz pedagogy. Rather, they either suggest that jazz education is bad – proposing that it stifles creativity – or that its presence cannot do any harm: hardly a glowing endorsement of educational method by the jazz fraternity. These perspectives are typified by the following musicians' responses in an interview with Paul Haines:

STEVE SWALLOW: My experience tends to support Paul Desmond's remark to the effect that jazz can be learned but not taught. Nevertheless, I think jazz schools are a good idea. They're valuable because they serve as a nexus for young musicians. Players and writers hopeful of a career in jazz can find each other in a nice place, funded by their parents (who likely approve of a school more than of a cheap apartment in a bad neighborhood), or by financial aid programs. A few months or years focused on learning music, without the draining obligation to find money for food and rent, could be a good thing. When attending school it's important to stay up late, to do the real work of becoming a good player in the company of like-minded fellow students, away from the paternal order of instructors ...

BOB BROOKMEYER: Paul, I am afraid we are stuck with the music schools. 'Real life' – as my generation knew and experienced it – does not exist anymore, so the teachers remain the last bastion of assistance before expelling the student out into the cruel world. My concern is the quality of teaching and the way that information is given ... Much needs to be done, but we are running out of people who can do it ...

AMY DENIO: Well, I have very little experience in jazz studies, so I can't really say if institutes/conservatories work or not. Here's my hypothetical reply:
YES THEY (can) WORK, especially if they include jazz musicians on the faculty. For those interested in jazz theory, history, philosophy, conservatories are quite good. Those who focus on praxis, on playing, on exploration and improvisation are the strongest.
NO THEY DON'T WORK (very well), because historically jazz is a musical form growing independently from academia, one which relies on the foundations of intuition, inherent musicality and a free spirit, elements not usually stressed in academia.[7]

Whilst not offering an entirely negative view of jazz education, these responses typify the value judgements found within the wider jazz community. Swallow's response perpetuates the idea that jazz cannot be taught; 'real jazz' is something that takes place outside the institution. The 'paternal order', it is suggested, is something which stifles creativity. This is echoed in Brookmeyer's comments, where 'real life' is separate from the world of education. Coupled with this comes the implication that only jazz musicians of a certain age make good teachers; nothing is as good as it used to be. Finally, Denio's opening remarks do not prevent her from passing judgement on the value of jazz education; jazz, intuition, inherent musicality and free spirit, she argues, are not compatible with academia.

There is a certain irony associated with the comments from these three professionals, as jazz pedagogy becomes increasingly reliant on established jazz professionals to spearhead developments in education. Indeed, within the current context of jazz in higher education, it is unusual for established jazz musicians not to have an institutional affiliation or visiting professorship.[8] However, the myth of the instinctive musician who is at odds with academia retains a degree of credibility even when the claimants have established track records in education and music pedagogy. Arguably, the jazz scene could be viewed either as in denial or proliferated with teachers who are just along for the ride, feeling or claiming that jazz cannot be taught.

## Deconstructing jazz education

The questions surrounding the value of jazz education and these typically ambivalent attitudes towards the subject can be understood more clearly when placed within the wider context of jazz today. Indeed, there are unique social and cultural conditions that help to account for the fact that, in jazz, education is treated with hostility and apprehension. As a cultural and historical artform, jazz is a deeply social music, linked to the everyday world and, in many cases, born out of oppression, politics and the entertainment industry. Mainstream histories of jazz obviously attempt to illustrate the environment in which the music was produced, and the music's social function is often emphasised together with a portrayal of its underlying political or cultural significance. However, this sense of the social is often constructed to create a romanticised depiction of the jazz icon, and serves further to support common mythologies. Indeed, the construction and celebration of a jazz canon have placed many jazz artists into the mythologised world of autonomous art, where music is deemed to transcend the social. This ideology of autonomous art creates a romanticised narrative where the iconic genius figure (typically male) transcends time and context; his work is treated in isolation and his music is regarded as conveying universal appeal. The construction and celebration of a jazz canon have dominated both pedagogy and the broader context of arts production and reception, arguably restricting the representation of iconic figures and limiting educational methods. Scott DeVeaux explains why the construction of a jazz canon embodies jazz's aspiration to enhance its cultural status, and comments on the desire to 'classicise' jazz along the lines of western art music:

> Only by acquiring the prestige, the 'cultural capital' (in Pierre Bourdieu's phrase) of an artistic tradition can the music hope to be heard, and its practitioners receive the support commensurate with their training and accomplishments. The accepted historical narrative for jazz serves this purpose. It is a pedigree, showing contemporary jazz to be not a fad or a mere popular music, subject to the whims of fashion, but an autonomous art of some substance … that has in its own way recapitulated the evolutionary progress of western art.[9]

However, as writers such as Krin Gabbard have observed, the celebration and construction of a jazz canon rides against the current trend in the broader arts and humanities sector, which seeks to deconstruct the grounds on which canons are formed.[10] This approach attempts to gain a critical understanding of artistic texts through social and political analysis, reinstilling a sense of the social into canonical discourses. By examining art's social function and significance, scholars aim to dispel the canon's widely accepted doctrines of universality and transcendence. Social readings of art have sought to expose dominant cultural and political hierarchies whilst questioning traditional assumptions of art music as autonomous or 'asocial', existing outside the reaches of the everyday world. This trend has not been welcomed by all musicologists; John Shepherd describes the traditional response of musical elites when faced with the challenge of a social reading of music: 'For the centralized dissemination of knowledge to remain intact in the face of challenge, knowledge is conceived according to the canons of an *absolute* or *objective idealism*. Reality is thought of as "given" and essentially independent of the vagaries of human volition.'[11] Here, the belief that 'high art' conveys universal meaning and inherent value is challenged and deconstructed by social theory. Indeed, sociological approaches have also sought to undermine elitism and have enabled other cultural forms, such as jazz and popular music, to gain a degree of legitimacy within the academic world. However, within a jazz context, this method of deconstruction would at first appear futile, as jazz is widely understood as a deeply *social* music; to deconstruct the canon and replace it with an appraisal of the music as 'social text' would be, in many respects, to leave the discourse unchallenged. This is where the paradox lies within the framework of jazz studies; the traditional opposition between the ideology of autonomous art and music as social text is immediately problematised. Jazz *is* a deeply social music and yet, as 'art', it is discussed in autonomous terms, reinforcing mythologies and canonical hierarchies. This goes some way to explaining why jazz pedagogy is regarded as complex and problematic, education having the potential to occupy the uncomfortable position between music as autonomous art and as social text. The potential power of jazz pedagogy to expose some of these embodied mythologies results in the value of jazz education being either discredited or neutralised in five broad ways.

### (i) The jazz institution is divorced from both 'art' and 'reality'

In her essay 'The Ideology of Autonomous Art', Janet Wolff discusses some of the problems encountered in the relationship between the worlds of fine art and industry, and comments on the uncomfortable place education assumes within society at large:

In England during the past few years there have been heated debates about the nature, and the future, of art education. A major focus of argument, for example at the Royal College of Art in London, has been the relationship between art and design, and between art and industry. Any suggestions that art education should be relevant to the needs of industry and business have been met with that outraged reaction which invariably occurs when the sanctity and purity of Art seem challenged. A practical art education is incompatible with the still dominant notion that Art is an individual creation, the result of creative talent and particular inspiration, which could only be contaminated and impeded by any extra-aesthetic concerns.[12]

Wolff's comments illustrate how an institution concerned with creating 'art' can seek to establish itself as the antithesis of the social, and describes the uncomfortable cultural position that education occupies. This perspective is supported by the idea that the academy is an 'ivory tower', divorced from the everyday world. Within a jazz education context, many of these issues are further complicated owing to the social nature of the music, creating a significant paradox. Jazz pedagogical institutions are, on the one hand, linked to the fabric of society, in that they are funded by government to provide training for students, and yet they are criticised for not being part of 'real life' (as expressed in the earlier quotations); the authentic jazz artist is portrayed as a product of the social, *not* the institution. Paradoxically, pedagogical institutions cannot be seen to be creating 'artists', as the genius figure is born out of nature; the institution is a *social* phenomenon, not a conduit for the divine to speak. In other words, the autonomous artist would not need an institution in order to create 'great' artworks; they are divorced from the institutional pillars of society. Within this context, therefore, education can be understood as incompatible with *both* music as social phenomenon *and* music as autonomous art. I would suggest, however, that in occupying the space between 'art' and 'society', education should not be viewed as being in some kind of social and cultural purgatory. Instead, I would argue that education is ideally placed to expose many mythologised assumptions within the jazz world.[13] Indeed, rather than leading us to view the autonomous artwork as the antithesis of art as social product, education's uncomfortable cultural position can identify that, in jazz, the ideology of autonomous art *is rooted in the social*, albeit a romanticised view of what the social represents. As stated earlier, conventional readings of jazz appear to be grounded in social and political contexts. However, these jazz narratives must adhere to a number of romanticised traits in order to remain valid and acceptable; as demonstrated in the previous chapter, those riding against the dominant narrative of jazz tend to be discredited, or accused of clouding the music with unnecessary ideology.

## (ii)  Anti-academic approaches to jazz

KEITH SMITH: Great jazz isn't compatible with academic studies. Ignorance is
    bliss!
GEORGE MELLY: I guess there's no harm in it [jazz education] as long as it doesn't
    try and impose taste.[14]

Smith and Melly's comments typify the position of the anti-academic: the belief that pure, unadulterated musical essence is antithetical to intellectualism. The claim that the academy breeds intellectualism, crammed full of unnecessary ideology, can itself be seen as an ideological position; Melly's comment is a clear example of an expression of ideology beneath the façade of anti-ideology. This echoes Terry Eagleton's observation that to claim that knowledge should be 'value-free' is itself a value judgement.[15] On a more practical level, anti-intellectual approaches to education manifest themselves in the promotion of the jazz artist as 'practitioner' as opposed to 'thinker'. Within this widely held mythology, the jazz musician is portrayed as an instinctive, emotive and corporeal musician as opposed to the rational, cerebral and theory-based jazz academic. David Ake articulates this perception when discussing the iconic reception of the jazz artist:

[T]he first mode of natural expression … that jazz passes from The Great Beyond through select musicians – endures in many circles. For instance, the solemn, ritual-like aura that surrounds Keith Jarrett's solo-piano concerts stems in large measure from audience understandings that Jarrett uniquely connects to a type of universal/musical consciousness … We can even see that the oft-bandied dictum about jazz to the effect that 'if you have to ask what it is, you'll never know' also supports understandings of the music as somehow outside the realm of general and rational understanding.[16]

I should stress here that the discussion of jazz in more critical and socio-cultural terms is not always dismissed by the broader community of historians, performers and enthusiasts as irrelevant; indeed, the quotations by Smith and Melly represent one extremity of the argument. However, previous attempts to theorise jazz in a way that deviates from the norm are usually construed as an infiltration of 'outside' influences – such as European cultural values or social science methodologies – resulting in fierce anti-academic sentiment. Examples include Sonny Rollins's dismissal of Gunther Schuller's analysis of 'Blue 7' and the ridiculing and questioning of Anthony Braxton's conceptual and philosophical approach to improvisation: 'stop Messiaen about' was the advice of one critic.[17] Within this context, 'theorising' jazz goes against the grain of the music's fundamental tenets of intuition and impulse. On a more subtle level, anti-academic sentiment frequently enters jazz discourse when the dominant ideology is threatened. As we have seen in previous chapters, a challenge to the dominant ideology results either in being ignored (it is *the music* that matters), being ridiculed (why discuss such irrelevant things?) or being accused of crowding the jazz narrative with unnecessary ideology; all three responses result in the dismissal of the supposedly 'academic' in jazz.

### (iii)  Celebrating the values of the 'pre-institutional' world

Critiques of jazz education often express the desire to return to the 'natural' values of the pre-institutionalised jazz world. As Bob Brookmeyer articulated above, authenticity is something to be found in the past: the present is a 'cruel world' devoid of great masters. This seems to ignore the fact that musicians throughout the jazz community, historically and in the present, have used both educational methodology and social institutions for personal development. Paul Berliner's *Thinking in Jazz*, for example, explores how institutions such as the jazz club and big band are governed by their own set of institutionalised codes and conventions. Furthermore, these codes and conventions could be regarded as stifling and restricting, given an appropriate context. Similarly, the historical notion of the jazz musician as uneducated and self-taught is a long-standing mythology. For example, Roger Trodre's 1998 article on jazz education opens: 'Louis Armstrong and Ornette Coleman taught themselves, but the next generation of jazz stars could be practising scales and sitting exams ...'[18] This quotation reinforces the stereotypical view of the jazz genius as a naturally gifted, self-taught musician. However, in his book *Chicago Jazz: A Cultural History, 1904–1930*, William Howland Kenney portrays a very different view of the early decades of jazz, including strong traits of discipline, regimentation, professionalism and dedication. On the musical training of Louis Armstrong, for example, Kenney states:

Armstrong's remarkable solos depended upon an exceptionally high level of instrumental virtuosity, one that appeared more often in the concert hall. Armstrong developed an exceedingly wide instrumental range, impressive power, and technical dexterity with which to demonstrate sweeping, dramatic jazz solos of grand proportions. Although he never described how he did it, the solo star did mention practice lessons with Lil Hardin, who had studied music at Fisk University before coming to Chicago and continued to earn her teaching certificate at the Chicago College of Music. Songwriter Hoagy Carmichael claimed that Lil Hardin 'got a book of the standard cornet solos and drilled him. He really worked, even taking lessons from a German down at Kimball Hall, who showed Louis all the European cornet clutches.'[19]

Kenney's historical research clearly contradicts the notion of Armstrong as the natural, self-taught player. His citation of Hoagy Carmichael in 1965 does nothing to dispel the myth of the jazz genius divorced from everyday rigours of education. Indeed, even when presented as part of the African American heroic ideal, which focuses on learning, intellect and discipline, alongside an array of signifyin(g) qualities, Armstrong's authenticity is still firmly rooted in 'natural', soulful, intuitive sounds and individual brilliance, traits that are, albeit misguidedly, established as the antithesis of the educational establishment.

### (iv)  Pedagogy stifles individualism and creativity

Jazz education is discredited through claims that it is responsible for stifling creativity and the development of jazz. Indeed, the so-called institutionalisation of jazz is viewed not as a by-product of a wider cultural sea-change – where jazz is celebrated as a canonical artform – but as the *cause* of the music's gradual shift away from the popular or socially significant. As discussed earlier, pedagogy has the critical potential to expose jazz myths such as the celebration of autonomous art hidden beneath the guise of jazz as social text. It is therefore understandable that education has a threatening potential, and thus tends to be either rigorously controlled or discredited by certain sectors of the jazz community. Neil Leonard's description of 'pollution behavior' within the writings of critics of early jazz could equally be applied to the tactics employed in discrediting the value of jazz education today:

Predictably, the orthodoxy turned its full wrath against jazz and its dilutions, finding allies among those ordinarily little moved by any kind of music. Thus fortified, establishmentarians condemned anything that sounded like jazz as ugly, cheap, degenerating and threatening. Anthropologist Mary Douglas calls this kind of treatment 'pollution behavior'. She points out that anything which captures or casts doubt on the received order seems dirty and arouses demands for expurgation and that ideas of defilement are not isolated complaints but an integral part of overall cultural values, keeping deviants in line and otherwise reinforcing notions of right and wrong as well as claims of class and status.[20]

We could easily replace the word 'jazz' with 'jazz education' in this quotation to illustrate the tactics employed to discredit the jazz institution. 'Pollution behavior' seeks to undermine the potential of education to develop innovative and individual thinking. The majority of arts programmes in higher education use the descriptors 'innovation', 'creativity', 'originality' and 'creative thinking' in the aims and objectives of individual courses, yet the stereotypical view of the institution remains a 'stifling' one.

### (v)  The jazz canon as a neutralising force

The canon plays a subtle role in neutralising the effectiveness of education as a subversive or critical tool; the canon's homogenising tendencies smooth over the potential conflict between critical scholarship and jazz as romanticised social text. In this respect, the construction and celebration of a jazz canon facilitates a quasi-hegemonic form of control over the discourse, in which education is used as a support mechanism to disseminate its power to the wider jazz community. From an educational perspective, it is perhaps understandable that the canon maintains such a seductive power. From establishing archives to designing curricula with supporting materials, the canon's promotion of objective standards and a single-strand chronological narrative allows for benchmarking and uniformity both within and across institutional boundaries. However, in buying into the ideology of the canon, educators not only run the risk of relegating jazz to a fossilised museum piece, they also lose the power of critical insight that is afforded education by its unique place in society. With this in mind, the power and influence of education projects that promote a canonical approach to jazz education should not be underestimated or viewed in isolation. Canonically based education programmes represent a much broader sea-change in American culture, where jazz education spans the arts and cultural sector. For example, educational projects and initiatives now reach beyond organisations traditionally linked to education, including archives, museums, venues and festivals. This integral relationship between canon and education is illustrated in a range of arts projects and music publications, from Jazz at Lincoln Center in New York, explored in the last chapter, to the Aebersold catalogue discussed in Chapter 2. Nationally funded initiatives such as the Smithsonian Institution's educational outreach programme, for example, work in a similar vein to Lincoln Center, promoting Ellington education, and issuing lesson plans and background information for teachers, online quizzes for students, recorded soundbites from musicians and scholars, and general resource lists. Programmes such as the Duke Ellington Youth Project at the Smithsonian Institution mirror the *Essentially Ellington* programme in seeking to preserve the history of jazz and 'extend the legacy of Ellington by disseminating his music'.[21] Within this context, as John Gennari stresses, iconic figures such as Duke Ellington play a significant part in our cultural landscape both in terms of the dominance of their artistic legacy and as a growth industry.[22] To demonstrate the educational links to these broader canonical issues and the restricted representation of iconic figures, consider the overarching aim of the first lesson plan on the music of Duke Ellington featured on the Smithsonian website. The first line of advice for music teachers is to: 'Encourage your students to consider the life and music of Duke Ellington in the same manner as that of any other great composer or person of accomplishment; that is, within the context of his times and the work he produced that has stood the test of time.'[23] Here, we are not only invited to view Ellington in relation to classical music (and, by implication, the educational methodologies bound up with classical music); the notion that the music 'has stood the test of time' removes any possibility of evaluating jazz as a social construct. In contrast to the comparison of Ellington to European masters, the Smithsonian Institution's education programme co-ordinator, Luvenia A. George, presents a hagiographic representation of Ellington that includes a sample lesson plan and a procedural instruction for tutors to read that prefaces Ellington's music with a talk about African slaves and West African music.[24] Here, we have two lesson plans on Ellington produced by the same institution that on the surface appear to create a critical tension between Ellington as European master and Ellington as embodied spirit of West African slaves. However, rather than encouraging a dialogue between these representations, the material is presented as fact, as an objective preface to the discovery of Ellington's music. These seemingly contradictory approaches serve to reinforce the multifaceted representation of the jazz icon as outlined in Chapter 1, and the dominant and simultaneous representation of Ellington both as great American composer and African American trickster, discussed in the previous chapter. Where Ellington is concerned, there is no conflict between Afrocentrism and Eurocentrism; the music is both social and transcendent and reinforces the same ideological message.[25]

In his criticism of jazz education methods in America, David Ake suggests that the emergence of the jazz canon has resulted in swing music losing its primitive denotation. Indeed, as part of Lincoln Center, jazz is instilled with a high level of sophistication and refinement. Ake, however, is also mindful of what is lost within these new settings, as the classicising of jazz inevitably leads to a favouring of harmony, the score and individuality over rhythm, timbre, intonation and collective musicianship.[26] Within this context, educational methods such as these are clearly restrictive in failing to enable students to find their own way into the music or in presenting a critical discourse surrounding great artists. Ultimately, this means that students are unlikely to interrogate the iconic legacies of jazz musicians in a critical way and, instead, inherit existing educational tools as a benchmark for good educational practices.

## Contemporary contexts: performance practice meets social theory

Reflecting on the original question regarding the contrasts between American and European jazz pedagogy, my initial observation was that although the geographical polarities were too simplistic, there were some cases that suggested clear differences between educational methods. It still amazes me when American jazz scholars say they *have* to come to Europe in order to have a meaningful discussion or engage in critical exchanges about jazz. For example, Barry Kernfeld reiterated this point in his keynote speech at a European jazz conference in Finland in 2003.[27] Equally, for European academics writing about jazz, critical appreciation among US publishers and scholars serves as an endorsement of work that is often felt to be on the margins of jazz discourse. However, to overplay the essentialism of the European–American divide is, I believe, unhelpful and potentially problematic, as it serves to widen the perceived gulf rather than addressing it. Despite this, I was still interested to explore ways in which the implications of differences between European and American jazz education could provide a useful theoretical methodology for other, more meaningful investigations. Rather than distinguishing between a European and American framework for jazz education, I felt a more useful delineation would be between different approaches to jazz scholarship, as educational methods are not necessarily defined geographically. Indeed, many European and American courses tend to reinforce the same myths and methodologies. With this in mind, rather than focusing on geography, I suggest that the 'canonical approach' could be classified as one that seeks to unify and underline jazz as a transcendent artform, celebrating the contributions of a handful of iconic individuals at the expense of a more pluralistic perspective, no matter where it is taught. In contrast to the 'canonical approach', the 'critical and cultural approach' to jazz could be characterised as more eclectic, reflecting both the multinational perspectives of different jazz communities and a lesser fixation with the idea of one 'authentic' canon. Although a distinction between these clearly recognisable educational philosophies can be helpful for the purposes of discussion, we should also be mindful of the fact that there are many other methods of jazz training that fall either outside or within these categories, and we should avoid falling into the trap of ideological essentialism, be it in terms of geography, race or educational method. Indeed, the further we continue to describe jazz in polar terms, the more fuel it adds to those who would caricature European jazz as white, cerebral and effeminate, in contrast to the soulful, black, masculine and, therefore, authentic jazz of America. The polarity is belied by the cross-fertilisation of ideas between Europe and the USA, as European institutions continue to look to the USA as the 'authentic home' of jazz, whilst US jazz scholars and musicians alike, whether consciously or subconsciously, look towards Europe for inspiration. An altogether healthier approach, I would argue, attempts not to force a choice between different schools of thought but to create a discourse between them. Within this context, it is useful to explore some of the perceived differences between established pedagogical methodologies in jazz. Within UK and US higher education sectors, 'jazz studies' tends to split between institutions that run performance-based programmes (typically in conservatoires and music departments) and those that view the subject from a more socio-critical perspective (in the university sector, usually within faculties of sociology, American studies and cultural studies). The former have a tendency to approach jazz using the 'canonical' model, focusing on repertoire studies, using bebop and the 'ABC' methodology – Aebersold–Baker–Coker – as the formulaic model for success. The latter seek to place jazz in its social context, aiming to examine critically the social and cultural impact of music. This approach places jazz in the context of other disciplines such as film and literature, and this interdisciplinary methodology is explored in texts such as Graham Lock and David Murray's recent volumes, *Thriving on a Riff* and *The Hearing Eye*.[28] In many respects, the different institutional contexts for practice-based and socio-critical jazz studies have created another unhelpful polarity, the perception that the study of jazz performance is somehow removed from the study of jazz culture; the study of jazz as verb is separate from the study of jazz as noun. As a scholar involved in the development of jazz education programmes, and having worked in environments where the performance-based and socio-critical sectors collide, I have tried to bridge the perceived differences between these approaches by demonstrating that they are integrally linked. For example, by examining jazz in the context of twentieth- and twenty-first-century developments, including other media and artforms, students can be encouraged to examine jazz history not just as a linear chronology (moving from clearly defined historical 'moments' – swing, bebop, cool etc.), but as a site for the cross-fertilisation of ideas. Through non-linear approaches to the subject, currents and cross-currents can be extracted from history, which encourage students to recognise that debates and ideas are ongoing. For example, looking at jazz history through the perspective of the influence of technology or the politics of jazz and its place within popular culture has enabled useful cross-referencing between different musical eras, and semiotic analysis has provided performers with a heightened awareness of codes and conventions that exist within musical practice.

In the context of the complexities surrounding jazz education and the cultural place of the institution, I argue that it is important to develop an integrated methodology that maintains a degree of critical distance at the same time as engaging with the subject matter first-hand. This integrated approach can effectively be demonstrated through the analysis of established jazz texts and documentaries that seek to present jazz as a linear and objective canonical narrative. For example, the discussion of Ken Burns's documentary *Jazz* in the previous chapter showed how supposedly unproblematic jazz texts can be read and reread to enable broader critical understandings of the discourse, offering a working model for the critical analysis of jazz through established 'canonical' works. However, the PBS documentary provides the critic with a contemporary example of the conventional jazz narrative and, as a text, it can be interpreted as the embodiment of the canonical jazz work. Rather than dismiss Burns's *Jazz* as a valueless addition to the repertoire of historical works, as an educator I suggest that it is important to place works such as these at the heart of jazz studies, in order to develop a critical understanding of the cultural framework within which the music operates. Indeed, like other standard jazz histories and biographies, the Burns narrative offers a good example of a conventional portrayal of jazz history on one level. And yet, within an integrated methodological approach to jazz education, texts such as these can be considered a valuable tool for both constructing and deconstructing jazz canons, enabling students to gain an insight into dominant ideologies and an understanding of current values in jazz. Receiving established jazz texts as mediated artefacts in this way can help us understand the complex nature of iconic representation and the extent to which musicians participate in constructing idealised images of themselves and the jazz greats. Krin Gabbard's study of Miles Davis's autobiography, for example, raises a number of interesting and problematic issues for those seeking a unified version of jazz history.[29] Gabbard not only illustrates the way in which writers and editors embellish autobiographical texts to portray an idealised or stereotypical view of artists and their music but also demonstrates the role musicians play in managing their own media representation. The creation of iconic personas both by artists themselves and the broader jazz superstructure might work to iron out conflict within the unproblematic world of the homogenous jazz tradition. However, accepting mediated representations as absolute truths avoids a critical reading of jazz history that, like icons themselves, involves conflict and contradiction. Understanding the many different representations of Miles Davis, from musical genius, to loveable romantic, to violent bully, forces us to treat jazz as a discursive subject at the same time as recognising the complexities of icon–audience relationships. This approach creates a powerful pedagogical tool that can encourage students to think critically even if many of the issues at play remain irreconcilable. Within this new methodology, a flexibility of approach would be necessary to encourage jazz as a discursive practice. As a critical tool, the methodology could obviously unsettle educators invested in the notion of canon, the inherent qualities of music and supposedly objective standards. However, this model provides a more inclusive approach to scholarship that resists the trend of simply rejecting one canonised discourse and replacing it with another.[30] Transforming jazz education from within in this way echoes Ajay Heble's observations on the music of John Zorn, which is said to draw 'its power and force from the very logic it works to unsettle', and this concept can be adopted by tutors when considering how the subversion of dominant ideologies can form part of the pedagogical process. This somewhat unsettling position presents many issues for jazz educators but has the potential to impact on jazz studies in both practical and theoretical settings.[31]

The canonical approach to jazz education obviously has advantages for those who seek to legitimise jazz as a serious artform, with its own set of objective standards and definable history. As jazz has gained an increased degree of legitimacy in the academy, the ability to classify and objectify the music and its history can prove extremely beneficial when seeking funding for libraries, education initiatives or publications. Equally, from an African American perspective, the desire to construct and celebrate a rich, definable cultural history is understandable in the broader frame-work of American history. This is echoed in African American studies, where authors such as Henry Louis Gates Jr have argued for recognition and celebration of African American canons of literature, and sensitivity to the political backdrop to American history when understanding the motivations behind canon formation.[32] The down side of this approach is that it encourages the presentation of history as a defined entity con-structed in the present, rather than something in constant flux, and can lead to the exclusion of approaches that do not conform to the defined benchmark. By contrast, a more socio-critical approach to jazz enables the subject to be deconstructed and viewed from a number of perspec-tives, acknowledging the idea of jazz *histories* in the plural and the idea of 'greatness' as a socially located term. This approach enables fluid debates on the nature of canons and iconic figures, although it still requires some grounding in the 'American textbook of jazz' in order to put deconstruc-tion into context. However, these critical readings of history inevitably lead to the questioning of established discourses and readings of music and, therefore, within a jazz context, this causes several problems. A critical approach to jazz studies in today's teaching environment can be seen as going against the grain of a subject that has only recently been 'historicised', legitimised and brought into the academy. Critical readings seek to challenge and undermine the inherent classification, objectifying and creation of a jazz lineage, although, echoing the words of Scott DeVeaux and Krin Gabbard, the immediate question troubling several jazz enthusiasts is 'why seek to destroy something that has just been created?'[33] However, these writings are now over fifteen years old and the disciplinary context for jazz studies has radically altered and strengthened since the early 1990s, as have the power and influence of the canon itself. Here, I argue that establishing a discursive framework from which to evaluate conventional and non-conventional approaches to jazz avoids discrediting the canon altogether. Rather than dismiss the established canon of jazz, the critical model I suggest aims to introduce a more inclusive, comparative and interdisciplinary approach to jazz studies, where the canon is subject to continual appraisal and discursive methodologies. By exposing the constructed and often unhelpful dualisms in jazz – the polarities of power – within the wider social order, jazz education can clearly perform a number of roles, from the critical to subversive, creative to political. In this sense, jazz pedagogy has the potential to embed itself in the realities of the social, whilst exposing ideologies that support the romanticised conception of jazz culture.

## Birth of the school: education and the New Jazz Studies

What we need is not to construct more institutions but instead to de-institutionalize the canons we have, to strip away the structures of power in which they are enmeshed and reveal them as the congeries of personal choices they are. We need, in other words, to turn our attention from the self-bolstering search for personal canons similar to our own to the less comforting scrutiny of and dialogue with canons divergent from ours.[34]

Gary Tomlinson's words are part of a much broader critique of the canonisation of jazz and the limitations of jazz education that, arguably, is as relevant today as it was in the early 1990s. In this text Tomlinson suggested that, more often than not, jazz studies were founded on the principles of aestheticism, transcendentalism and formalism found most often in the validation of European classical music. Moreover, he suggested that, even when theories of the African American vernacular such as signifyin(g) were invoked, they tended to be limited in approach, being used to assert the authority of an essential black canon of literature/jazz rather than a process of constant revision and dialogue. Tomlinson argued that instead of historians and educators exploring a truly complex and multi-dimensional approach to jazz scholarship they have instead offered a form of monological imitation, the result of which 'is a brand of narrowly based value judgment that cannot do justice to the complex dialogues of self and other in which culture is created'.[35] Borrowing from the writings of Mikhail Bakhtin in his discussion of dialogism and moving beyond Henry Louis Gates's somewhat limited use of signifyin(g) in African American literature, Tomlinson presented a refreshing view of jazz studies that was based on constant revision, challenging widely accepted notions of 'reality' in jazz history, and injecting a degree of complexity and contestation into the music and its context. Using the critical reception of Miles Davis's electric period as a case study, Tomlinson demonstrated how, in treating Davis's late music as 'selling out' or as a deviation from the authentic jazz of the past, different writings could be understood as ideologically motivated, favouring a monological view of history instead of a complex and dialogical understanding of jazz. The arguments presented in Tomlison's article formed a significant part of a new wave of jazz scholarship that was later dubbed the New Jazz Studies, with writings from the 1990s onwards being immersed in interdisciplinary theory and discursive approaches to jazz history. The diversity and complexity of criticism during this period has been neatly summarised by John Gennari as part of the conclusions to his impressive study of jazz criticism past and present, *Blowin' Hot and Cool: Jazz and Its Critics*:

The questions and issues that have riven jazz criticism over the last twenty years – on matters of race, culture, aesthetics, history, and power – are knotty and difficult. They constitute a dissonant 'noise' that is a necessary antidote to the emptily pious jazz hero-worship that threatens to reduce a fiercely complex music to feel-good Muzak. Jazz and its history are full of dislocations, heresy, iconoclasm, and stupendous feats of imagination. Jazz criticism should be no less gloriously messy.[36]

Gennari suggests that conflict and contestation, or the dissonances of jazz, have resulted in a relatively healthy New Jazz Studies that is both incisive and challenging in nature. Although I agree with Gennari about the richness of different perspectives and the value of critical dissonance within writings on jazz at present, the 'gloriously messy' approach to jazz scholarship has not necessarily filtered down to the level of jazz programmes, which offer practical, critical and theoretical studies within their curricula. Indeed, at several points over the last ten years, I have been frustrated by the reluctance of cultural theorists or New Jazz Studies scholars to engage with the music itself, as if understanding the mechanics of music itself is an irrelevant aside to social and cultural concerns.

More significantly, however, I find jazz practitioners' reluctance to apply discursive methods to musical training as deeply problematic, not enabling students to reflect on the processes of learning or the political and cultural context in which their music is played. Tomlinson, for example, suggests that this refusal to engage with music as a discursive or dialogical form is another manifestation of the Eurocentric notion of autonomous art. To suggest that the music should 'speak for itself', or that listening should be the primary route to understanding, reinforces the notion that meaning is found in the music itself and that inherent value is separate from the context in which music is created. Tomlinson argues that, by placing the music first, there will always be a distance from the complexities and cultural negotiations that created it in the first place and continue to sustain it and, as an alternative, asks:

Instead of repeating such Western myths of the noncontingency of artworks, why not search for jazz meanings *behind* the music, in the life-shapes that gave rise to it and that continue to sustain it? Why not, in other words, scrutinize the interactions between our own rules of formation and those we impute to the makers of jazz as the source of our evaluations of it?[37]

Here, Tomlinson stresses the importance of social context and the dialogical in generating a complex and multifaceted understanding of jazz history. However, whereas Tomlinson dismisses the primacy of performance and listening in developing a dialogical understanding of jazz, I would suggest that this approach continues to place performance-based jazz pedagogy at the margins and at a distance from dialogical investigation, as aspiring musicians obviously need to foreground performance skills as part of their studies. With this in mind, I would suggest that one of the major challenges for New Jazz Studies over the coming years is to discover ways in which the discursive methods of both theory *and* practice can interact. In other words, rather than allowing cultural criticism to work as an abstraction, we should explore the way in which writing could take on a performative dimension, engaging with the music itself as the primary text. More significantly, I would suggest that practical jazz pedagogy seeks to devise methodologies that can be considered discursive and dialogical. This approach would serve to avoid the way in which musicians tend to retreat into their own world either by suggesting that the music should do the talking or that jazz scholars cannot possibly understand the true value of jazz unless they themselves can cut it on the bandstand.

With this in mind, several educational methods have surfaced in recent years that, although still marginal and most often centred around the pedagogy of 'free jazz', demonstrate a more discursive approach to jazz studies, challenging existing convention by focusing on the processes of learning for both the practical and theoretical study of jazz.[38] Consider the following statement from writer-saxophonist David Borgo: 'By conceiving musical "knowledge" as individual, abstract, relatively fixed, and unaffected by the activity through which it is acquired and used, music programmes have devalued the experiential, exploratory, and collective qualities that make for compelling improvisation and, more generally, that inform the development of musical ears, memory, instincts, sensitivity, and, ultimately, creativity.'[39] Within this context, Borgo's ecological model of jazz education mirrors Bakhtin's dialogism on one level in that it presents the idea of knowledge as a process rather than something fixed and essential. Knowledge in this educational setting relies on the situated position of the subject; where people are placed contextually changes the way in which they perceive and are perceived. Bakhtin, for example, suggests that identities can be made or unmade according to the situated position of the subject, and that knowledge of the self is never stable, relying instead on the dialogical relationship between the self and others.[40] This echoes the discussion of community and identity in Chapter 3 where identities can now be understood as acts of becoming, part of a relational process between identity (who we are) and identification (how we relate to others) that exists only within discourse. Within the context of jazz pedagogy, Borgo suggests that educators need to develop strategies that are sensitive to the discursive nature of music, encouraging students to explore the interpersonal dimension of improvised music and facilitating learning that is negotiated by the participants themselves. As Borgo proposes, '[r]ather than simply imparting problem solving skills in the abstract, they [instructors] must encourage students to develop problem finding approaches and create a context in which everyone feels comfortable exploring new ideas and experimenting together'.[41] This model resists the temptation to view jazz as a reified object with a 'master' teacher who imparts a fixed idea of knowledge to his or her passive and reverent students and instead promotes a mentoring system where educators act as the facilitators of learning, with knowledge in this context being understood as 'co-instituted', learners themselves forming a dynamic part of the process.

Moving away from the context of ecological psychology, I suggest that, as a basic strategy, educators can instil into jazz practice a dialogic or discursive character simply by feeding off some of the points of contestation and ideological control presented both in the examples used within this book and the related writings of New Jazz Studies scholars. Furthermore, this strategy would not have to include the introduction of free jazz methods alone or involve iconoclastic approaches that undermine the contributions of the jazz greats to jazz history. Indeed, the discursive or dialogical nature of jazz practice could arguably be more meaningful when performance projects include a different take on the work of jazz icons.

Therefore, the theoretical ideas proposed in this study and other jazz writings could easily work well as dialogic performance projects. For example, the representation of Ellington as the singular voice of a 'great composer' in the previous chapter could easily be challenged by a project that explored collaborative music making. Rather than transcribing the work of the great composer for students to recreate as classical musicians would a score, to confront musicians with a collaborative composition would provide a valuable insight into the working practices of Ellington and could subsequently challenge the ideological model of authorship as a singular enterprise linked to music's autonomous existence. Equally, students could be encouraged to use technology as part of a jazz remixing or overdubbing that, as with Kenny G's interaction with Louis Armstrong, would serve to question the assumption that iconic jazz is hallowed territory. In the broader context of New Jazz Studies, several critical writings lend themselves to practice-based pedagogical settings. Ake, for example, proposes educational projects that involve the late recordings of John Coltrane: music that is, ironically, bound up with the creation of Coltrane as spiritual icon, but material that is nonetheless frequently ignored by educators influenced by chord-scale theory.[42] To devise performance-based projects involving the late music of Coltrane would achieve several critical objectives that could be viewed as discursive acts. On the one hand, as Ake suggests, the strategy presents an immediate alternative to chord-scale theory, encouraging students to reconceptualise their approach to improvised music. On the other hand, I would suggest that this method shows another dimension to the work of an iconic jazz figure; to engage with Coltrane's late recordings is, in many respects, to enter into a dialogical relationship with the past, revising the teleological history of the neo-traditionalist mainstream that encourages us to view *Giant Steps* as the pinnacle of technical achievement and *A Love Supreme* as the last great spiritual masterwork. In this context, the relationship between past and present can be inverted; rather than a reified sense of history impacting on the practices of today, present strategies can reinform and revise our understanding of the past. This is the primary essence of dialogism. Other writings could include Tomlinson's own study of the dialogics of Miles Davis's electric period, which could easily be mapped onto performance-based settings, as could Nicholas Gebhardt's challenge to the ideology of bebop.[43] Gebhardt's work questions the ideological narratives that focus on the individual, the virtuosic and the fatalistic mythologies of evolutionary progress, typified in the biographical writings of icons such as Charlie Parker, and instead promotes an understanding of bebop that is rooted in ensemble playing, the dynamics of scene, and cultural and political context.

Whilst these discursive and dialogical methods of jazz pedagogy might well offer fascinating insights and produce a 'gloriously messy' approach to education, we should not lose sight of the reifying and naturalising tendencies of ideology that inevitably lead to the canon-formation and iconic representation seen so evidently within this book. However, the continued reification of jazz as a canonical artform alongside stereotypical understandings of categories such as gender and race need not cause alarm to critical scholars, especially when we develop an understanding of their culturally constructed nature. Indeed, as I have argued, it is possible to envisage a situation where singular or homogenous narratives are questioned even when they are deemed to be representative of the New Jazz Studies. Sherrie Tucker, for example, has made the convincing point that there is an inherent critical value in receiving different perspectives on jazz simultaneously, whether they are contradictory or tangential.[44] From Tucker's perspective, the process of thinking differently and drawing different conclusions from historical evidence is both a key aspect of interdisciplinary thinking and a process that is heard in music making itself. However, unlike inherent conflicts and contradictions in the perspectives of Murray, Crouch and Marsalis explored in the opening chapter, I suggest that these differing perspectives ultimately lead to a discursive understanding of jazz and its history where alternative readings of events are offered and iconic figures do not necessarily have authority or pride of place. From my perspective, the most significant challenge within this new environment is allowing the variety of voices to *be* heard, enabling creative dissonances to speak through the pleasant and uncomplicated harmonies of the jazz mainstream. As we have seen within this study, the naturalising tendencies of any dominant ideological viewpoint tend to favour a singular world view, and so a discursive approach to jazz theory and practice remains far from straightforward and somewhat idealistic. With this in mind, the discursive approach I propose here might not necessarily change the jazz world overnight; however, it would enable us to reconsider the centrality of 'great men' to the understanding of jazz at the same time as encouraging us to reflect upon, review and interrogate our own relationships to the icons of the music's history. Using dialogical methodologies and an integrated approach to examining jazz as both music and culture, the study of iconic figures can unlock doors to new ways of thinking critically, promoting critical jazz practice and discursive historiography over heroic jazz narratives and hagiographic representations of the past.

# Notes

## Introduction: Jazz narratives and sonic icons

1. Transcribed from *Collateral*, film, directed by Michael Mann (USA: Dreamworks Pictures, 2004).

2. Norman Mailer, 'The White Negro' in Walser, R. (ed.), *Keeping Time: Readings in Jazz History* (New York and Oxford: Oxford University Press, 1999), 242–6.

3. Krin Gabbard, 'Miles from Home: Miles Davis and the Movies', *The Source: Challenging Jazz Criticism* 1 (March 2004), 27–41.

4. Gabbard draws on Vance Bourjaily's concept of 'The Story' when comparing the pursuit and achievement of the American dream in Al Jolson's *The Jazz Singer* to black artists in Hollywood:

> For African American musicians, the basic narrative has been very different. Vance Bourjaily has called it 'The Story'. 'The Story' goes like this: a musician of genius, frustrated by the discrepancy between what he can achieve and the crummy life musicians lead (because of racial discrimination, or the demand that the music be made commercial, or because he has a potential he can't reach), goes mad, or destroys himself with alcohol and drugs. The Story might be a romance, but it is a valid one.

See Krin Gabbard, *Jammin' at the Margins: Jazz and the American Cinema* (Chicago and London: University of Chicago Press, 1996), 67.

5. To illustrate this point, writers such as David Ake and Michael Jarrett have used William Claxton's photograph of Sonny Rollins posing as a cowboy on the cover of his 1957 album *Way Out West* to discuss the signifying potential of jazz photography and album covers. On one level, the Rollins cover seems rather abstract and light-hearted, as we are not accustomed to seeing leading jazz figures dressed up in cowboy outfits in the middle of the Californian desert. And yet, the photograph moves beyond the jovial to encourage a connection between jazz and the American frontier, a connection that has perhaps remained implicit within written and verbal jazz discourses (I explore this relationship in more detail in Chapter 1). See David Ake, *Jazz Cultures* (Berkeley: University of California Press, 2002); and Michael Jarrett, 'The Tenor's Vehicle: Reading *Way Out West*' in Gabbard, K. (ed.), *Representing Jazz* (Durham, NC and London: Duke University Press, 1995),

260–82. For writings on the visual nature of jazz, see Robert O'Meally, *Seeing Jazz: Artists and Writers on Jazz* (San Francisco: Chronicle Books, 1997); Krin Gabbard, 'Images of Jazz' in Cooke, M. and Horn, D. (eds.), *The Cambridge Companion to Jazz* (Cambridge: Cambridge University Press, 2002), 332–46; and Graham Lock and David Murray (eds.), *The Hearing Eye: Jazz and Blues Influences in African American Visual Art* (New York and Oxford: Oxford University Press, 2009).

6. Several Blue Note designs owe a lot to the design aesthetic of European art movements such as Bauhaus and De Stijl. For example, compare the Bauhaus design on the cover of Magdalena Droste's *Bauhaus 1919–1933* (Cologne: Taschen, 1998) to the Blue Note album cover for Stanley Turrentine's *Up at Minton's*. Both designs employ exactly the same block-colour geometric layout, with the Blue Note cover differing only in terms of its blue colour palette and the addition of monochrome photography. For more examples of the Blue Note design aesthetic see Graham Marsh and Glyn Callingham, *The Cover Art of Blue Note Records* (London: Collins and Brown, 1991). See also Richard Cook, *Blue Note Records: The Biography* (London: Pimlico Press, 2003).

7. For example, Gabbard states, 'At their best, fiction, cinema and photography produce illuminating, often startling representations of jazz through different sets of metaphors appropriate to the history and aesthetics of each medium.' See Gabbard, 'Images of Jazz', 332.

8. Jed Rasula, 'The Media of Memory: The Seductive Menace of Records in Jazz History' in Gabbard, K. (ed.), *Jazz among the Discourses* (Durham, NC and London: Duke University Press, 1995), 134–64.

9. As a recent example, photographer Martin Parr has commented on the emotional nuances of sepia and monochrome photography and discusses Madonna's use of sepia to connote maternal instincts, authenticity and idealism. See Martin Parr, 'The Power of Sepia: An Expert's Take on That Madonna Image', *Guardian*, Comments and Features (15 April 2009), 2.

10. For more on the discussion of celebrity and stardom, see Richard Dyer, *Stars* (London: BFI, 1998); and Jessica Evans and David Hesmondalgh, *Understanding Media: Inside Celebrity* (Maidenhead and New York: Open University Press, 2005).

11. Evans and Hesmondalgh, *Understanding Media*, 23. For further reading on the mediated nature of performance, see Philip Auslander, *Liveness: Performance in a Mediatized Culture* (London and New York: Routledge, 1999).

12. Valerie Wilmer, *As Serious as Your Life: John Coltrane and Beyond* (London: Serpent's Tail, 1992), 31.

13. Gabbard, 'Images of Jazz', 340–6.

14. Frederick J. Spencer, *Jazz and Death: Medical Profiles of Jazz Greats* (Jackson: University of Mississippi Press, 2002).

15. Historian Scott DeVeaux has led the way in terms of New Jazz Studies scholars who have sought to uncover the ideological potential of jazz history. DeVeaux's hugely influential essay 'Constructing the Jazz Tradition' provides a compelling and influential account of the politics of jazz history, and his subsequent writings have also discussed the way in which the biographies of jazz greats play a central role in perpetuating mythologies, from melodramatic and romanticised depictions of tragic jazz lives to the idea of the music as an unmediated expression. See, for example, Scott DeVeaux, 'Constructing the Jazz Tradition' in O'Meally, R. (ed.), *The Jazz Cadence of American Culture* (New York: Columbia University Press, 1998), 484–514, and 'Struggling with *Jazz*', *Current Musicology* 71–3 (Spring 2001–Spring 2002), 353–74.

16. Roland Barthes, *Mythologies* (London: Vintage Classics, 1993).

17. For more on the semiotic theory of Peirce in music and art, see Philip Tagg and Bob Clarida, *10 Little Title Tunes* (New York and Montreal: Mass Media Scholars' Press, 2003); and Michael Leja, 'Peirce, Visuality, and Art', *Representation* 72 (Autumn 2000), 97–122.

18. James Lincoln Collier, *Duke Ellington* (London and New York: Penguin, 1987); and David Hajdu, 'A Jazz of Their Own', *Vanity Fair* 465 (May 1999), 188–96.

## 1  Jazz icons, heroes and myths

1. Albert Murray, 'The Function of the Heroic Image' in O'Meally, R. (ed.), *The Jazz Cadence of American Culture* (New York: Columbia University Press, 1998), 569–79 (571).

2. For example, see Sherrie Tucker, *Swing Shift:"All-Girl" Bands of the 1940s* (Durham, NC and London: Duke University Press, 2000); Krin Gabbard (ed.), *Jazz among the Discourses* (Durham, NC and London: Duke University Press, 1995); and David Ake, *Jazz Cultures* (Berkeley: University of California Press, 2002) for useful insights into the discursive and ideological nature of jazz canons.

3. Albert Murray, *The Omni-Americans: New Perspectives on Black Experience and American Culture* (New York: Outerbridge and Dienstfrey, 1970).

4. Murray, 'The Function of the Heroic Image', 578.

5. Ralph Ellison, 'Homage to Duke Ellington on His Birthday' in John F. Callahan (ed.), *The Collected Essays of Ralph Ellison* (New York: Modern Library Paperback 2003), 680–7 (682).

6. See Scott DeVeaux, 'Struggling with *Jazz*', *Current Musicology* 71–3 (Spring 2001–Spring 2002), 353–74 for a discussion of the involvement of Marsalis and Crouch in the Burns documentary.

7. Stuart Nicholson, *Is Jazz Dead? (Or Has It Moved to a New Address?)* (London and New York: Routledge, 2005), 26.

8. Eric Porter, *What Is This Thing Called Jazz? African American Musicians as Artists, Critics and Activists* (Berkeley: University of California Press, 2002), 287–334.

9. *Ibid.*, 289.

10. *Ibid.*, 317.

11. *Ibid.*, 328.

12. Wynton Marsalis and Frank Stewart, *Sweet Swing Blues on the Road* (New York: Thunder's Mouth Press, 1999), 152.

13. *Ibid.*, 153.

14. *Ibid.*, 153.

15. *Ibid.*, 163.

16. Consider, for example, the explicit use of the word 'genius' in Wynton Marsalis and John Edward Hasse, *Beyond Category: The Life and Genius of Duke Ellington* (New York: Da Capo Press, 1995); and Stanley Crouch, *Considering Genius: Writings on Music* (New York: Basic Civitas Books, 2006).

17. Crouch, *Considering Genius*, 196.

18. *Ibid.*, 196.

19. See, for example, Crouch's 'Body and Soul' in *ibid.*, 193.

20. Penelope Murray (ed.), *Genius: The History of an Idea* (Oxford: Blackwell, 1989).

21. For typical examples of the invocation of genius see Gary Giddins, *Satchmo: The Genius of Louis Armstrong*, 2nd edn (New York: Da Capo Press, 2000); John Edward Hasse, *Duke Ellington beyond Genius* (New York: Simon and Schuster, 1993); and Leslie Gourse, *Straight, No Chaser: The Life and Genius of Thelonious Monk* (London: Books with Attitude, 1997).

22. Janet Wolff, *The Social Production of Art*, 2nd edn (London: Macmillan, 1993), 10.

23. *Ibid.*, 11.

24. See, for example, Alan Merriam and Raymond Mack, 'The Jazz Community', *Social Forces* 38.3 (1960), 211–22; and Nat Hentoff, *The Jazz Life* (London: Hamilton and Co., 1964) for romanticised descriptions of the Outsider qualities of jazzmen.

25. Henry Louis Gates Jr, *The Signifyin(g) Monkey: A Theory of African-American Literary Criticism* (Oxford and New York: Oxford University Press, 1990). For examples of jazz writings that draw on Gates's work see Gary Tomlinson, 'Cultural Dialogics and Jazz: A White Historian Signifies', *Black Music Research Journal* 11.2 (Autumn 1991), 229–64; and George Burrows, 'Black, Brown and Beige and the Politics of Signifyin(g)', *Jazz Research Journal* 1.1 (March 2007), 45–71.

26. Derek Scott, *From the Erotic to the Demonic: On Critical Musicology* (New York: Oxford University Press, 2003), 199.

27. Robert Walser, '"Out of Notes": Signification, Interpretation and the Problem of Miles Davis', *The Musical Quarterly* 77.2 (Summer 1993), 343–65.

28. Tomlinson, 'Cultural Dialogics', 242.

29. See, for example, Krin Gabbard, 'Signifyin' the Phallus: Mo' Better Blues and Representations of the Jazz Trumpet' in Gabbard, K. (ed.), *Representing Jazz* (Durham, NC and London: Duke University Press, 1995), 104–30; and Robert O'Meally, 'Checking Our Balances: Louis Armstrong, Ralph Ellison and Betty Boop', *The Source: Challenging Jazz Criticism* 1 (March 2004), 44–59.

30. Albert Murray, *From the Briarpatch File: On Context, Procedure and American Identity* (New York: Pantheon Books, 2001), 6.

31. Murray, 'The Function of the Heroic Image', 576.

32. Michael Jarrett, 'The Tenor's Vehicle: Reading *Way Out West*' in Gabbard, *Representing Jazz*, 260–282.

33. David Hamilton Murdoch, *The American West: The Invention of a Myth* (Cardiff: Welsh Academic Press, 1999), 21.

34. Nicholas Gebhardt, *Going for Jazz: Musical Practices and American Ideology* (Chicago and London: University of Chicago Press, 2001).

35. *Ibid.*, 102–5.

36. Lawrence Levine, *High Brow Low Brow: The Emergence of Cultural Hierarchy in America* (Cambridge, MA: Harvard University Press, 1990), 132.

37. See, for example, Matthew Arnold, *Culture and Anarchy* (Oxford and New York: Oxford University Press, 1990); and F. R. Leavis, 'Mass Civilisation and Minority Culture' in Storey, J. (ed.), *Cultural Theory and Popular Culture: A Reader* (Hemel Hempstead: Harvester Wheatsheaf, 1994), 12–20.

38. Levine, *High Brow Low Brow*, 177.

39. Hamilton Murdoch, *The American West*, 84.

40. *Ibid.*, 1.

41. For example, see Larry Kart, 'Miles Davis Biography Fails to Unravel Strands of Art and Image' in Kirchner, B. (ed.), *A Miles Davis Reader* (Washington and London: Smithsonian Institution Press, 1997), 229–33; and John Szwed, 'The Man' in O'Meally, R., Hayes Edwards, B. and Jasmine Griffin, F. (eds.), *Uptown Conversation: The New Jazz Studies* (New York: Columbia University Press, 2004), 166–86 for tributes to Davis's character and music that largely ignore the problematic elements of his biography. Kart, for example, argues that it is important to distinguish between the facts and the gossip in artist biographies but only goes on to focus on the importance of the pain of Davis's sickle-cell anaemia and the overcoming of his drug addiction.

42. See Howard Brofsky's 'Miles Davis and "My Funny Valentine": The Evolution of a Solo' in Kirchner, *A Miles Davis Reader*, 140–63 for a discussion of the differences between media representations of Miles Davis and Chet Baker. Similarly, Jon Panish, *The Color of Jazz: Race and Representation in Postwar American Culture* (Jackson: University of Mississippi Press, 1997) offers some interesting examples of the prejudiced and politicised nature of the American media in relation to black artists.

43. Ajay Heble, *Landing on the Wrong Note: Jazz, Dissonance and Critical Practice* (London and New York: Routledge, 2000), 144.

44. Krin Gabbard, *Jammin' at the Margins: Jazz and the American Cinema* (Chicago and London: University of Chicago Press, 1996), 7.

45. Peter J. Martin, 'The Jazz Community as an Art World', *The Source: Challenging Jazz Criticism* 2 (March 2005), 5–13.

46. Anthony Easthope, *What a Man's Gotta Do: Masculine Myth in Popular Culture* (New York: Routledge, 1990).

47. Wynton Marsalis quoted in Francis Davis, *In the Moment: Jazz in the 1980s* (New York: Oxford University Press, 1986), 32.

48. Even though Francis Davis suggests that Marsalis might have been referring to dashikis worn by Black Nationalist musicians in the 1970s, I would argue that the use of the word 'dress' in this context is used to assert masculine norms and the dominance of stereotypically male representations regardless of whether the reference is to nationalism or gendered stereotypes in jazz. The gendered norms of the neo-traditionalist mainstream can also be seen in the rhetorical statements of Stanley Crouch. For example, Crouch not only equated the criticisms of Marsalis to jealousy over Marsalis's sexual prowess but also described free jazz as being analogous to transvestism. See Nicholson, *Is Jazz Dead?*, 61–4.

49. See Orrin E. Klapp, *Heroes, Villains and Fools* (Harlow: Prentice Hall, 1962); and Richard Dyer, *Stars* (London: BFI, 1998). For an analysis of heroic narratives see Joseph Campbell, *The Hero with a Thousand Faces* (London: Fontana Press, 1993); and Christopher Vogler, *The Writer's Journey: Mythic Structure for Writers*, 3rd edn (Studio City, CA: Michael Wiese Productions, 2007).

50. Although it could be argued that the biographies of artists such as Billie Holiday follow a similar trajectory to Charlie Parker's Faustian narrative, I suggest that there is no female equivalent for the masculine myth in jazz, and that the way in which male artists are mythologised posthumously is bound up with masculine ideals.

51. Frederick Garber, 'Fabulating Jazz' in Gabbard, *Representing Jazz*, 70–103 (83).

## 2 Jazz and the disembodied voice

1. Evan Eisenberg, *The Recording Angel: Music, Records and Culture from Aristotle to Zappa*, 2nd edn (New Haven: Yale University Press, 2005), 120.

2. Jacques Attali, *Noise: The Political Economy of Music* (Minneapolis: University of Minnesota Press, 1985), 85.

3. Frederick Garber, 'Fabulating Jazz' in Gabbard, K. (ed.), *Representing Jazz* (Durham, NC and London: Duke University Press, 1995), 70–103 (83).

4. Christopher Washburne, 'Does Kenny G Play Bad Jazz?' in Washburne, C. J. and Derno, M. (eds.), *Bad Music: The Music We Love to Hate* (New York and London: Routledge, 2004), 123–47.

5. For more on this subject, see Jed Rasula, 'The Media of Memory: The Seductive Menace of Records in Jazz History' in Gabbard, K. (ed.), *Jazz among the Discourses* (Durham, NC and London: Duke University Press, 1995), 134–64. Rasula comments on the way in which records are essential to historians in constructing a definable and legitimate history for jazz, yet, through their dominance, they have the ability to skew understandings of the past and concretise our perceptions of jazz history.

6. David Laing, 'A Voice without a Face: Popular Music and the Phonograph in the 1890s', *Popular Music* 10 (January 1991), 1–9.

7. Mark Katz, *Capturing Sound: How Technology Changed Music* (Berkeley: University of California Press, 2004), 48–71.

8. Walter Benjamin, 'The Work of Art in the Age of Mechanical Reproduction' in *Illuminations* (London: Pimlico Press, 1999), 211–44.

9. See, for example, Alastair Williams, *Constructing Musicology* (Aldershot: Ashgate, 2007), 80; and Richard Middleton, *Studying Popular Music* (Milton Keynes and Philadelphia: Open University Press, 1995), 64, for a comparison between Benjamin's 'aura' and the ideology of autonomous art.

10. See Middleton, *Studying Popular Music*, 64. For an account of the discourse between Adorno and Benjamin, see Robert W. Witkin, *Adorno on Popular Culture* (London and New York: Routledge, 2003), 50–67.

11. John Berger, *Ways of Seeing* (London: Penguin, 1990), 21.

12. Krin Gabbard, *Jammin' at the Margins: Jazz and the American Cinema* (Chicago and London: University of Chicago Press, 1996), 4.

13. Garber, 'Fabulating Jazz', 74.

14. Andy LaVerne, *Countdown to Giant Steps*, Play-A-Long book series no. 75 (New Albany, IN: Jamey Aebersold Jazz, 1996).

15. Katz, *Capturing Sound*, 3–7.

16. This argument is expanded by Eisenberg, who suggests that recordings have the power to 'inseminate' music, defining the way in which we view its history. Similarly, outside the recording, Marshall McLuhan and Jean Baudrillard have explored how our understandings of the world are constructed through various media. See Marshall McLuhan, *Understanding Media: The Extensions of Man* (New York: Routledge, 2001); and Jean Baudrillard, 'The Work of Art in the Electronic Age' in Gane, M. (ed.), *Baudrillard Live: Selected Interviews* (London and New York: Routledge, 1993), 145–51.

17. For example, Georgina Born has demonstrated how jazz recordings can undermine the concept of the musical work in western art music, with the ephemeral qualities of recordings serving to challenge fixed interpretations. See Georgina Born, 'On Musical Mediation: Ontology, Technology and

Creativity,' *Twentieth-Century Music* 2 (March 2005), 7–36. For studies on recordings as trophies, see Eisenberg, *The Recording Angel*, 14–18; and for a discussion of 'nerdy' jazz fan culture, see Will Straw, 'Sizing Up Record Collections: Gender and Connoisseurship in Rock Music Culture' in Whiteley, S. (ed.), *Sexing the Groove: Popular Music and Gender* (London: Routledge, 1997), 3–16; and Krin Gabbard, *Black Magic: White Hollywood and African American Culture* (New Brunswick: Rutgers University Press, 2004), 199–232.

18. John Coltrane, *A Love Supreme*, Impulse! IMP 11552, LP (1964), reissued as Impulse B000061002, CD (2003).

19. For more on the Church of St John Coltrane, see David Ake, *Jazz Cultures* (Berkeley: University of California Press, 2002), 112–45.

20. See, for example, Bill Cole, *John Coltrane* (New York: Da Capo Press, 2001); Lewis Porter, *John Coltrane: His Life and Music* (Ann Arbor: University of Michigan Press, 1998); Eric Nisenson, *Ascension: John Coltrane and His Quest* (New York: Da Capo Press, 1995); and John Gennari, *Blowin' Hot and Cool: Jazz and Its Critics* (Chicago and London: University of Chicago Press, 2006).

21. Ashley Kahn, *A Love Supreme: The Creation of John Coltrane's Classic Album* (London: Granta Books, 2002), xix.

22. Cited in Neil Leonard, *Jazz: Myth and Religion* (New York and Oxford: Oxford University Press, 1987), 55. In the case of John Coltrane, this magical or iconic influence has not only led to his music being interpreted as an act of mysterious and religious creation, but has also compelled some listeners to act like quasi-religious disciples following their exposure to his music. Paul Berliner, for example, documents the testimony of musicians who have been profoundly affected by the music of Coltrane; see Paul Berliner, *Thinking in Jazz: The Infinite Art of Improvisation* (Chicago and London: University of Chicago Press, 1994), 30–2. See also Charles Keil and Stephen Feld, *Music Grooves: Essays and Dialogues* (Chicago and London: University of Chicago Press, 1994), 5 for further accounts of the impact and influence of Coltrane on listeners.

23. See Christopher Small, *Musicking: The Meanings of Performance and Listening* (Middletown, CT: Wesleyan University Press, 1998) for a valuable insight into the way in which communities construct myths through the ritualistic practices of performance. See also Eisenberg, *The Recording Angel*, 89–131 for a discussion of the rituals of recordings and the construction of mystery.

24. Ake, *Jazz Cultures*, 83–111.

25. For examples of the promotion of jazz as a romanticised, unmediated aesthetic, see Martin Williams, *The Jazz Tradition* (Oxford: Oxford University Press, 1993); and Gary Giddins, *Satchmo: The Genius of Louis Armstrong*, 2nd edn (New York: Da Capo Press, 2000).

26. Small, for example, suggests that audiences need to believe in the metaphysical qualities of music in order to perpetuate certain paradigms of values and behaviour. See Small, *Musicking*, 87–93. For an example of how traditional

approaches to music have been deconstructed to demonstrate the artifice of mystery, see Janet Wolff, 'The Ideology of Autonomous Art' in Leppert, R. and McClary, S. (eds.), *Music and Society: The Politics of Composition, Performance and Reception* (Cambridge: Cambridge University Press, 1994), 1–12.

27. See Berliner, *Thinking in Jazz*; Cole, *John Coltrane*; and Porter, *John Coltrane* for accounts of Coltrane's influence on musicians and the jazz community.

28. For instance, Krin Gabbard discusses the way in which Spike Lee's *Mo' Better Blues* (Universal, 1990) was originally to be named *A Love Supreme* after the Coltrane album. Coltrane's widow would only grant permission on the condition that all foul language be removed from the film, a condition that Lee chose not to meet. See Gabbard, *Jammin' at the Margins*, 151.

29. Kahn, *A Love Supreme*, xix.

30. Carolyn Abbate, 'Music: Drastic or Gnostic', *Critical Enquiry* 30 (Spring 2004), 505–36.

31. John Corbett has similarly discussed the way in which the disembodied nature of recordings engenders fetishistic tendencies in consumers. See Corbett, *Extended Play: From John Cage to Dr Funkenstein* (Durham, NC and London: Duke University Press, 1994), 38–42.

32. I suggest that we could align Abbate's and Vladimir Jankelevich's notion of the 'drastic' with Roland Barthes's 'text', in that both terms signal a resistance to fixed interpretations and advocate every performance or reading as a unique event. See Roland Barthes, *Image-Music-Text* (London: Fontana Press, 1977), 155–64.

33. John Coltrane, *The Classic Quartet: Complete Impulse! Studio Recordings*, IMPD8-280, CD (1998). Somewhat unsurprisingly, the futility of the fetishistic collector's quest for the definitive recordings was demonstrated four years after the release of the *Complete Impulse! Studio Recordings*, when Impulse! issued additional 'new' material as part of subsequent Coltrane releases, *Coltrane [Deluxe Edition]*, Impulse! 3145895672 (2002) and *Ballads [Deluxe Edition]*, Impulse! 3145895482 (2002). See my discussion of Coltrane reissues in Chapter 4; and also Ashley Kahn, 'The House that Trane Built', *JazzTimes* (September 2002), 128–9, or his book of the same name (London: Granta Books, 2006), 276.

34. John Coltrane, radio interview by Carl-Erik Lindgren, 22 March 1960, Stockholm (British Library National Sound Archive); and *The World according to John Coltrane*, DVD, directed by Robert Palmer (New York: BMG, 1991).

35. For example, Ashley Kahn discusses such an instance in *A Love Supreme*, which is the only commercial album that explicitly introduces Coltrane's voice. Kahn suggests that the presence of Coltrane's voice in this release is another reason why the album has gained a symbolic and religious value. Kahn further describes how this official use of Coltrane's voice is taken as a representation of divinity by cultish collectors and enthusiasts. Compare, for example,

Coltrane's limited exposure within the media to the dissemination of Louis Armstrong's voice in recording, film and television. Whereas Armstrong's voice has featured prominently in film and television, becoming synonymous with his music, Coltrane is typically represented by the sounds of his saxophone, or portrayed in spiritual, non-performative poses in publicity photographs for Impulse! records.

36. Richard Dyer, *Heavenly Bodies: Film Stars and Society* (Basingstoke: Palgrave Macmillan, 1987).

37. For example, Gracyk states: 'The audience feels like a witness to independent reality even when they understand it [the recording] is a "fiction".' Theodore Gracyk, *Rhythm and Noise: An Aesthetics of Rock* (Durham, NC and London: Duke University Press, 1996), 84.

38. Michael Chanan, *Repeated Takes: A Short History of Recording and Its Effects on Music* (London: Verso, 1995), 18–19.

39. Garber, 'Fabulating Jazz', 75.

40. See Berliner, *Thinking in Jazz*, 36–59 for discussions of jazz community and master–apprentice relationships.

41. LaVerne, *Countdown to Giant Steps*.

42. While LaVerne's *Countdown to Giant Steps* offers some interesting insights into the recording and its influence on musicians, it is useful to explore the influence of the disembodied voice in a wider context. For example, John Corbett suggests that teenage air guitar gestures relate directly to the desire to fill the physical void with a sexualised, phallic self. See Corbett, *Extended Play*, 55. Further, John Mowitt draws reference to the way in which *Downbeat*'s famous 'blindfold tests' exploit the absence of the body, encouraging contemporary musicians to recognise the artist on record without reference to any visual aids. See John Mowitt, 'The Sound of Music In the Era of Its Electronic Reproducibility' in Leppert, R. and McClary, S. (eds.), *Music and Society: The Politics of Composition, Performance and Reception* (Cambridge: Cambridge University Press, 1994), 173–97 (174).

43. For a cross-section of perspectives on imitation, signification and intertextuality in musical practice, see Robert Walser, '"Out of Notes": Signification, Interpretation and the Problem of Miles Davis', *The Musical Quarterly* 77.2 (Summer 1993), 343–65; Daniel Fischlin and Ajay Heble (eds.), *The Other Side of Nowhere: Jazz, Improvisation and Communities in Dialogue* (Middletown, CT: Wesleyan University Press, 2004); John Zorn (ed.), *Arcana: Musicians on Music* (New York: Granary Books, 2000); and Ulrike H. Meinhof and Jonathan Smith (eds.), *Intertextuality and the Media: From Genre to Everyday Life* (Manchester: Manchester University Press, 2000).

44. Richard Dyer, *Stars* (London: BFI, 1998), 17–18.

45. Leonard, *Jazz: Myth and Religion*, 42.

46. *Ibid.*, 42.

47. Rex Stewart, quoted in Nat Shapiro and Nat Hentoff, *Hear Me Talkin' to Ya: The Classic Story of Jazz as Told by the Men who Made It* (London: Souvenir Press, 1992), 206.

48. The promotion of the unmediated experience is widespread in jazz folklore. The claim, credited to Charlie Parker, that 'if you haven't lived it, it won't come out of your horn' epitomises this well-trodden mythology. Paul Berliner discusses the way in which the ideal of 'jazz as a way of life' proliferates among the jazz community in his *Thinking in Jazz*, 485–504. Similarly, romanticised notions of the jazz life are often found within Hollywood biopics. For instance, Clint Eastwood's *Bird* (Warner Bros., 1988) plays on the mythology of Charlie Parker's drug addiction through the portrayal of Red Rodney and his desire to 'shoot like Bird, play like Bird'. For more on Hollywood depictions of the jazz life, see Gabbard, *Jammin' at the Margins*.

49. For examples of writings on the relationship between art and religion in the nineteenth century, see Derek Scott, *From the Erotic to the Demonic: On Critical Musicology* (New York: Oxford University Press, 2003). Nicholas Cook also discusses the power of live performance in relation to classical music, and compares the entering of a concert hall to the entering of a cathedral, placing audiences under the spell of nineteenth-century communal rituals and the awe of magnificent architecture. See Nicholas Cook, *Music: A Very Short Introduction* (Oxford and New York: Oxford University Press, 2000), 33.

50. Leonard, *Jazz: Myth and Religion*, 179.

51. Michael Molasky has described the ritualised world of jazz coffee shops in Japan, where listeners seek an incredibly fetishised and autonomous listening experience. These coffee shops enable individuals to request individual vinyl recordings to be played over the speaker system; however, customers do not talk, interact or share in their choices of record requests; Michael Molasky, 'Jazz Coffee Shops in Japan', unpublished conference paper, presented at Leeds International Jazz Conference, March 2005. For detailed discussion of the ritualistic nature of music, see Small, *Musicking*, and Christopher Small, *Music of the Common Tongue* (London: Calder Press, 1987); and, although problematic in terms of its limited treatment of jazz and popular music, Roger Scruton, *The Aesthetics of Music* (Oxford and New York: Oxford University Press, 1999). I also acknowledge that rituals can fulfil a number of functions within musical practice, from intensifying a sense of political struggle, to the construction of a sense of meaning, place and community. For alternative readings of ritual in music, see Ron Eyerman and Andrew Jamison, *Music and Social Movements: Mobilizing Traditions in the Twentieth Century* (Cambridge: Cambridge University Press, 1998).

52. For example, in the quest for jazz to gain an enhanced cultural status, commercialism is often presented as a corrupting or polluting influence, and the music's link to popular culture is subverted. For an example of this type of cultural positioning, see Gunther Schuller, 'The State of Our Art' in *Musings: the Musical*

*Worlds of Gunther Schuller. A Collection of His Writings* (Oxford and New York: Oxford University Press, 1986), 258–71; and Wynton Marsalis's anti-commercial sentiment in 'What Jazz Is and Isn't' in Walser, R. (ed.), *Keeping Time: Readings in Jazz History* (New York and Oxford: Oxford University Press, 1999), 334–8.

53. Sonny Rollins's famous self-imposed exile from the jazz scene is a good example of how wood-shedding practices of musicians are both understood and promoted as acts of cleansing. Rollins spent approximately two years away from the professional scene from 1959 to 1961. For further discussion of wood-shedding, see Berliner, *Thinking in Jazz*, 54; and Ake, *Jazz Cultures*, 129–34.

54. Branford Marsalis, *Footsteps of Our Fathers*, Marsalis Music MARCD3301, CD (2002).

55. *Branford Marsalis Quartet Performs Coltrane's* A Love Supreme *in Amsterdam Live*, Marsalis Music 11661–3310–9, DVD (2004).

56. Delfeayo Marsalis, liner notes to B. Marsalis, *Footsteps of Our Fathers*.

57. For example, Donald Harrison's *Kind of New*, Candid CCD79768, CD (2002), is an album that re-works Miles Davis's *Kind of Blue* without laying claim to the intense homage relationship inherent in the Branford Marsalis album. Obviously, the significant differences in the symbolism and status of these two albums are a key factor in their different approaches to appropriation and re-presentation.

58. Gunther Schuller subsequently left the group in the mid 1990s. Baker went on record in 2000 as part of the Smithsonian Oral History projects and stated:

> We had different ideas about how the music should be done. Gunther tended to be a little more – he thought of the music in a more – as precious, a kind of museum music. For instance, he wanted to ask people not to clap for the short solos and things, because he wanted to hear every note of the written solo. That was the first time that we were at odds about what the scope should be, how it should be approached. (David Baker, Smithsonian Jazz Oral History Project, interviews of 19, 20 and 23 June 2000 (20 June segment))

59. *The Cotton Club Band Featuring Keith Nichols*, JRC Records JR40001-C, CD (1997).

60. The equivalent practice within a classical setting would be for a conductor to interpret the work of a composer via a previous recording; it would be impossible to envisage, for example, a classical album entitled *Sir Simon Rattle Records Haitink's Mahler*.

61. Ted Gioia, *The Imperfect Art: Reflections on Jazz and Modern Culture* (Oxford: Oxford University Press, 1988), 13.

62. For instance, Timothy D. Taylor gives examples of the humanising tendencies of other contemporary music forms, such as New Age: 'One of the biggest differences between New Age musicians and other musicians who make electronic musics is that New Age musicians usually foreground themselves

as selves.' Timothy D. Taylor, *Strange Sounds: Music, Technology and Culture* (New York: Routledge, 2001), 143.

### 3  Not a wonderful world: Louis Armstrong meets Kenny G

1. Studies of community are widespread in the literature of jazz, ranging from general enquiries into the nature of performers, audiences and scenes, to studies that deconstruct myths associated with jazz community. See, for example, Paul Berliner, *Thinking in Jazz: The Infinite Art of Improvisation* (Chicago and London, University of Chicago Press, 1994); Peter Townsend, *Jazz in American Culture* (Edinburgh: Edinburgh University Press, 2000); and Peter J. Martin, 'The Jazz Community as an Art World', *The Source: Challenging Jazz Criticism* 2 (March 2005), 5–13 for examples of these approaches.

2. During a recent trip to a jazz club in Prague, I was amazed at the degree of obeisance shown by the audience to performers on stage. A journalist friend explained to me that the club's audience had a reputation for policing their own behaviour by producing notes that could be passed around the club requesting patrons to be quiet. Whilst this quirky set-up seemed a little controlling from an audience perspective, I was really surprised during the performance to see the drummer on stage take time out from his playing also to hand out a note requesting silence!

3. Francis Davis reiterates this by commenting on the way in which both sleeve notes and reissues have the potential to mythologise jazz, encouraging audiences to buy into the continuum of jazz history and the legacy of past masters. See Francis Davis, *Like Young: Jazz, Pop, Youth and Middle Age* (New York: Da Capo Press, 2001), xi–xx.

4. The unofficial biography was Graham Lord, *Dick Francis: A Racing Life* (London: Little, Brown and Co., 1999).

5. Roland Barthes, 'The Death of the Author' in *Image-Music-Text* (London: Fontana Press, 1977), 142–8.

6. The work featured as part of an exhibition entitled 'The Rape of Creativity' at the Museum of Modern Art, Oxford in April 2003. See Philip Shaw, 'Abjection Sustained: Goya, the Chapman Brothers and the *Disasters of War*', *Art History* 26.4 (September 2003), 479–504.

7. Jonathan Jones, 'Look What We Did', *Guardian*, G2 supplement (31 March 2003), 2–4 (2).

8. David Hajdu, *Lush Life: A Biography of Billy Strayhorn* (New York: Granta Books, 1998).

9. *Ibid.*, 169–70.

10. Walter Benjamin, 'The Work of Art in the Age of Mechanical Reproduction' in *Illuminations* (London: Pimlico Press, 1999), 211–44.

11. At the *Criss Cross* conference on African American influences in art, Nottingham 2004, Robert O'Meally gave an example of the obsessive nature of record collection. He cited an example of a collector who had moved beyond the mere collection of different versions of *Kind of Blue* to an obsession with the editions pressed in different factories.

12. For a discussion of the authority of the score and the problems of authenticity in classical music, see Stanley Boorman, 'The Musical Text' in Cook, N. and Everist, M. (eds.), *Rethinking Music* (Oxford and New York: Oxford University Press, 2001), 403–42.

13. Geoff Dyer, *But Beautiful: A Book about Jazz* (London: Abacus, 2000), 189.

14. Pat Metheny, 'Pat Metheny on Kenny G', www.jazzoasis.com/methenyonkennyg.htm, last accessed 5 April 2009.

15. Kenny G, *Classics in the Key of G*, Arista/BMG 07822-19085-2, CD (1999).

16. See Christopher Washburne, 'Does Kenny G Play Bad Jazz?' in Washburne, C. J. and Derno, M. (eds.), *Bad Music: The Music We Love to Hate* (New York and London: Routledge, 2004), 123–47 for an appraisal of smooth jazz and an overview of the reception of Kenny G's *Classics in the Key of G* album in the jazz press.

17. Within the interview, Metheny cites other types of virtual collaboration between artists (such as Natalie Cole and Nat King Cole) and, whilst stating that some of these efforts have been misguided, excuses them for their artistic endeavours and/or for their sincerity in approach.

18. Gary Giddins, 'Cadenza: I Remember Chirpy', *JazzTimes* (January–February 2003), 88.

19. For example, Carmen McRae attributes the nickname to Parker's stint as an army recruit; see Nat Shapiro and Nat Hentoff, *Hear Me Talkin' to Ya: The Classic Story of Jazz as Told by the Men who Made It* (London: Souvenir Press, 1992), 353. Alternatively, Christopher Washburne cites Parker's road trip from Kansas City to Lincoln, Nebraska, where Parker retrieved and cooked the carcass of a chicken (a yardbird) hit by a car; see Washburne, 'Does Kenny G Play Bad Jazz?', 144 n. 10.

20. Washburne, 'Does Kenny G Play Bad Jazz?', 124–8.

21. Pat Metheny, keynote address at the IAJE conference (New York, January 2001).

22. Liner notes to G[orelick], *Classics in the Key of G*.

23. Robert Walser, 'Valuing Jazz' in Cooke, M. and Horn, D. (eds.), *The Cambridge Companion to Jazz* (Cambridge: Cambridge University Press, 2002), 301–20.

24. Alastair Williams, *Constructing Musicology* (Aldershot: Ashgate, 2007), 76.

25. Scott DeVeaux's balanced appriasal of Ken Burns's *Jazz* explores these issues in more detail, examining the way in which the film constructs an art narrative and is selective in its choice of content. See Scott DeVeaux, 'Struggling with Jazz', *Current Musicology* 71–3 (Spring 2001–Spring 2002), 353–74.

26. Grover Sales, *Jazz: America's Classical Music* (New York: Da Capo Press, 1992).

27. Wynton Marsalis, 'What Jazz Is and Isn't' in Walser, R. (ed.), *Keeping Time: Readings in Jazz History* (New York and Oxford: Oxford University Press, 1999), 334–8 (334–5).

28. Walser, *Keeping Time*, 334.

29. See, for example, Walser, 'Valuing Jazz'; DeVeaux, 'Constructing the Jazz Tradition' in O'Meally, R. (ed.), *The Jazz Cadence of American Culture* (New York: Columbia University Press, 1998), 484–514; and Stuart Nicholson, *Is Jazz Dead? (Or Has It Moved to a New Address?)* (London and New York: Routledge, 2005) for further discussions of the contradictions of the neo-traditionalist agenda.

30. For example, Gabbard states: 'Jazz is a construct. Nothing can be called jazz simply because of its "nature" … If today we call something jazz, it has much more to do with the utterances of critics, journalists, record companies and club owners than with the music itself …' See Krin Gabbard, 'The Word Jazz' in Cooke and Horn, *The Cambridge Companion to Jazz*, 1–6 (1).

31. Marsalis, 'What Jazz Is and Isn't', 335.

32. The forum took place as part of the IAJE conference, Toronto, 2003.

33. Christopher Washburne makes a similar point in his study of Kenny G, suggesting that popular notions of jazz help to shape what jazz is. This point is emphasised through Berklee School of Music's (among others) development of courses in smooth jazz. See Washburne, 'Does Kenny G Play Bad Jazz?', 141.

34. Bernard Gendron, '"Moldy Figs" and Modernists: Jazz at War (1942–1946)' in Gabbard. K. (ed.), *Jazz among the Discourses* (Durham, NC and London: Duke University Press, 1995), 31–56.

35. Alan Stanbridge, 'Burns Baby Burns: Jazz History as a Contested Cultural Site', *The Source: Challenging Jazz Criticism* 1 (March 2004), 81–99 (83).

36. Neil Leonard, *Jazz: Myth and Religion* (New York and Oxford: Oxford University Press, 1987), 30–1.

37. Writings on the constitution and function of jazz community are numerous, tackling the subject from different ideological and methodological perspectives. Examples of these include Alan Merriam and Raymond Mack, 'The Jazz Community', *Social Forces* 38.3 (1960), 211–22, to more recent studies including Daniel Fischlin and Ajay Heble (eds.), *The Other Side of Nowhere: Jazz, Improvisation and Communities in Dialogue* (Middletown, CT: Wesleyan University Press, 2004); Ingrid Monson, *Saying Something: Jazz Improvisation and Interaction* (Chicago and London: University of Chicago Press, 1996); and Scott DeVeaux, *Jazz in America: Who's Listening?*, Research Division Report, National Endowment for the Arts no. 31 (Carson, CA: Seven Locks Press, 1995).

38. Martin, 'The Jazz Community as an Art World'.

39. *Ibid.*, 9.

40. Anthony Cohen, *The Symbolic Construction of Community* (London and New York: Routledge, 1993), 98.

41. For further discussion of identity within popular music see Simon Frith, 'Music and Identity' in S. Hall and P. du Gay (eds.), *Questions of Cultural Identity* (London: Sage Publications, 2000), 108–27; Stan Hawkins, *Settling the Pop Score: Pop Texts and Identity Politics* (Aldershot: Ashgate, 2002); and Sheila Whiteley, Andy Bennett and Stan Hawkins (eds.), *Music, Space and Place: Popular Music and Cultural Identity* (Aldershot: Ashgate, 2005).

42. See numerous contributions to Hall and du Gay, *Questions of Cultural Identity*.

43. Stuart Hall, 'Who Needs Identity?' in *ibid.*, 1–17.

44. Christopher Small, *Musicking: The Meanings of Performance and Listening* (Middletown, CT: Wesleyan University Press, 1998), 94–5.

45. See, for example, work on gender and performativity including Judith Butler, *Gender Trouble: Feminism and the Subversion of Identity* (London and New York: Routledge, 1990); and various contributions in Sheila Whiteley (ed.), *Sexing the Groove: Popular Music and Gender* (London and New York: Routledge, 1997).

46. Christopher Small, *Music of the Common Tongue* (London: Calder Press, 1987), 75.

47. Ron Eyerman and Andrew Jamison, *Music and Social Movements: Mobilizing Traditions in the Twentieth Century* (Cambridge: Cambridge University Press, 1998), 36.

48. Roger Scruton, *The Aesthetics of Music* (Oxford and New York: Oxford University Press, 1999), 461.

49. Scott DeVeaux has discussed the friction between fixed and ever-changing interpretations of jazz history. His study of jazz's core and boundaries illustrates how historical writing is written from the values of the present, with the concept of boundary being something that ties directly into understandings of jazz community. DeVeaux argues that, on closer inspection, boundaries in jazz can be considered contradictory and fluid entities, quite often founded on arbitrary principles. See Scott DeVeaux, 'Core and Boundaries', *The Source: Challenging Jazz Criticism* 2.1 (March 2005), 15–30.

50. John Corbett, *Extended Play: From John Cage to Dr Funkenstein* (Durham, NC and London: Duke University Press, 1994), 34. This point is also explored further in Chapter 4.

51. Hall, 'Who Needs Identity?', 4.

52. See, for example, Leonard, *Jazz: Myth and Religion*; Small, *Music of the Common Tongue*; and Frith, 'Music and Identity'.

53. Frith, 'Music and Identity', 124.

54. Simon Frith, *Music for Pleasure: Essays on the Sociology of Pop* (Cambridge: Polity Press, 1988), 46.

55. Washburne, 'Does Kenny G Play Bad Jazz?', 135.

## 4  Men can't help acting on Impulse!

1. Mica Nava, Andrew Blake, Iain MacCrury and Barry Richards (eds.), *Buy This Book: Studies in Advertising and Consumption* (London and New York: Routledge, 2001), 2. Other texts that demonstrate the growing importance of theories of advertising in music include Michael Jarrett, 'The Tenor's Vehicle: Reading *Way Out West*' in Gabbard, K. (ed.), *Representing Jazz* (Durham, NC and London: Duke University Press, 1995), 260–82; and Nicholas Cook, *Analysing Musical Multimedia* (Oxford and New York: Oxford University Press, 2001). Further texts that show how theories of consumption can contrast with traditional theories of production include John Shepherd, *Music as Social Text* (Cambridge: Polity Press, 1991); Jim Collins, *Uncommon Cultures: Popular Culture and Postmodernism* (London and New York: Routledge, 1989); and Robert Walser, '"Out of Notes": Signification, Interpretation and the Problem of Miles Davis', *The Musical Quarterly* 77.2 (Summer 1993), 343–65.

2. See Gary Giddins, *Satchmo: The Genius of Louis Armstrong*, 2nd edn (New York: Da Capo Press, 2000); and Wynton Marsalis and Frank Stewart, *Sweet Swing Blues on the Road* (New York: Thunder's Mouth Press, 1999) for examples of this type of approach.

3. Jose Bowen, for example, explores the canonisation of jazz largely through a discussion of musical performances and their relationship to lead sheets or 'real' books. Bowen acknowledges the differences and complexities of jazz performance in comparison to classical music; however, when discussing the concept of musical works, the significance of recordings in jazz is underplayed, as jazz is compared to the notated forms of classical music. Within this context, Robert Walser has demonstrated how analytical writings on jazz that mirror methodologies established in classical music are problematic, in that they both undermine the value of jazz as an artform with its own discernible history, and also fail to capture jazz's signifyin(g) and intertextual qualities. See Jose Bowen, 'The History of Remembered Innovation: Tradition and Its Role in the Relationship between Musical Works and Their Performances', *The Journal of Musicology* 11.2 (Spring 1993), 139–73; and Walser, 'Out of Notes'.

4. Georgina Born, 'On Musical Mediation: Ontology, Technology and Creativity', *Twentieth-Century Music* 2 (March 2005), 7–36.

5. See Christopher Small, *Musicking: The Meanings of Performance and Listening* (Middletown, CT: Wesleyan University Press, 1998); and Lydia Goehr, *The Imaginary Museum of Musical Works: An Essay in the Philosophy of Music* (Oxford and New York: Oxford University Press, 1992). For an overview of the contextual and political issues surrounding the canonisation of jazz, see Krin Gabbard, 'The Jazz Canon and Its Consequences' in *Jazz among the Discourses* (Durham, NC and London: Duke University Press, 1995), 1–28;

and Scott DeVeaux, 'Constructing the Jazz Tradition' in O'Meally, R. (ed.), *The Jazz Cadence of American Culture* (New York: Columbia University Press, 1998), 484–514.

6. Frank Kermode, 'Canon and Period' in Walder, D. (ed.), *Literature in the Modern World* (Oxford and New York: Oxford University Press, 1993), 17–20.

7. *Jazz: A Film by Ken Burns*, directed by Ken Burns, The Jazz Film Project, PBS DD4721, DVD (2001); and Scott DeVeaux, 'Struggling with *Jazz*', *Current Musicology* 71–3 (Spring 2001–Spring 2002), 353–74.

8. For further studies on the ideology of autonomous art in jazz, see DeVeaux, 'Constructing the Jazz Tradition'; and David Ake, *Jazz Cultures* (Berkeley: University of California Press, 2002).

9. Giddins, *Satchmo*, 147.

10. Ted Panken, 'Approaching Enlightenment', *Downbeat* (February 2001), 22–7. Moreover, in the introduction to his book *Jazz and Death: Medical Profiles of Jazz Greats* (Jackson: University of Mississippi Press, 2002), Frederick J. Spencer examines the discourse's fascination with dead artists, and how the portrayal of these artists differs from that of the living.

11. Small, *Musicking*, 87.

12. See, for example, Thomas Owens, *Bebop: The Music and Its Players* (Oxford and New York: Oxford University Press, 1995); and Lewis Porter, *John Coltrane: His Life and Music* (Ann Arbor: University of Michigan Press, 1998).

13. Michael Cuscuna, '"Strictly on the Record": The Art of Jazz and the Recording Industry', *The Source: Challenging Jazz Criticism* 2 (March 2005), 63–70.

14. John Coltrane, *The Classic Quartet: Complete Impulse! Studio Recordings*, Impulse! IMPD8-280, CD (1998).

15. Donald Harrison, *Nouveau Swing*, IMPD209, CD (1997).

16. DeVeaux, 'Constructing the Jazz Tradition', 485–6.

17. Evan Eisenberg, *The Recording Angel: Music, Records and Culture from Aristotle to Zappa*, 2nd edn (New Haven: Yale University Press, 2005).

18. David Ake, 'Learning Jazz, Teaching Jazz' in Cooke, M. and Horn, D. (eds.), *The Cambridge Companion to Jazz* (Cambridge: Cambridge University Press, 2002), 255–69 (257).

19. Eisenberg elaborates on the ownership of records in his chapter 'Music Becomes a Thing' in *The Recording Angel*, 9–28.

20. Roland Barthes, *Image-Music-Text* (London: Fontana Press, 1977), 155–64.

21. John Corbett, 'Free, Single and Disengaged' in *Extended Play: From John Cage to Dr Funkenstein* (Durham, NC and London: Duke University Press, 1994), 32–55 (41).

22. Andrew Wernick, 'Resort to Nostalgia: Mountains, Memories and Myths of Time' in Nava, Richards and MacCrury, *Buy This Book*, 207–23.

23. Corbett, *Extended Play*, 34.

24. Eisenberg, *The Recording Angel*, 15.

25. Ashley Kahn, 'The House that Trane Built', *JazzTimes* (September 2002), 128–9.

26. Phil Schapp, 'Jazz Records Are Our Books!', paper presented at the IAJE conference, Toronto, 10 January 2003.

27. The Impulse! label made an exception for Coltrane's *A Love Supreme*, which carried a white and black spine, symbolising its otherness, sense of purity and explicit spirituality.

28. Whereas Blue Note Records has become associated with quintessential jazz imagery – for example, see Graham Marsh and Glyn Callingham, *The Cover Art of Blue Note Records* (London: Collins and Brown, 1991) – Impulse! Records provides an ideal model for comparative analysis as, since the company's inception, it has adopted an explicit visual strategy as part of its marketing activities.

29. Ashley Kahn, *A Love Supreme: The Creation of John Coltrane's Classic Album* (London: Granta Books, 2002), 53–4.

30. This pattern of new releases does not include the vocal music of Diana Krall, who continued to produce albums for Impulse! around and beyond this period.

31. This personal interpretation can be read in the context of other works on the representation of blackness and primitivism, such as Krin Gabbard, *Black Magic: White Hollywood and African American Culture* (New Brunswick: Rutgers University Press, 2004); Ted Gioia, *The Imperfect Art: Reflections on Jazz and Modern Culture* (Oxford: Oxford University Press, 1988); and Jon Panish, *The Color of Jazz: Race and Representation in Postwar American Culture* (Jackson: University of Mississippi Press, 1997).

32. As I will mention later on, this differs from Impulse!'s earlier marketing strategies. During the first decade of the label's history, advertising was more explicitly commercial, encouraging collectors to 'go out and buy' without delay. The label's change in strategy should, of course, be read in the historical context of an overall shift in marketing and advertising strategies in all spheres of everyday life.

33. From an Impulse! advert in *Downbeat* magazine, April 1961.

34. Geoff Dyer, *But Beautiful: A Book about Jazz* (London: Abacus, 2000), 202–7.

35. Andreas Huyssen, *After the Great Divide: Modernism, Mass Culture and Postmodernism* (London and New York: Routledge, 1986), 178–221.

36. John Berger, *Ways of Seeing* (London: Penguin, 1990), 21.

37. Will Straw, 'Organized Disorder: The Changing Space of the Record Shop' in Redhead, S. (ed.), *The Clubcultures Reader: Readings in Popular Cultural Studies* (Oxford and Malden: Blackwell, 1998), 39–47.

38. Small, *Musicking*, 87–9.

39. See, for example, Eisenberg, *The Recording Angel*; and Mark Katz, *Capturing Sound: How Technology Changed Music* (Berkeley: University of California Press, 2004) for detailed analyses of the impact and influence of recordings on society.

## 5  Witnessing and the jazz anecdote

1. Ngugi wa Thiong'o, 'The Language of African Literature' in Ashcroft, B., Griffiths, G. and Tiffin, H. (eds.), *A Post Colonial Studies Reader* (London and New York: Routledge, 1999), 285–90 (289).

2. Solomon Volkov, *Testimony: The Memoirs of Dimitri Shostakovich* (London: Faber and Faber, 1981), 1.

3. Ekkehard Jost, *Free Jazz* (New York: Da Capo Press, 1994), 8.

4. For example, see Roland Barthes, *Image-Music-Text* (London: Fontana Press, 1977); Anthony Easthope and Kate McGowan (eds.), *A Critical and Cultural Theory Reader* (Buckingham: Open University Press, 1997); Jane Gallop, *Anecdotal Theory* (Durham, NC and London: Duke University Press, 2002); George Steiner, *Language and Silence: Essays on Language, Literature and the Inhuman* (New Haven: Yale University Press, 1998); and Elizabeth Tonkin, *Narrating Our Pasts: The Social Construction of Oral History* (Cambridge: Cambridge University Press, 1995) for an overview of both current and historic discourses on various aspects of the power and nature of language.

5. The majority of jazz publications cite informal stories from musicians. However, some jazz texts place the stories and anecdotes of jazz musicians at the centre of their narrative. See Bill Crow, *Jazz Anecdotes* (Oxford and New York: Oxford University Press, 1990); Nat Shapiro and Nat Hentoff, *Hear Me Talkin' to Ya: The Classic Story of Jazz as Told by the Men who Made It* (London: Souvenir Press, 1992); and Arthur Taylor, *Notes and Tones: Musician-to-Musician Interviews*, 2nd edn (New York: Da Capo Press, 1993) for examples of this.

6. Ross Russell, *Bird Lives! The High Life and Hard Times of Charlie (Yardbird) Parker* (New York: Da Capo Press, 1996), 51. John Gennari provides an interesting analysis of Russell's writings on Parker, suggesting that his work turns Parker's mouth into a fetish object, linking his sexual self with music, speech and eating habits. See John Gennari, *Blowin' Hot and Cool: Jazz and Its Critics* (Chicago and London: University of Chicago Press, 2006), 325–6. Taken in this context, this anecdote about Parker eating chicken does not just explain his genius but is also a fetish linked to the artist's masculine prowess.

7. Louis Armstrong, *Louis Armstrong Plays W. C. Handy*, Columbia/Legacy CK64925, CD (1997). For an alternative version of this anecdote, linking Armstrong's humour to memories of Louisiana, see Max Jones and John Chilton, *Louis: The Louis Armstrong Story* (St Albans: Mayflower, 1975), 227.

8. Crow, *Jazz Anecdotes*, ix.

9. Krin Gabbard, 'The Jazz Canon and Its Consequences' in *Jazz among the Discourses* (Durham, NC and London: Duke University Press, 1995), 11–12.

10. Consider, for example, Gabbard's analysis of Gunther Schuller's influential *Early Jazz: Its Roots and Musical Development* (Oxford: Oxford University Press, 1968), and *The Swing Era: The Development of Jazz, 1930–1945* (Oxford: Oxford University Press, 1989), texts that tend to mystify rather than clarify:

"In both books, however, he [Schuller] rejects scholarly prose in favour of journalistic terms such as 'truly magnificent', 'totally unredeemable', and 'heartrendingly moving'. Because Schuller is also devoted to the myth of jazz's autonomy, he seldom considers the music's contextual and historical relationships. His consistent reluctance in *The Swing Era* to press his analyses beyond his own impressions is most explicit when he states, for example, that Billie Holiday's talent is 'in the deepest sense inexplicable', or when he writes of Ben Webster, 'as with most truly great art, Webster's cannot be fully explained', or when, after a few words on Lester Young's mastery of understatement, he calls Young 'The Gandhi of American jazz'."

See Gabbard, 'The Jazz Canon and Its Consequences', 11–12.

11. See, for example, Michael Cogswell, *Louis Armstrong: The Offstage Story of Satchmo* (Portland, OR: Collectors Press, 2003) for examples of Armstrong's writings. It should also be noted that Armstrong's final recording was of a reading of 'The Night before Christmas' in 1971.

12. Crow, *Jazz Anecdotes*, xi.

13. Christopher Harlos, 'Jazz Autobiography: Theory, Practice, Politics' in Gabbard, K. (ed.), *Representing Jazz* (Durham, NC and London: Duke University Press, 1995), 131–66.

14. Taylor, *Notes and Tones*.

15. *Ibid.*, 5.

16. Howard Brofsky, 'Miles Davis and "My Funny Valentine": The Evolution of a Solo' in Kirchner, B. (ed.), *A Miles Davis Reader* (Washington and London: Smithsonian Institution Press, 1997), 140–63.

17. *Ibid.*, 144.

18. Miles Davis and Quincy Troupe, *Miles: The Autobiography* (London and New York: Picador, 1989), 163–4.

19. See Kirchner, *A Miles Davis Reader*, 140.

20. Morgenstern presented a keynote address at the Leeds International Jazz Education Conference, April 2000.

21. Transcribed from Matthew Seig, *Thelonious Monk: American composer*, NTV Entertainment NTV0017, VHS (1991).

22. Transcribed from *Jazz: A Film by Ken Burns*, directed by Ken Burns, The Jazz Film Project, PBS DD4721, DVD (2001).

23. In *Sweet Swing Blues on the Road*, Marsalis describes the impact and influence of Bolden in overly romanticised terms: 'Buddy Bolden, then Bunk Johnson, Freddie Keppard, then King Oliver, and then Louis. That's the roll call … Buddy Bolden could play so loud, he could make the rain stay up in the sky'; see Wynton Marsalis and Frank Stewart, *Sweet Swing Blues on the Road* (New York: Thunder's Mouth Press, 1999), 17. The text also serves to place Marsalis within the continuum of jazz 'masters' of the past, adding himself to the 'roll call' of great New Orleans jazz trumpeters. Arguably, this type of

documentary work should be treated with caution, as the poetic use of language and interpretation of the past are placed within a supposedly serious historical narrative. This differs from the more overtly poetic and fictional interpretations of the Bolden legend featured in books such as Michael Ondaatje, *Coming through Slaughter* (Oxford: Picador, 1984); or Ray Bisso, *Buddy Bolden of New Orleans: A Jazz Poem* (Santa Barbara: Fithian Press, 1998).

24. Claude Lanzmann, *Shoah*, BFI CAV020, VHS (1994).

25. For a further example, see Thelonious Monk, *Monk Alone: The Complete Columbia Solo Studio Recordings of Thelonious Monk 1962–1968*, Columbia/Legacy C2K 65495, CD (1998).

26. Shoshana Felman and Dori Laub (eds.), *Testimony: Crises of Witnessing in Literature, Psychoanalysis, and History* (New York and London: Routledge, 1992), 1–56.

27. *Ibid.*, 9.

28. Lawrence Langer, *Holocaust Testimonies: The Ruins of Memory* (New Haven and London: Yale University Press, 1991), xiv.

29. Transcribed from Seig, *Thelonious Monk*.

30. Langer, *Holocaust Testimonies*, xv.

31. Albert Camus, quoted in Felman and Laub, *Testimony*, xi.

## 6 Dispelling the myth: essentialist Ellington

1. Derek Scott, *From the Erotic to the Demonic: On Critical Musicology* (New York: Oxford University Press, 2003), 4.

2. Christopher Small, *Musicking: The Meanings of Performance and Listening* (Middletown, CT: Wesleyan University Press, 1998), 13.

3. James Lincoln Collier, *Duke Ellington* (London and New York: Penguin Books, 1987), vii.

4. For example, see Janet Wolff, *The Social Production of Art*, 2nd edn (London: Macmillan, 1993); and Lawrence Levine, *High Brow Low Brow: The Emergence of Cultural Hierarchy in America* (Cambridge, MA: Harvard University Press, 1990) for studies that expose traditional concepts of art through social commentary and analysis.

5. See writings on different aspects of history from Walter Benjamin, *Illuminations* (London: Pimlico Press, 1999), to Elizabeth Tonkin, *Narrating Our Pasts: The Social Construction of Oral History* (Cambridge: Cambridge University Press, 1995), to Eric Hobsbawm and Terence Ranger (eds.), *The Invention of Tradition* (Cambridge: Cambridge University Press, 1992).

6. See, for example, Scott DeVeaux, 'Constructing the Jazz Tradition' in O'Meally, R. (ed.), *The Jazz Cadence of American Culture* (New York: Columbia University Press, 1998), 484–514; Alyn Shipton, *A New History of Jazz* (New York and London: Continuum, 2007); and the introduction to Richard Walser (ed.),

*Keeping Time: Readings in Jazz History* (Oxford and New York: Oxford University Press, 1999).

7. Krin Gabbard, 'The Jazz Canon and Its Consequences' in *Jazz among the Discourses* (Durham, NC and London: Duke University Press, 1995), 9.

8. See Sherrie Tucker, 'Deconstructing the Jazz Tradition: The "Subjectless Subject" of New Jazz Studies', *The Source: Challenging Jazz Criticism* 2 (March 2005), 31–46; and Ajay Heble, *Landing on the Wrong Note: Jazz, Dissonance and Critical Practice* (London and New York: Routledge, 2000).

9. See Gendron, '"Moldy Figs" and Modernists: Jazz at War (1942–1946)' in Gabbard, *Jazz among the Discourses*, 31–56.

10. See Krin Gabbard, *Jammin' at the Margins: Jazz and the American Cinema* (Chicago and London: University of Chicago Press, 1996), 104–6.

11. Scott DeVeaux, 'Core and Boundaries', *The Source: Challenging Jazz Criticism* 2.1 (March 2005), 15–30 (15–16).

12. Small, *Musicking*, 31.

13. DeVeaux, 'Core and Boundaries', 16–20.

14. Jack Kerouac, *On The Road* (New York and London: Penguin, 1972), 166–7.

15. For further discussion of the relationship between beat writers and bebop, see Jon Panish, *The Color of Jazz: Race and Representation in Postwar American Culture* (Jackson: University of Mississippi Press, 1997).

16. See, for example, Small, *Musicking*; and Claude Lévi-Strauss, *Myth and Meaning* (London and New York: Routledge Classics, 2005) for a broader discussion of mythology as a cultural paradigm.

17. Small, *Musicking*, 100.

18. *Ibid.*, 141.

19. In his introduction to his book *Free Jazz*, Ekkehard Jost describes the way in which all improvisation is codified including supposedly 'free forms'. To illustrate this point, Jost cites an anecdote by Ian Carr in which a musician is thrown out of a free jazz session because after being told to express himself 'freely' he repeatedly performs 'I do like to be beside the seaside'. See Ekkehard Jost, *Free Jazz* (New York: Da Capo Press, 1994), 8.

20. Peter Townsend, *Jazz in American Culture* (Edinburgh: Edinburgh University Press, 2000), 140.

21. Stuart Nicholson, *Is Jazz Dead? (Or Has It Moved to a New Address?)* (London and New York: Routledge, 2005), 64.

22. Small, *Musicking*, 27.

23. Townsend, *Jazz in American Culture*, 169.

24. For examples of Ellington's writings and a picture of the surrounding discourse see Mark Tucker (ed.), *The Duke Ellington Reader* (Oxford and New York: Oxford University Press, 1999); and, to a lesser extent, Duke Ellington's autobiography: Edward Kennedy [Duke] Ellington, *Music Is My Mistress* (New York: Da Capo Press, 1976).

25. Peter Gammond, *Duke Ellington* (London: Apollo Press, 1987), 76.

26. For 'insider' biographies of Ellington, see Stanley Dance, *The World of Duke Ellington* (New York: Da Capo Press, 1981); and A. H. Lawrence, *Duke Ellington and His World* (New York and London: Routledge, 2001); or Stuart Nicholson's *A Portrait of Duke Ellington: Reminiscing in Tempo* (London: Sidgwick and Jackson Press, 1999), which provide a variety of insider perspectives on Ellington's life. For hagiographic accounts of Ellington, and studies of his status as a great composer, see Wynton Marsalis and John Edward Hasse, *Beyond Category: The Life and Genius of Duke Ellington* (New York: Da Capo Press, 1995); and Ken Rattenbury, *Duke Ellington Jazz Composer* (London and New Haven: Yale University Press, 1990).

27. See Gunther Schuller, 'Duke Ellington in the Pantheon', in *Musings: The Musical Worlds of Gunther Schuller. A Collection of His Writings* (Oxford and New York: Oxford University Press, 1986), 47–50; and Albert Murray, 'The Vernacular Imperative: Duke Ellington's Place within the National Pantheon', *Boundary 2* 22.2 (Summer, 1995), 19–24.

28. Schuller, *Musings*, 56–9.

29. Derek Jewell, *Duke: A Portrait of Duke Ellington* (London: Elm Tree Books, 1977), 24.

30. Wynton Marsalis and Robert O'Meally, 'Duke Ellington: "Music like a Big Pot of Good Gumbo"' in O'Meally, *Jazz Cadence*, 144.

31. See Jazz at Lincoln Center, *Essentially Ellington* resources: 'Duke Leadsheet' and the supporting 'Ellington 101', www.jalc.org/jazzED/ee/resources.html, last accessed 13 April 2009.

32. Jewell, *Duke*, 24.

33. See Roland Barthes, 'The Brain of Einstein' in *Mythologies* (London: Vintage Classics, 1993), 68–70. Arguably, this divine romanticism could explain why audiences and critics alike have struggled to get to grips with the late works of John Coltrane post *A Love Supreme*. I argue that, from the romanticised perspective of the constructed jazz tradition, *A Love Supreme* would have been more fitting as Coltrane's last work and, in many respects, is treated as such within mainstream jazz histories. Whilst the most common appraisal of the neglect of the late works stems from their use of free jazz and inaccessible musical language, I suggest that the symbolic nature of *A Love Supreme* and the romantic ideal of the divine artist go some way to explaining why the late works are often discounted or infrequently discussed. As Eric Nisenson states, 'At a recent concert co-produced by [Wynton] Marsalis devoted to Coltrane's work, all his accomplishments after 1964 were ignored, as if Trane had died after recording *A Love Supreme*.' See Eric Nisenson, *Ascension: John Coltrane and His Quest* (New York: Da Capo Press, 1995), 222.

34. For examples of heroic writings on Ellington, see Ralph Ellison, 'Homage to Duke Ellington on His Birthday' in John F. Callahan (ed.), *The Collected Essays of Ralph Ellison* (New York: Modern Library Paperback, 2003), 680–7; Albert Murray, 'Made in America: The Achievement of Duke Ellington' in *From the*

*Briarpatch File: On Context, Procedure and American Identity* (New York: Pantheon Books, 2001), 41–58; and Stanley Crouch, 'Duke Ellington: Transcontinental Swing' in *Considering Genius: Writings on Music* (New York: Basic Civitas Books, 2006), 133–52.

35. See Mercer Ellington with Stanley Dance, *Duke Ellington in Person: An Intimate Memoir* (New York: Da Capo Press, 1979), 105; and also the discussion of Ellington, Strayhorn and Joe Morgen in this volume, Chapter 3.

36. Albert Murray and Ralph Ellison's correspondence often drew reference to Ellington as the upholder of standards in an age of musical decline. Take, for example, Ellison's letter to Murray in 1958, which comments on his involvement in a critics' symposium at Newport Jazz Festival. Here, Ellison describes the music of Miles Davis and John Coltrane as 'fucking up the blues' and, on the participation of Ellington and his band, stresses, 'Duke signified on Davis all through his numbers and his trumpeters and saxophonists went after him like a bunch of hustlers in a Georgia skin game fighting with razors.' See Albert Murray and John F. Callahan (eds.), *Trading Twelves: The Selected Letters of Ralph Ellison and Albert Murray* (New York: Vintage Books, 2000), 193–4.

37. Jewell, *Duke*, 21.

38. Graham Lock, *Blutopia: Visions of the Future and Revisions of the Past in the Work of Sun Ra, Duke Ellington, and Anthony Braxton* (Durham, NC and London: Duke University Press, 1999), 122.

39. George Burrows, 'Black, Brown and Beige and the Politics of Signifyin(g)', *Jazz Research Journal* 1.1 (March 2007), 45–71 (55).

40. Collier, *Duke Ellington*.

41. For examples of the critical reviews of Collier's Duke Ellington biography see Peter J. Martin, 'Review: *Duke Ellington* by James Lincoln Collier, *The Reception of Jazz in America* by James Lincoln Collier, *Ellingtonia: The Recorded Music of Duke Ellington and His Sidemen* by W. R. Timner', *Popular Music* 9.1 (January 1990), 139–44; Mark Tucker, 'Review: *Duke Ellington* by James Lincoln Collier', *Notes*, 2nd series 45.3 (March 1989), 499–502; and Martin Williams, 'Review: *Duke Ellington* by James Lincoln Collier', *American Music* 6.3 (Autumn 1988), 338–42. For the comparison between Collier and Hitler, see Krin Gabbard's appraisal of the reception of Collier's work in 'Krin Gabbard Replies', *American Music* 8.3 (Autumn 1990), 360–2.

42. Wynton Marsalis, James Lincoln Collier and Andre Craddock-Willis, 'Jazz People', *Transition* 65 (1995), 140–78 (141).

43. *Ibid.*, 154.

44. See Lawrence Gushee's review article, 'The Reception of Jazz in America', *American Music* 8.3 (Autumn 1990), 359–60; and Krin Gabbard's response, 'Krin Gabbard Replies'.

45. See Lock, *Blutopia*, 262; and for Mercer Ellington's account of his father's supposed hatred of women, see Ellington with Dance, *Duke Ellington in Person*, 128.

46. David Hajdu, 'A Jazz of Their Own', *Vanity Fair* 465 (May 1999), 188–96.

47. *Jazz: A Film by Ken Burns*, directed by Ken Burns, The Jazz Film Project, PBS DD4721, DVD (2001).

48. See, for example, Alan Stanbridge, 'Burns Baby Burns: Jazz History as a Contested Cultural Site', *The Source: Challenging Jazz Criticism* 1 (March 2004), 81–99; and Scott DeVeaux, 'Struggling with *Jazz*', *Current Musicology* 71–3 (Spring 2001–Spring 2002), 353–74.

## 7 Birth of the school

1. Randall Allsup, 'Transformational Education and Critical Music Pedagogy: Examining the Link between Culture and Learning', *Music Education Research* 5.1 (January 2003), 5–12 (7).

2. For example, see a variety of articles on the politics of education in Bill Ashcroft, Gareth Griffiths and Helen Tiffin (eds.), *The Post-Colonial Studies Reader* (London and New York: Routledge, 1995), 425–62.

3. Christopher Small, *Music, Society, Education*, 2nd edn (Hanover and London: Wesleyan University Press, 1996), 162–3.

4. See, for example, Simon Frith, *Performing Rites: Evaluating Popular Music* (Oxford and New York: Oxford University Press, 2002); and Philip Tagg, 'Analyzing Popular Music: Theory, Method and Practice', *Popular Music* 2 (1982), 37–48.

5. Krin Gabbard, 'The Word Jazz' in Cooke, M. and Horn, D. (eds.), *The Cambridge Companion to Jazz* (Cambridge: Cambridge University Press, 2002), 1–6 (5).

6. Stuart Nicholson, *Is Jazz Dead? (Or Has It Moved to a New Address?)* (London and New York: Routledge, 2005).

7. Paul Hainer, 'Sienna/Symposium', *Coda: The Journal of Jazz and Improvised Music* (January–February 2003), 39–40.

8. For example, many renowned jazz musicians, including Anthony Braxton, Billy Taylor and Jon Hendricks, have aspired to positions of academic authority within the American university sector.

9. Scott DeVeaux, 'Constructing the Jazz Tradition' in O'Meally, R. (ed.), *The Jazz Cadence of American Culture* (New York: Columbia University Press, 1998), 484–514 (484).

10. See, for example, Krin Gabbard, 'The Jazz Canon and Its Consequences' in *Jazz among the Discourses* (Durham, NC and London: Duke University Press, 1995); and Sherrie Tucker, 'Deconstructing the Jazz Tradition: The "Subjectless Subject" of New Jazz Studies', *The Source: Challenging Jazz Criticism* 2 (March 2005), 31–46.

11. John Shepherd, *Music as Social Text* (Cambridge: Polity Press, 1991), 49.

12. Janet Wolff, 'The Ideology of Autonomous Art' in Leppert, R. and McClary, S. (eds.), *Music and Society: The Politics of Composition, Performance and Reception* (Cambridge: Cambridge University Press, 1994), 1–12 (2).

13. Within this context, I argue that education is both implicitly ideological and equipped to expose underlying ideologies. As Bill Ashcroft states, 'Education thus remains one of the most powerful discourses within the complex of colonialism and neo-colonialism. A powerful technology of social control, it also offers one of the most potentially fruitful routes to a dis/mantling of that old author/ity.' See Ashcroft, Griffiths and Tiffin, *The Post-Colonial Studies Reader*, 427.

14. Roger Trodre, 'Professor Jazz Opens Cool School', *The Observer* (15 February 1998), 20.

15. Terry Eagleton, *Literary Theory* (Oxford: Blackwell Publishing, 1993), 14.

16. David Ake, 'Learning Jazz, Teaching Jazz' in Cooke and Horn, *The Cambridge Companion to Jazz*, 255–69 (257).

17. Ronald M. Radano, *New Musical Configurations: Anthony Braxton's Cultural Critique* (Chicago and London: University of Chicago Press, 1993), 255.

18. Trodre, 'Professor Jazz'.

19. William Howland Kenney, *Chicago Jazz: A Cultural History, 1904–1930* (Oxford and New York: Oxford University Press, 1995), 59.

20. Neil Leonard, *Jazz: Myth and Religion* (New York and Oxford: Oxford University Press, 1987), 9.

21. See www.smithsonianjazz.org/flash/module.html, last accessed 30 March 2009; and Jazz at Lincoln Center, *Jazz Ed*, J@LC 2003 Educational Program brochure, 2003.

22. John Gennari, *Blowin' Hot and Cool: Jazz and Its Critics* (Chicago and London: University of Chicago Press, 2006), 370.

23. See www.smithsonianjazz.org/class/ellington/de_teacher.asp, last accessed 23 March 2009.

24. Luvenia A. George, 'Duke Ellington: The Man and His Music', *Music Educators Journal* 85.6 (May 1999), 15–21.

25. This conflation of the great composer with slave narratives feeds directly into Scott DeVeaux's analysis of the constructed jazz tradition where he discusses the fact that jazz's autonomy mirrors that of western art music. However, as DeVeaux states: 'The added twist is that this new American classical music openly acknowledges its debt not to Europe, but to Africa. There is a sense of triumphant reversal as the music of a formerly enslaved people is designated a "rare and valuable national American treasure" by the Congress, and beamed overseas as a weapon of the Cold War.' DeVeaux, 'Constructing the Jazz Tradition', 484.

26. David Ake, *Jazz Cultures* (Berkeley: University of California Press, 2002), 119.

27. Kernfeld made this comment as part of the Jyvaskyla Summer Jazz Conference in 2003. I also recognise that, as an appreciative guest, Kernfeld might well have been flattering his European audience.

28. See the two edited volumes by Graham Lock and David Murray (eds.), *Thriving on a Riff: Jazz and Blues Influences in African American Literature*

*and Film* (New York: Oxford University Press, 2009); and *The Hearing Eye: Jazz and Blues Influences in African American Visual Art* (Oxford and New York: Oxford University Press, 2009).

29. Krin Gabbard, 'How Many Miles? Alternate Takes on the Jazz Life' in Lock and Murray, *Thriving on a Riff*, 184–200.

30. For example, Richard Sudhalter's *Lost Chords: White Musicians and Their Contribution to Jazz 1915–1945* (Oxford and New York: Oxford University Press, 1999) provides an alternative reading of jazz history, with accounts of white musicians from New Orleans to the Swing Era. However, this selective view of history only serves to invert the African American exceptionalism found within the neo-traditionalist mainstream in recent years, and does nothing to create a discourse between versions of the past.

31. See Ajay Heble, *Landing on the Wrong Note: Jazz, Dissonance and Critical Practice* (London and New York: Routledge, 2000), 186. From a practitioner's perspective, for example, a discursive approach to education can also be understood at the symbolic level. Within this framework, an acclaimed jazz musician's positive attitude towards the educational environment and its flexible methodologies can be read as a discursive statement in its own right; to be an innovative, fresh and original musician commenting on the positive attributes of education goes against the established norms of 'professional' convention. In other words, supporting the merits of jazz education could be construed as a discursive act in its own right, kicking back against the norm of anti-education sentiment within the dominant jazz culture.

32. See Henry Louis Gates Jr, *Loose Canons: Notes on the Culture Wars* (Oxford and New York: Oxford University Press, 1993). This point is similar to John Gennari's comment on the negative reception of Wynton Marsalis and the African American exceptionalism of the Jazz at Lincoln Center programme. Gennari argues convincingly that we should not underestimate the political significance of having an African American such as Wynton Marsalis in charge of a major arts organisation, and that neo-traditionalist agendas plague the entire institutionalised arts establishment, not just the jazz world. See Gennari, *Blowin' Hot and Cool*, 364.

33. Gabbard, *Jazz among the Discourses*, 18.

34. Gary Tomlinson, 'Cultural Dialogics and Jazz: A White Historian Signifies', *Black Music Research Journal* 11.2 (Autumn 1991), 229–64 (243).

35. *Ibid.*, 248–9.

36. Gennari, *Blowin' Hot and Cool*, 371.

37. Tomlinson, 'Cultural Dialogics', 247.

38. See, for example, Ake, 'Learning Jazz, Teaching Jazz' in Cooke and Horn, *The Cambridge Companion to Jazz*, 255–69; Catherine Parsonage, Petter Fadnes and James Taylor, 'Integrating Theory and Practice in Conservatoires: Formulating Holistic Models for Teaching and Learning Improvisation', *British Journal of*

*Music Education* 24.3 (November 2007), 295–312; and Simon Purcell, 'Moving from Learning as Transmission to Learning as Process', research paper presented at the AEC Pop/Jazz Platform, Amsterdam, 13 February 2009, www.aecinfo.org/Content.aspx?id=2237, last accessed 13 April 2009.

39. David Borgo, 'Free Jazz in the Classroom', *Jazz Perspectives* 1.1 (May 2007), 61–88 (66).

40. See, for example, Lakshimi Bandlamudi, 'Dialogics of Understanding Self/Culture', *Ethos* 22.4 (December 1994), 460–93; or Pam Morris (ed.), *The Bakhtin Reader: Selected Writings of Bakhtin, Medvedev and Voloshinov* (London: Edward Arnold, 1994).

41. Borgo, 'Free Jazz in the Classroom', 69.

42. Ake, *Jazz Cultures*, 127–32.

43. See Tomlinson, 'Cultural Dialogics'; and Nicholas Gebhardt, *Going for Jazz: Musical Practices and American Ideology* (Chicago and London: University of Chicago Press, 2001), 77–122.

44. Sherrie Tucker, 'Deconstructing the Jazz Tradition', 44–6.

# Bibliography

Abbate, C., 'Music: Drastic or Gnostic', *Critical Enquiry* 30 (Spring 2004), 505–36

Ake, D., *Jazz Cultures*, Berkeley: University of California Press, 2002

    'Learning Jazz, Teaching Jazz' in Cooke, M. and Horn, D. (eds.), *The Cambridge Companion to Jazz*, Cambridge: Cambridge University Press, 2002, 255–69

Allsup, R., 'Transformational Education and Critical Music Pedagogy: Examining the Link between Culture and Learning', *Music Education Research* 5.1 (January 2003), 5–12

Arnold, M., *Culture and Anarchy*, Oxford and New York: Oxford University Press, 1990

Ashcroft, B., Griffiths, B. and Tiffin, H. (eds.), *The Post-Colonial Studies Reader*, London and New York: Routledge, 1995

Attali, J., *Noise: The Political Economy of Music*, Minneapolis: University of Minnesota Press, 1985

Auslander, P., *Liveness: Performance in a Mediatized Culture*, London and New York: Routledge, 1999

Bandlamudi, L., 'Dialogics of Understanding Self/Culture', *Ethos* 22.4 (December 1994), 460–93

Barthes, R., *Image-Music-Text*, London: Fontana Press, 1977

    *Mythologies*, London: Vintage Classics, 1993

Baudrillard, J., 'The Work of Art in the Electronic Age' in Gane, M. (ed.), *Baudrillard Live: Selected Interviews*, London and New York: Routledge, 1993, 145–51

Benjamin, W., *Illuminations*, London: Pimlico Press, 1999

Berger, J., *Ways of Seeing*, London: Penguin, 1990

Berliner, P., *Thinking in Jazz: The Infinite Art of Improvisation*, Chicago and London, University of Chicago Press, 1994

Bisso, R., *Buddy Bolden of New Orleans: A Jazz Poem*, Santa Barbara: Fithian Press, 1998

Boorman, S., 'The Musical Text' in Cook, N. and Everist, M. (eds.), *Rethinking Music*, Oxford and New York: Oxford University Press, 2001, 403–42

Borgo, D., 'Free Jazz in the Classroom', *Jazz Perspectives* 1.1 (May 2007), 61–88

Born, G., 'On Musical Mediation: Ontology, Technology and Creativity', *Twentieth-Century Music* 2 (March 2005), 7–36

Bowen, J., 'The History of Remembered Innovation: Tradition and Its Role in the Relationship between Musical Works and Their Performances', *The Journal of Musicology* 11.2 (Spring 1993), 139–73

Brofsky, H., 'Miles Davis and "My Funny Valentine": The Evolution of a Solo' in Kirchner, B. (ed.), *A Miles Davis Reader*, Washington and London: Smithsonian Institution Press, 1997, 140–63

Burrows, G., 'Black, Brown and Beige and the Politics of Signifyin(g)', *Jazz Research Journal* 1.1 (March 2007), 45–71

Butler, J., *Gender Trouble: Feminism and the Subversion of Identity*, London and New York: Routledge, 1990

Callahan, J. F. (ed.), *The Collected Essays of Ralph Ellison*, New York: Modern Library Paperback, 2003

Campbell, J., *The Hero with a Thousand Faces*, London: Fontana Press, 1993

Chanan, M., *Repeated Takes: A Short History of Recording and Its Effects on Music*, London: Verso, 1995

Cogswell, M., *Louis Armstrong: The Offstage Story of Satchmo*, Portland, OR: Collectors Press, 2003

Cohen, A., *The Symbolic Construction of Community*, London and New York: Routledge, 1993

Cole, B., *John Coltrane*, New York: Da Capo Press, 2001

Collier, J. L., *Duke Ellington*, London and New York: Penguin, 1987

Collins, J., *Uncommon Cultures: Popular Culture and Postmodernism*, London and New York: Routledge, 1989

Cook, N., *Analysing Musical Multimedia*, Oxford and New York: Oxford University Press, 2001

 *Music: A Very Short Introduction*, Oxford and New York: Oxford University Press, 2000

Cook, R., *Blue Note Records: The Biography*, London: Pimlico Press, 2003

Cooke, M. and Horn, D. (eds.), *The Cambridge Companion to Jazz*, Cambridge: Cambridge University Press, 2002

Corbett, J., *Extended Play: From John Cage to Dr Funkenstein*, Durham, NC and London: Duke University Press, 1994

Crouch, S., *Considering Genius: Writings on Music*, New York: Basic Civitas Books, 2006

Crow, B., *Jazz Anecdotes*, Oxford and New York: Oxford University Press, 1990

Cuscuna, M., '"Strictly on the Record": The Art of Jazz and the Recording Industry', *The Source: Challenging Jazz Criticism* 2 (March 2005), 63–70

Dance, S., *The World of Duke Ellington*, New York: Da Capo Press, 1981

Davis, F., *In the Moment: Jazz in the 1980s*, New York: Oxford University Press, 1986

 *Like Young: Jazz, Pop, Youth and Middle Age*, New York: Da Capo Press, 2001

Davis, M. and Troupe, Q., *Miles: The Autobiography*, London and New York: Picador, 1989

DeVeaux, S., *The Birth of Bebop: A Social and Musical History*, Berkeley: University of California Press, 1997

'Constructing the Jazz Tradition' in O'Meally, R. (ed.), *The Jazz Cadence of American Culture*, New York: Columbia University Press, 1998, 484–514

'Core and Boundaries', *The Source: Challenging Jazz Criticism* 2.1 (March 2005), 15–30

*Jazz in America: Who's Listening?*, Research Division Report, National Endowment for the Arts no. 31, Carson, CA: Seven Locks Press, 1995

'Struggling with *Jazz*', *Current Musicology* 71–3 (Spring 2001–Spring 2002), 353–74

Droste, M., *Bauhaus 1919–1933*, Cologne: Taschen, 1998

Dyer, G., *But Beautiful: A Book about Jazz*, London: Abacus, 2000

Dyer, R., *Heavenly Bodies: Film Stars and Society*, Basingstoke: Palgrave Macmillan, 1987

*Stars*, London: BFI, 1998

Eagleton, T., *Literary Theory*, Oxford: Blackwell Publishing, 1993

Easthope, A., *What a Man's Gotta Do: Masculine Myth in Popular Culture*, New York: Routledge, 1990

Easthope, A. and McGowan, K. (eds.), *A Critical and Cultural Theory Reader*, Buckingham: Open University Press, 1997

Eisenberg, E., *The Recording Angel: Music, Records and Culture from Aristotle to Zappa*, 2nd edn, New Haven: Yale University Press, 2005

Ellington, E. K., *Music Is My Mistress*, New York: Da Capo Press, 1976

Ellington, M. with Dance, S., *Duke Ellington in Person: An Intimate Memoir*, New York: Da Capo Press, 1979

Ellison, R., 'Homage to Duke Ellington on His Birthday' in John F. Callahan (ed.), *The Collected Essays of Ralph Ellison*, New York: Modern Library Paperback, 2003, 680–7

Evans, J. and Hesmondalgh, D., *Understanding Media: Inside Celebrity*, Maidenhead and New York: Open University Press, 2005

Eyerman, R. and Jamison, A., *Music and Social Movements: Mobilizing Traditions in the Twentieth Century*, Cambridge: Cambridge University Press, 1998

Felman, S. and Laub, D. (eds.), *Testimony: Crises of Witnessing in Literature, Psychoanalysis, and History*, New York and London: Routledge, 1992

Fischlin, D. and Heble, A. (eds.), *The Other Side of Nowhere: Jazz, Improvisation and Communities in Dialogue*, Middletown, CT: Wesleyan University Press, 2004

Franceschina, J., *Duke Ellington's Music for the Theatre*, Jefferson, NC and London: McFarland and Co., 2001

Frith, S., 'Music and Identity' in S. Hall and P. du Gay (eds.), *Questions of Cultural Identity*, London: Sage Publications, 2000, 108–27

*Music for Pleasure: Essays on the Sociology of Pop*, Cambridge: Polity Press, 1988

*Performing Rites: Evaluating Popular Music*, Oxford and New York: Oxford University Press, 2002

Gabbard, K., *Black Magic: White Hollywood and African American Culture*, New Brunswick: Rutgers University Press, 2004

'How Many Miles? Alternate Takes on the Jazz Life' in Lock, G. and Murray, D. (eds.), *Thriving on a Riff: Jazz and Blues Influences in African American Literature and Film*, Oxford and New York: Oxford University Press, 2009, 184–200

'Images of Jazz' in Cooke, M. and Horn, D. (eds.), *The Cambridge Companion to Jazz*, Cambridge: Cambridge University Press, 2002, 332–46

*Jammin' at the Margins: Jazz and the American Cinema*, Chicago and London: University of Chicago Press, 1996

(ed.), *Jazz among the Discourses*, Durham, NC and London: Duke University Press, 1995

'The Jazz Canon and Its Consequences' in *Jazz among the Discourses*, Durham, NC and London: Duke University Press, 1995, 1–28

'Krin Gabbard Replies', *American Music* 8.3 (Autumn 1990), 360–2

'Miles from Home: Miles Davis and the Movies', *The Source: Challenging Jazz Criticism* 1 (March 2004), 27–41

(ed.), *Representing Jazz*, Durham, NC and London: Duke University Press, 1995

'The Word Jazz' in Cooke, M. and Horn, D. (eds.), *The Cambridge Companion to Jazz*, Cambridge: Cambridge University Press, 2002, 1–6

Gallop, J., *Anecdotal Theory*, Durham, NC and London: Duke University Press, 2002

Gammond, P., *Duke Ellington*, London: Apollo Press, 1987

Garber, F., 'Fabulating Jazz' in Gabbard, K. (ed.), *Representing Jazz*, Durham, NC and London: Duke University Press, 1995, 70–103

Gates, H. L., Jr, *Loose Canons: Notes on the Culture Wars*, Oxford and New York, Oxford University Press, 1993

*The Signifyin(g) Monkey: A Theory of African-American Literary Criticism*, Oxford and New York: Oxford University Press, 1990

Gebhardt, N., *Going for Jazz: Musical Practices and American Ideology*, Chicago and London: University of Chicago Press, 2001

Gendron, B., '"Moldy Figs" and Modernists: Jazz at War (1942–1946)' in Gabbard, K. (ed.), *Jazz among the Discourses*, Durham, NC and London: Duke University Press, 1995, 31–56

Gennari, J., *Blowin' Hot and Cool: Jazz and Its Critics*, Chicago and London: University of Chicago Press, 2006

George, L. A., 'Duke Ellington: The Man and His Music', *Music Educators Journal* 85.6 (May 1999), 15–21

Giddins, G., 'Cadenza: I Remember Chirpy', *JazzTimes* (January–February 2003), 88

*Satchmo: The Genius of Louis Armstrong*, 2nd edn, New York: Da Capo Press, 2000

Gioia, T., *The Imperfect Art: Reflections on Jazz and Modern Culture*, Oxford: Oxford University Press, 1988

Goehr, L., *The Imaginary Museum of Musical Works: An Essay in the Philosophy of Music*, Oxford and New York: Oxford University Press, 1992

Gourse, L., *Straight, No Chaser: The Life and Genius of Thelonious Monk*, London: Books with Attitude, 1997

Gracyk, T., *Rhythm and Noise: An Aesthetics of Rock*, Durham, NC and London: Duke University Press, 1996

Gushee, L., 'The Reception of Jazz in America', *American Music* 8.3 (Autumn 1990), 359–60

Haines, P., 'Sienna/Symposium', *Coda: The Journal of Jazz and Improvised Music* (January–February 2003), 39–40.

Hajdu, D., 'A Jazz of Their Own', *Vanity Fair* 465 (May 1999), 188–96
    *Lush Life: A Biography of Billy Strayhorn*, New York: Granta Books, 1998

Hall, S., 'Who Needs Identity?' in S. Hall and P. du Gay (eds.), *Questions of Cultural Identity*, London: Sage Publications, 2000, 1–17

Hall, S. and du Gay, P. (eds.), *Questions of Cultural Identity*, London: Sage Publications, 2000

Hamilton Murdoch, D., *The American West: The Invention of a Myth*, Cardiff: Welsh Academic Press, 1999

Harlos, C., 'Jazz Autobiography: Theory, Practice, Politics' in Gabbard, K. (ed.), *Representing Jazz*, Durham, NC and London: Duke University Press, 1995, 131–66

Hasse, J. E., *Duke Ellington beyond Genius*, New York: Simon and Schuster, 1993

Hawkins, S., *Settling the Pop Score: Pop Texts and Identity Politics*, Aldershot: Ashgate, 2002

Heble, A., *Landing on the Wrong Note: Jazz, Dissonance and Critical Practice*, London and New York: Routledge, 2000

Hentoff, N., *The Jazz Life*, London: Hamilton and Co., 1964

Hobsbawm, E. and Ranger, T. (eds.), *The Invention of Tradition*, Cambridge: Cambridge University Press, 1992

Huyssen, A., *After the Great Divide: Modernism, Mass Culture and Postmodernism*, London and New York: Routledge, 1986

Jarrett, M., 'The Tenor's Vehicle: Reading *Way Out West*' in Gabbard, K. (ed.), *Representing Jazz*, Durham, NC and London: Duke University Press, 1995, 260–82

Jewell, D., *Duke: A Portrait of Duke Ellington*, London: Elm Tree Books, 1977

Jones, J., 'Look What We Did', *Guardian*, G2 supplement (31 March 2003), 2–4

Jones, M. and Chilton, J., *Louis: The Louis Armstrong Story*, St Albans: Mayflower, 1975

Jost, E., *Free Jazz*, New York: Da Capo Press, 1994

Kahn, A., 'The House that Trane Built', *JazzTimes* (September 2002), 128–9

*The House that Trane Built*, London: Granta Books, 2006

*A Love Supreme: The Creation of John Coltrane's Classic Album*, London: Granta Books, 2002

Kart, L., 'Miles Davis Biography Fails to Unravel Strands of Art and Image' in Kirchner, B. (ed.), *A Miles Davis Reader*, Washington and London: Smithsonian Institution Press, 1997, 229–33

Katz, M., *Capturing Sound: How Technology Changed Music*, Berkeley: University of California Press, 2004

Keil, C. and Feld, S., *Music Grooves: Essays and Dialogues*, Chicago and London: University of Chicago Press, 1994

Kenney, W. H., *Chicago Jazz: A Cultural History, 1904–1930*, Oxford and New York: Oxford University Press, 1995

Kermode, F., 'Canon and Period' in Walder, D. (ed.), *Literature in the Modern World*, Oxford and New York: Oxford University Press, 1993, 17–20

Kerouac, J., *On the Road*, New York and London: Penguin, 1972

Kirchner, B. (ed.), *A Miles Davis Reader*, Washington and London: Smithsonian Institution Press, 1997

Klapp, O. E., *Heroes, Villains and Fools*, Harlow: Prentice Hall, 1962

Laing, D., 'A Voice without a Face: Popular Music and the Phonograph in the 1890s', *Popular Music* 10 (January 1991), 1–9

Langer, L., *Holocaust Testimonies: The Ruins of Memory*, New Haven and London: Yale University Press, 1991

LaVerne, A., *Countdown to Giant Steps*, Play-A-Long book series no. 75, New Albany, IN: Jamey Aebersold Jazz, 1996

Lawrence, A. H., *Duke Ellington and His World*, New York and London: Routledge, 2001

Leavis, F. R., 'Mass Civilisation and Minority Culture' in Storey, J. (ed.), *Cultural Theory and Popular Culture: A Reader*, Hemel Hempstead: Harvester Wheatsheaf, 1994, 12–20

Leja, M., 'Peirce, Visuality, and Art', *Representation* 72 (Autumn 2000), 97–122

Leonard, N., *Jazz: Myth and Religion*, New York and Oxford: Oxford University Press, 1987

Lévi-Strauss, C., *Myth and Meaning*, London and New York: Routledge Classics, 2005

Levine, L., *High Brow Low Brow: The Emergence of Cultural Hierarchy in America*, Cambridge, MA: Harvard University Press, 1990

Lock, G., *Blutopia: Visions of the Future and Revisions of the Past in the Work of Sun Ra, Duke Ellington, and Anthony Braxton*, Durham, NC and London: Duke University Press, 1999

Lock, G. and Murray, D. (eds.), *The Hearing Eye: Jazz and Blues Influences in African American Visual Art*, Oxford and New York: Oxford University Press, 2009 (eds.), *Thriving on a Riff. Jazz and Blues Influences in African American Literature and Film*, New York: Oxford University Press, 2009

Lord G., *Dick Francis: A Racing Life*, London: Little, Brown and Co., 1999

Mailer, N., 'The White Negro' in Walser, R. (ed.), *Keeping Time: Readings in Jazz History*, New York and Oxford: Oxford University Press, 1999, 242–6

Marsalis, W., 'What Jazz Is and Isn't' in Walser, R. (ed.) *Keeping Time: Readings in Jazz History*, New York and Oxford: Oxford University Press, 1999, 334–8

Marsalis, W., Collier, J. L. and Craddock-Willis, A., 'Jazz People', *Transition* 65 (1995), 140–78

Marsalis, W. and Hasse, J. E., *Beyond Category: The Life and Genius of Duke Ellington*, New York: Da Capo Press, 1995

Marsalis, W. and O'Meally, R., 'Duke Ellington: "Music like a Big Pot of Good Gumbo"' in O'Meally, R. (ed.), *The Jazz Cadence of American Culture*, New York: Columbia University Press, 1999, 143–53

Marsalis, W. and Stewart, F., *Sweet Swing Blues on the Road*, New York: Thunder's Mouth Press, 1999

Marsh, G. and Callingham, G., *The Cover Art of Blue Note Records*, London: Collins and Brown, 1991

Martin, P. J., 'The Jazz Community as an Art World', *The Source: Challenging Jazz Criticism* 2 (March 2005), 5–13

'Review: *Duke Ellington* by James Lincoln Collier, *The Reception of Jazz in America* by James Lincoln Collier, *Ellingtonia: The Recorded Music of Duke Ellington and His Sidemen* by W. R. Timner', *Popular Music* 9.1 (January 1990), 139–44

McLuhan, M., *Understanding Media: The Extensions of Man*, New York: Routledge, 2001

Meinhof, U. H. and Smith, J. (eds.), *Intertextuality and the Media: From Genre to Everyday Life*, Manchester: Manchester University Press, 2000

Merriam, A. and Mack, R., 'The Jazz Community', *Social Forces* 38.3 (1960), 211–22

Metheny, P., 'Pat Metheny on Kenny G', www.jazzoasis.com/methenyonkennyg.htm, last accessed 5 April 2009

Middleton, R., *Studying Popular Music*, Milton Keynes and Philadelphia: Open University Press, 1995

Monson, I., *Saying Something: Jazz Improvisation and Interaction*, Chicago and London: University of Chicago Press, 1996

Morris, P. (ed.), *The Bakhtin Reader: Selected Writings of Bakhtin, Medvedev and Voloshinov*, London: Edward Arnold, 1994

Mowitt, J., 'The Sound of Music in the Era of Its Electronic Reproducibility' in Leppert, R. and McClary, S. (eds.), *Music and Society: The Politics of Composition, Performance and Reception,* Cambridge: Cambridge University Press, 1994, 173–97

Murray, A., *From the Briarpatch File: On Context, Procedure and American Identity*, New York: Pantheon Books, 2001

   'The Function of the Heroic Image' in O'Meally, R. (ed.), *The Jazz Cadence of American Culture*, New York: Columbia University Press, 1998, 569–79

   *The Omni-Americans: New Perspectives on Black Experience and American Culture*, New York: Outerbridge and Dienstfrey, 1970

   *Stomping the Blues*, London: Quartet Books, 1978

   'The Vernacular Imperative: Duke Ellington's Place within the National Pantheon', *Boundary 2* 22.2 (Summer 1995), 19–24

Murray, A. and Callahan, J. F. (eds.), *Trading Twelves: The Selected Letters of Ralph Ellison and Albert Murray*, New York: Vintage Books, 2000

Murray, P. (ed.), *Genius: The History of an Idea*, Oxford: Blackwell, 1989

Nava, M., Blake, A., MacCrury, I. and Richards, B. (eds.), *Buy This Book: Studies in Advertising and Consumption*, London and New York: Routledge, 2001

Nicholson, S., *Is Jazz Dead? (Or Has It Moved to a New Address?)*, London and New York: Routledge, 2005

   *A Portrait of Duke Ellington: Reminiscing in Tempo*, London: Sidgwick and Jackson Press, 1999

Nisenson, E., *Ascension: John Coltrane and His Quest*, New York: Da Capo Press, 1995

O'Meally, R., 'Checking Our Balances: Louis Armstrong, Ralph Ellison and Betty Boop', *The Source: Challenging Jazz Criticism* 1 (March 2004), 44–59

   (ed.), *The Jazz Cadence of American Culture*, New York: Columbia University Press, 1998

   *Seeing Jazz: Artists and Writers on Jazz*, San Francisco: Chronicle Books, 1997

O'Meally, R., Hayes Edwards, B. and Jasmine Griffin, F. (eds.), *Uptown Conversation: The New Jazz Studies*, New York: Columbia University Press, 2004

Ondaatje, M., *Coming through Slaughter*, Oxford: Picador, 1984

Owens, T., *Bebop: The Music and Its Players*, Oxford and New York: Oxford University Press, 1995

Panish, J., *The Color of Jazz: Race and Representation in Postwar American Culture*, Jackson: University of Mississippi Press, 1997

Panken, T., 'Approaching Enlightenment', *Downbeat* (February 2001), 22–7

Parr, M., 'The Power of Sepia: An Expert's Take on That Madonna Image', *Guardian*, Comments and Features (15 April 2009), 2

Parsonage, C., Fadnes, P. and Taylor, J., 'Integrating Theory and Practice in Conservatoires: Formulating Holistic Models for Teaching and Learning Improvisation', *British Journal of Music Education* 24.3 (November 2007), 295–312

Porter, E., *What Is This Thing Called Jazz? African American Musicians as Artists, Critics and Activists*, Berkeley: University of California Press, 2002

Porter, L., *John Coltrane: His Life and Music*, Ann Arbor: University of Michigan Press, 1998

Radano, R. M., *New Musical Configurations: Anthony Braxton's Cultural Critique*, Chicago and London, University of Chicago Press, 1993

Rasula, J., 'The Media of Memory: The Seductive Menace of Records in Jazz History' in Gabbard, K. (ed.), *Jazz among the Discourses*, Durham, NC and London: Duke University Press, 1995, 134–64

Rattenbury, K., *Duke Ellington Jazz Composer*, London and New Haven: Yale University Press, 1990

Russell, R., *Bird Lives! The High Life and Hard Times of Charlie (Yardbird) Parker*, New York: Da Capo Press, 1996

Sales, G., *Jazz: America's Classical Music*, New York: Da Capo Press, 1992

Schuller, G., *Early Jazz: Its Roots and Musical Development*, Oxford: Oxford University Press, 1968

　*Musings: The Musical Worlds of Gunther Schuller. A Collection of His Writings*, Oxford and New York: Oxford University Press, 1986

　*The Swing Era: The Development of Jazz, 1930–1945*, Oxford: Oxford University Press, 1989

Scott, D., *From the Erotic to the Demonic: On Critical Musicology*, New York: Oxford University Press, 2003

Scruton, R., *The Aesthetics of Music*, Oxford and New York: Oxford University Press, 1999

Shapiro, N. and Hentoff, N., *Hear Me Talkin' to Ya: The Classic Story of Jazz as Told by the Men who Made It*, London: Souvenir Press, 1992

Shaw, P., 'Abjection Sustained: Goya, the Chapman Brothers and the *Disasters of War*', *Art History* 26.4 (September 2003), 479–504

Shepherd, J., *Music as Social Text*, Cambridge: Polity Press, 1991

Shipton, A., *A New History of Jazz*, New York and London: Continuum, 2007

Small, G., *Music of the Common Tongue*, London: Calder Press, 1987

　*Music, Society, Education*, 2nd edn, Hanover and London: Wesleyan University Press, 1996

　*Musicking: The Meanings of Performance and Listening*, Middletown, CT: Wesleyan University Press, 1998

Spencer, F. J., *Jazz and Death: Medical Profiles of Jazz Greats*, Jackson: University of Mississippi Press, 2002

Stanbridge, A., 'Burns Baby Burns: Jazz History as a Contested Cultural Site', *The Source: Challenging Jazz Criticism* 1 (March 2004), 81–99

Steiner, G., *Language and Silence: Essays on Language, Literature and the Inhuman*, New Haven: Yale University Press, 1998

Storey, J. (ed.), *Cultural Theory and Popular Culture: A Reader*, Hemel Hempstead: Harvester Wheatsheaf, 1994

Straw, W., 'Organized Disorder: The Changing Space of the Record Shop' in Redhead, S. (ed.), *The Clubcultures Reader: Readings in Popular Cultural Studies*, Oxford and Malden: Blackwell, 1998, 39–47

'Sizing Up Record Collections: Gender and Connoisseurship in Rock Music Culture' in Whiteley, S. (ed.), *Sexing the Groove: Popular Music and Gender*, London: Routledge, 1997, 3–16

Sudhalter, R., *Lost Chords: White Musicians and Their Contribution to Jazz 1915–1945*, Oxford and New York: Oxford University Press, 1999

Szwed, J., 'The Man' in O'Meally, R., Hayes Edwards, B. and Jasmine Griffin, F. (eds.), *Uptown Conversation: The New Jazz Studies*, New York: Columbia University Press, 2004, 166–86

Tagg, P., 'Analyzing Popular Music: Theory, Method and Practice', *Popular Music* 2 (1982), 37–48

Tagg, P. and Clarida, B., *10 Little Title Tunes*, New York and Montreal: Mass Media Scholars' Press, 2003

Taylor, A., *Notes and Tones: Musician-to-Musician Interviews*, 2nd edn, New York: Da Capo Press, 1993

Taylor, T. D., *Strange Sounds: Music, Technology and Culture*, New York: Routledge, 2001

Thiong'o, N. wa, 'The Language of African Literature' in Ashcroft, B., Griffiths, G. and Tiffin, H. (eds.), *A Post Colonial Studies Reader*, London and New York: Routledge, 1999, 285–90

Tomlinson, G., 'Cultural Dialogics and Jazz: A White Historian Signifies', *Black Music Research Journal* 11.2 (Autumn 1991), 229–64

Tonkin, E., *Narrating Our Pasts: The Social Construction of Oral History*, Cambridge: Cambridge University Press, 1995

Townsend, P., *Jazz in American Culture*, Edinburgh: Edinburgh University Press, 2000

Trodre, R., 'Professor Jazz Opens Cool School', *The Observer* (15 February 1998), 20

Tucker, M. (ed.), *The Duke Ellington Reader*, Oxford and New York: Oxford University Press, 1999

'Review: *Duke Ellington* by James Lincoln Collier', *Notes*, 2nd series 45.3 (March 1989), 499–502

Tucker, S., 'Deconstructing the Jazz Tradition: The "Subjectless Subject" of New Jazz Studies', *The Source: Challenging Jazz Criticism* 2 (March 2005), 31–46

*Swing Shift:"All-Girl" Bands of the 1940s*, Durham, NC and London: Duke University Press, 2000

Vogler, C., *The Writer's Journey: Mythic Structure for Writers*, 3rd edn, Studio City, CA: Michael Wiese Productions, 2007

Volkov, S., *Testimony: The Memoirs of Dimitri Shostakovich*, London: Faber and Faber, 1981

Walser, R. (ed.), *Keeping Time: Readings in Jazz History*, Oxford and New York: Oxford University Press, 1999

'"Out of Notes": Signification, Interpretation and the Problem of Miles Davis', *The Musical Quarterly* 77.2 (Summer 1993), 343–65

'Valuing Jazz' in Cooke, M. and Horn, D. (eds.), *The Cambridge Companion to Jazz*, Cambridge: Cambridge University Press, 2002, 301–20

Washburne, C. J., 'Does Kenny G Play Bad Jazz?' in Washburne, C. J. and Derno, M. (eds.), *Bad Music: The Music We Love to Hate*, New York and London: Routledge, 2004, 123–47

Washburne, C. J. and Derno, M. (eds.), *Bad Music: The Music We Love to Hate*, New York and London: Routledge, 2004

Wernick, A., 'Resort to Nostalgia: Mountains, Memories and Myths of Time' in Nava, M., Richards, B., and MacCrury, I. (eds.), *Buy This Book: Studies in Advertising and Consumption*, London and New York: Routledge, 1997, 207–23

Whiteley, S. (ed.), *Sexing the Groove: Popular Music and Gender*, London and New York: Routledge, 1997

Whiteley, S., Bennett, A. and Hawkins, S. (eds.), *Music, Space and Place: Popular Music and Cultural Identity*, Aldershot: Ashgate, 2005

Whyton, T., 'Acting on Impulse! Recordings and the Reification of Jazz' in M. Dogantan-Dack (ed.), *Recorded Music: Philosophical and Critical Reflections*, London: Middlesex University Press, 2008, 155–71

   'Birth of the School: Discursive Methodologies in Jazz Education', *Music Education Research* 8.2 (March 2006), 65–81

   'Four for Trane: Jazz and the Disembodied Voice', *Jazz Perspectives* 1.2 (October 2007), 115–32

   'Telling Tales: Witnessing and the Jazz Anecdote', *The Source: Challenging Jazz Criticism* 1 (March 2004), 115–31

Williams, A., *Constructing Musicology*, Aldershot: Ashgate, 2007

Williams, M., *The Jazz Tradition*, Oxford: Oxford University Press, 1993

   'Review: *Duke Ellington* by James Lincoln Collier', *American Music* 6.3 (Autumn 1988), 338–42

Wilmer, V., *As Serious as Your Life: John Coltrane and Beyond*, London: Serpent's Tail, 1992

Witkin, R., *Adorno on Popular Culture*, London and New York: Routledge, 2003

Wolff, J., 'The Ideology of Autonomous Art' in Leppert, R. and McClary, S. (eds.), *Music and Society: The Politics of Composition, Performance and Reception*, Cambridge: Cambridge University Press, 1994, 1–12

   *The Social Production of Art*, 2nd edn, London: Macmillan, 1993

Zorn, J. (ed.), *Arcana: Musicians on Music*, New York: Granary Books, 2000

# Index

Adorno, Theodor, 41
Aebersold, Jamey, 13, 49–51, 53, 154, 166, 169
Ake, David, 44, 91, 133, 162, 167, 176
Armstrong, Louis, 13, 16, 39, 51, 70, 79, 86, 94,
    119, 129, 147, 176
  and education, 164
  as African American hero, 19
  as musical genius, 23, 55, 86
  as signifyin(g) artist, 26, 37
  *Louis Armstrong Plays W. C. Handy*, 111
  'West End Blues', (imitations of), 54
  'What a Wonderful World', (Kenny G),
    64–5, 66, 77
Associated Board of the Royal Schools of Music
    (ABRSM), 154

Baker, Chet, 114
Baker, David, 54, 169
Bakhtin, Mikhail, 172, 175
Barthes, Roland, 11, 60, 92
Benjamin, Walter, 40–1, 55, 62
Berliner, Paul, 163
Bimhuis (Amsterdam), 138, 139
Blue Note Records, 6–7
Bolden, Buddy, vi, 11, 37, 117–18
Borgo, David, 174–5
Braxton, Anthony, 163
Brofsky, Howard, 114–15, 123
Brookmeyer, Bob, 158, 163
Burns, Ken (*Jazz*), 14, 19, 24, 72, 86, 117, 125,
    149–52, 169–70

Chapman Brothers, 60–2
chord-scale theory, 176
*Collateral* (Michael Mann), 2–5, 10
Collier, James Lincoln, 14, 147–50, 151
Coltrane, Alice, 47, 95
Coltrane, John, 9, 12–13, 16, 34, 42–54, 86–99,
    102, 108, 116, 176
  *A Love Supreme*, 11, 42–5, 67, 89
    imitations of, 53–4
  as spiritual master, 11, 17, 24, 37, 86, 91
  *Complete Impulse! Studio Recordings*, 88
  fetish character of voice, 11

Coltrane, The Church of St John, 43, 91
Corbett, John, 78, 92–3
Crouch, Stanley, 18, 19–23, 30, 69, 137, 144, 177
Crow, Bill, 110, 112
Cuscuna, Michael, 87, 92

Davis, Miles, 10, 16, 34, 37, 47, 123, 173, 176
  and commercialism, 22, 134
  as signifyin(g) artist, 25–6
  *Bitches Brew*, 5
  controversial biography, 32–3, 149, 170
  *Kind of Blue*, 5, 62, 71
  'My Funny Valentine', 114–15
  representation in film, 2–5
Davis, Steve, 50
Denio, Amy, 158–9
DeVeaux, Scott, 70, 86, 89, 132, 133, 137,
    160, 171
Dyer, Geoff, 63–5, 102
Dyer, Richard, 36, 47, 50–1

Easthope, Anthony, 34–5
Eisenberg, Evan, 39, 51, 55, 89–90, 93
Ellington, Duke, 14, 16, 37, 74, 127–8,
    129, 176
  and jazz education, 166–7
  as African American hero, 18–20, 143–5
  as art composer, 137, 141–3
  as enigmatic, 145–7
  as musical genius, 23, 24, 61–2, 134
  controversial writings on, 147–52
  dominant representations of, 140–1
  *Sacred Concerts*, 11
Ellington, Mercer, 144, 149–50
Ellison, Ralph, 17, 18–19, 22, 69, 141, 143–4

Fitzgerald, Ella, 94
Francis, Dick, 59–61

Gabbard, Krin, ix, 5, 7, 10, 26, 41, 71, 110, 129,
    130, 148, 157, 160, 170, 171
Gaillard, Slim, 133–4
Garber, Frederick, 37, 39, 41–2, 48
Gates Jr, Henry Louis, 25–7, 79, 171, 172

Gebhardt, Nicholas, 28, 176–7
Gennari, John, 166, 173
Giddins, Gary, 65, 86
Gioia, Ted, 41, 55–6
Gorelick, Kenny (Kenny G), 13, 39, 58, 64–71,
    74, 77–81, 86, 176
Gramsci, Antonio, 155

Hajdu, David, 14, 61, 149–51
Hall, Stuart, 75, 78
Harlos, Christopher, 113
Harrison, Donald, 89, 96, 104
Heble, Ajay, 33, 133, 170
Holiday, Billie, 116–17, 183

Impulse! Records, 13, 87–104
International Association for Jazz Education
    (IAJE), 66, 94, 154

Jarrett, Keith, 44, 136, 163
Jarrett, Michael, 27
Jones, Elvin, 90–1
Julliard School of Music, 3, 4

Kahn, Ashley, 43–5, 94
Katz, Mark, 40–3
Kenney, William Howland, 164
Kernfeld, Barry, 167
Kerouac, Jack, 133–4

LaVerne, Andy, 42, 48–50, 53
Leonard, Neil, 50–2, 165
Levine, Lawrence, 29–31
Lincoln Center, 19, 20, 29, 67–9, 130, 138–40,
    142, 148, 166–7
  architectural design, 138–40
  Essentially Ellington programme, 14, 142–3,
    166
  Lincoln Center Jazz Orchestra, 54
Lock, Graham, 145–6, 149, 169

Marsalis, Branford, 13, 42, 52–3, 67
Marsalis, Wynton, 18–19, 35–6, 69, 72, 98, 117,
    138, 142, 144, 148, 151
Martin, Peter, 34, 73–4
Metheny, Pat, 13, 58, 64–8, 70, 74, 77–81, 86
Miles, Reid, 6

Mingus, Charles, 95
Monk, Thelonious, 116–17, 121–2
Morgen, Joe, 61
Morgenstern, Dan, 94, 116
Murray, Albert, 16–24, 26–7, 30, 32, 69, 137,
    141–4, 177
Murray, David, 169

National Jazz Ensemble, 54
Nicholson, Stuart, 70, 138, 157

O'Meally, Robert, 26

Parker, Charlie 'Bird', 3, 11, 16, 22–3, 28–9, 39,
    65, 74, 87, 108, 129, 133–4, 144, 176
  Faustian mythology, 37
Patitucci, John, 49–50
Peirce, Charles Sanders, 12
Porter, Eric, 19–20

Rasula, Jed, 7, 85
Riley, Ben, 121–2
Rollins, Sonny, 27, 46, 53, 86, 163

Schapp, Phil, 94
Schuller, Gunther, 142, 163
Small, Christopher, 76–7, 85, 86, 105, 132, 135,
    138–9, 156
Smithsonian Institution, 166
  Smithsonian Jazz Masterworks Orchestra, 54
Strayhorn, Billy, 14, 61–2, 144, 149–51
Swallow, Steve, 158

Taylor, Creed, 95, 113–14
Third Stream, 89, 130
Tomlinson, Gary, 26, 172–6
Tucker, Sherrie, 35, 177
Tyner, McCoy, 44, 95, 102

Walser, Robert, 25–6, 35, 68, 70
Washburne, Christopher, 66, 79
Weston, Randy, 116–17
Whiteman, Paul, 136
Wolff, Francis, 6
Wolff, Janet, 24, 29, 161

Zorn, John, 171